CW00621774

Open Mind

Upper Intermediate Student's Book

Mickey Rogers

Joanne Taylore-Knowles

Steve Taylore-Knowles

with Ingrid Wisniewska

Concept development:
Mariela Gil Vierma

Contents

PRONUNCIATION	GRAMMAR	VOCABULARY	LIFESKILLS
WORDS: emphatic *do/did* for contrast	**REVIEW OF PAST TENSES** **FUNCTION** talking about a past experience ***WOULD, USED TO, BE + ALWAYS + -ING*** **FUNCTION** talking about family identity	**PERSONAL IDENTITY** **FUNCTION** talking about your family background ***SENSE*** **FUNCTION** talking about learning a new language	**SELF & SOCIETY:** Understanding stereotypes **FUNCTION** discussing the consequences of negative stereotypes
		LANGUAGE WRAP-UP	
SOUNDS: voiced and voiceless consonant sounds	**VERBS WITH STATIVE AND DYNAMIC USES** **FUNCTION** talking about the spread of multinational corporations **REPEATED AND DOUBLE COMPARATIVES** **FUNCTION** talking about the growth of social media	**GLOBALISATION** **FUNCTION** talking about the positive and negative aspects of a global market **VERBS FOR TAKING SOCIAL ACTION** **FUNCTION** talking about ways of supporting your local economy	**STUDY & LEARNING:** Understanding internet search terms **FUNCTION** studying the effect of globalisation on your local economy
		LANGUAGE WRAP-UP	
SOUNDS: silent letters – consonants	**REPORTED SPEECH – MODAL VERBS AND PAST PERFECT** **FUNCTION** talking about 15 minutes of fame **REPORTED SPEECH – OPTIONAL BACK-SHIFTING** **FUNCTION** talking about lookalikes	**WAYS TO BECOME FAMOUS** **FUNCTION** talking about famous people in your country **GUESSING MEANING FROM CONTEXT** **FUNCTION** talking about the effects of celebrity	**WORK & CAREER:** Evaluating arguments **FUNCTION** discussing a proposal
		LANGUAGE WRAP-UP	
WORDS: reduced forms of *would you* and *did you*	**NOUN CLAUSES AS OBJECTS** **FUNCTION** talking about laughter therapy **REVIEW OF CONDITIONAL FORMS** **FUNCTION** talking about taking a year off before university	**LIFE SATISFACTION** **FUNCTION** talking about wealth and happiness **MOOD** **FUNCTION** talking about your state of well-being	**WORK & CAREER:** Being a positive team member **FUNCTION** focusing on solutions to problems
		LANGUAGE WRAP-UP	
SOUNDS: word stress in adjective + compound noun phrases	**THE PASSIVE** **FUNCTION** talking about problems caused by the monsoon season **EXPRESSIONS OF PURPOSE** **FUNCTION** understanding FAQs about water	**MARKETING** **FUNCTION** talking about how packaging can affect your buying decisions **ENVIRONMENTAL ISSUES** **FUNCTION** discussing responsibility for solving environmental problems	**SELF & SOCIETY:** Developing empathy **FUNCTION** discussing your water usage
		LANGUAGE WRAP-UP	
SOUNDS: stress in words with *-tion/-sion*	***BE USED TO / GET USED TO*** **FUNCTION** describing habits and customs **VERB + OBJECT + INFINITIVE** **FUNCTION** comparing traditional and non-traditional jobs	**INSTITUTIONAL TRADITIONS** **FUNCTION** discussing customs and rituals **PHRASAL VERBS FOR PERSONAL RITUALS** **FUNCTION** discussing why you have rituals	**STUDY & LEARNING:** Managing distractions **FUNCTION** making a plan to change your habits
		LANGUAGE WRAP-UP	

PRONUNCIATION	GRAMMAR	VOCABULARY	LIFESKILLS
WORDS: *'s* after names that end in /s/, /ʃ/ or /z/	**POSSESSIVE APOSTROPHE** **FUNCTION** talking about celebrities' clothing sale **PAST PERFECT VS PAST PERFECT CONTINUOUS** **FUNCTION** understanding a biography	**DESIGN** **FUNCTION** talking about revolutionising the design process **PHRASAL VERBS** **FUNCTION** talking about fashion design and trends	**WORK & CAREER:** Showing initiative **FUNCTION** identifying opportunities to show initiative
		LANGUAGE WRAP-UP	
WORDS: the contracted form of *would*	***WOULD RATHER* AND *WOULD PREFER*** **FUNCTION** talking about donating to charities **NOUN CLAUSES AS SUBJECTS** **FUNCTION** talking about unemployment	**SOCIAL ISSUES** **FUNCTION** talking about humanitarian causes **SOCIAL JUSTICE** **FUNCTION** talking about a fair society	**SELF & SOCIETY:** Understanding rights and responsibilities **FUNCTION** sharing your ideas on the rights and responsibilities in your country
		LANGUAGE WRAP-UP	
WORDS: nouns and verbs with different pronunciation	**GERUNDS AFTER PREPOSITIONS** **FUNCTION** talking about personality types **VERB + GERUND** **FUNCTION** talking about reality shows	**SCIENTIFIC NOUNS AND VERBS** **FUNCTION** talking about psychology and the effects of competition **EXPRESSIONS OF EMOTION** **FUNCTION** talking about feelings and desires	**STUDY & LEARNING:** Synthesising information **FUNCTION** preparing and presenting a report
		LANGUAGE WRAP-UP	
WORDS: reduction of *have*	**EXPRESSING ABILITY** **FUNCTION** talking about entrepreneurs **PAST MODALS OF DEDUCTION** **FUNCTION** working out how something happened	**SAFETY AND RISK** **FUNCTION** discussing freedom and security **EXPRESSIONS WITH *RISK*** **FUNCTION** talking about high-risk situations	**SELF & SOCIETY:** Managing stress **FUNCTION** creating strategies to help you relax
		LANGUAGE WRAP-UP	
SOUNDS: stress timing	**VERB + GERUND/INFINITIVE WITH A CHANGE IN MEANING** **FUNCTION** talking about a past memory **CONNECTORS OF ADDITION / CAUSE AND EFFECT** **FUNCTION** talking about image manipulation	**DESCRIBING PHOTOS** **FUNCTION** explaining what you like and dislike about photos **MAKING COMPARISONS** **FUNCTION** finding similarities and differences between photos	**WORK & CAREER:** Giving and receiving feedback **FUNCTION** discussing a campaign to boost local tourism
		LANGUAGE WRAP-UP	
SOUNDS: connected speech	**CONNECTORS OF CONTRAST** **FUNCTION** talking about a visit to a city **WAYS OF TALKING ABOUT THE FUTURE** **FUNCTION** talking about cities of the future	**FORMAL LETTERS** **FUNCTION** writing a letter of complaint **DESCRIBING PLACES** **FUNCTION** talking about a city that you know	**STUDY & LEARNING:** Recognising and avoiding plagiarism **FUNCTION** discussing strategies to make your work original
		LANGUAGE WRAP-UP	

Grammar review

1 Find and correct the mistake in each sentence.

1 I've taken all my holiday days this year yet.
2 He didn't used to be a troublemaker at school.
3 Did you use give presentations in your old job?
4 You should help your mother, should not you?
5 The happiness is important in life.
6 By the time I arrived, he left the office already.

2 Complete the sentences with one word.

1 How long has it _____ raining?
2 Why haven't you gone home _____? It's 5pm.
3 I _____ to have long hair when I was a child, but now it's short.
4 You're going to develop the marketing strategy, _____ you?
5 Only a few colleagues _____ signed up for the seminar when I spoke to them.
6 You registered online, _____ you?

3 Complete the sentences with the present prefect or present perfect continuous form of the verbs in brackets. In one case, both are possible.

1 Emily _____ (retrain) as a teacher. She's almost finished her training programme.
2 She _____ (study) part-time for her master's degree for six months.
3 My brother _____ (apply) to lots of colleges recently.
4 Is Tom OK? He _____ (push) himself really hard lately in his new job.
5 Our family _____ (not have) a pet before. It's a new thing for us.

4 Complete each sentence so that it has the same meaning as the first one.

1 Do you give refunds without a receipt?
Could you tell me _____?
2 What other models do you have?
Do you know _____?
3 I would like someone to create a website for me.
I would like to have _____.
4 My hair is too long.
I need to get _____.
5 Mark doesn't like that his friend always talks through films.
Mark wishes _____.

5 Choose the correct options to complete the sentences.

1 The interview was too long / long enough. It was over an hour and a half!
2 Sophia felt dissatisfied / dissatisfying with the poor-quality service.
3 It's a great book, but quite frustrated / frustrating at times.
4 I really enjoyed the film. It was such / so entertaining.
5 The flight was supposed / going to leave two hours ago, but there was a delay.

6 Complete the statements and questions in reported speech.

1 'I've worked on this project for a long time.'
Mark said _____.
2 'We'll give you a loan when the business plan is accepted.'
The bank's business advisor told Harry _____.
3 'This song reminds me of my school days.'
My aunt told me _____.
4 'Where are you going to take us for lunch tomorrow?'
Mike and Naomi asked me _____.
5 'Do you think many customers were dissatisfied with the sound quality?'
My manager asked me _____.

7 Complete the sentences with a modal verb: *must*, *might*, *could* or *can't*.

Amy: Have you seen Joe? He was supposed to be here an hour ago.

James: I can see his car outside. This (1) _____ be him now.

Amy: No, Joe left his car here last night.

James: He (2) _____ be at football club. He sometimes has practice on Sundays.

Amy: I've already called Tom and he told me he didn't go today. Do you think he (3) _____ be ill?

James: No, Joe's never ill. Wait! Do you think he (4) _____ be at Sara's house?

Amy: He (5) _____ be at Sara's; she's on holiday. I'm really worried!

8 Complete the sentences with the correct form of the verbs in brackets.

1 If only I _____ (buy) that dress when I saw it. Now it's sold out.

2 If I _____ (not feel) so tired, I would have remembered everyone's names.

3 More people would have bought the product if the company _____ (advertise) it better.

4 I _____ (not turn up) late if you had given me better directions.

5 I wish I _____ (study) Portuguese, so I could understand my colleagues in São Paolo.

9 Choose the correct options to complete the sentences.

1 I usually try to avoid using / use the internet late at night before I go to bed.

2 My colleague had to admit send / sending an embarrassing text to the wrong person.

3 I refuse to read / reading articles that have pointless arguments.

4 We finally persuaded Dad to go to the doctor when he admitted feel / feeling dizzy.

5 The magazine has denied start / starting the rumour and spreading gossip about the singer.

6 When you finish register / registering online, log in and look at the photos I uploaded.

10 Complete the sentences with a defining or non-defining relative clause. Remember to use correct punctuation.

1 *The Grapes of Wrath* is a famous American novel. It is set during the Great Depression.
The Grapes of Wrath _, which is a famous American novel, is set during the Great Depression_ .

2 There is a great restaurant in Bologna. You can eat the best minestrone soup there.
There is a great restaurant in Bologna _____.

3 The Burj al Khalifa is the world's tallest building. It is over 2716 feet high.
The Burj al Khalifa _____.

4 Jennifer Lawrence won Best Actress at the 2013 Oscar Award Ceremony. She had wanted to be a doctor.
Jennifer Lawrence _____.

11 What advice or criticism would you give in these situations? Complete the sentences with the words from the box and the correct form of the verbs in brackets. There may be more than one possible answer.

advisable   good   should have   shouldn't have   understandable

Your friend is coughing and sneezing after walking all day outside without warm clothes.

1 It's _____ _____ _____ the weather before you go out. (check)

2 You _____ _____ _____ a coat and scarf. (wear)

She clicked the 'reply to all' button when sending a friend a personal email at work.

3 It's _____ _____ _____ embarrassed about things like that. (feel)

4 You _____ _____ _____ a personal email at work. (send)

I feel really lonely and depressed at the moment.

5 It's _____ _____ _____ friends. (see)

6 You _____ _____ _____ me sooner. (tell)

12 Find the four incorrect sentences and rewrite them correctly.

1 Dan called. Did you call back him? _____

2 I promise to copy everyone in this time. _____

3 What about your essay? Did you hand in it? _____

4 Did you run Jonas into at the café this afternoon? _____

5 My parents like Susie. She gets on well with them. _____

6 That music is too loud. Can you turn down it? _____

UNIT 1 WHO DO YOU THINK YOU ARE?

IN THIS UNIT YOU

- learn language to talk about identity
- read about identity when speaking a second language
- talk about personal identity
- listen to an immigrant talking about how his identity has changed
- write a comment about peer pressure
- learn about stereotypes
- ▶ watch a video about personal identity

READING
for different purposes

Do you read different types of texts in different ways? How? Think about a novel, a dictionary, a magazine, etc.

SPEAKING
agreeing and disagreeing

In what situations might you need to disagree with someone politely?

LIFE SKILLS

SELF & SOCIETY

understanding stereotypes A stereotype is an idea we have about what someone, or a group of people, is like when we don't know them. What common stereotypes do people have about teenagers, or about elderly people?

A 🔊 Work in pairs. Identify each type of group in the photos and say which similar groups you belong to.

1

2

3

4

B 🔊 Think about each group you belong to and how important that group is to your identity. Choose the two groups you think have the biggest influence on your identity. Then compare with your partner and explain your choice.

5

A The following factors can all influence our personal identity. Number them 1–8 in order of importance to your identity. Number 1 is the most important.

clothes ☐   friends ☐   values ☐   language ☐
studies ☐   interests ☐   family ☐   job ☐

B 🎧 **1.01** Listen to the first part of a podcast interview with a Scottish man who has moved to Japan. Circle the things in the list in Exercise A that he says were important for his sense of identity in the past. Does he mention anything that is not on the list?

C 🎧 **1.02** Listen to the second part of the interview and answer the questions.

1   In general, how does Dylan feel he has changed since moving to Nagoya?
2   Which specific factors in his sense of identity have changed? Why?

D   VOCABULARY: PERSONAL IDENTITY
Match the phrases (1–6) to the definitions (a–f).

1   family values   a)   the kind of family you come from
2   sense of identity   b)   the things you hope to achieve in the future
3   social status   c)   beliefs that you learn from your family
4   family background   d)   position in society; class
5   life goals   e)   your friends
6   social group   f)   the feeling of who you are

E 🗣 **VOCABULARY: PERSONAL IDENTITY**
Work in groups. Ask and answer the questions.

1   Is family background important to your sense of identity? Which family values are important to you?
2   What's the difference between family background and social status? How might they be related to each other?
3   Do you and the people in your social group share the same life goals? Is that important?

⚙ There is a variety of words and phrases that you can use to express agreement, partial agreement, or disagreement. In more formal situations, we often apologise as we disagree.

A 🗣 Work in pairs. What phrases do you already know for agreeing, partially agreeing, and disagreeing? Make a list.

B 🎧 **1.03** Listen to part of a seminar on identity. What does Sean think about expressing personal identity?

C 🗣 Work in pairs. Listen again and complete the phrases from the conversation then compare your answers with another pair. Which phrases are used to agree, partially agree, or disagree?

1   Well, yes, to a _____ extent …
2   _____ and no.
3   I'm _____, but I just don't think that's true.
4   I'm _____ I can't agree.
5   In a _____, you're right, but …
6   I _____ agree more.

D 🗣 Work in small groups. Discuss the question.

Do you think it is important to 'be yourself' at all times, even if sometimes it may upset people?

GRAMMAR: review of past tenses

A LANGUAGE IN CONTEXT Read the blog extract. What was difficult for Akna when she moved to the city?

IDENTITY CRISIS

the blog of a woman living in two worlds   HOME   ABOUT ME   ARCHIVE   LINKS

ABOUT ME

Hi, I'm Akna! I grew up in remote northern Canada, as a member of an indigenous community. My people are Inuit, and up to the age of 18 I spent my days in a very traditional way: fishing and cooking, as well as attending a local school. And then my life changed completely when I met Jordan. Jordan had arrived in my area as an anthropologist a year before I met him, and he was studying our language and traditions. We fell in love and eventually we got married and moved to Montreal. I did try to fit in, but I really suffered from culture shock and felt out of place. I was scared of losing my identity and didn't know who I was anymore. After a long struggle I finally realised that my family background and community had made me who I was, but that my choices have made me who I am today.

NOTICE!

Underline all the past tense verbs in the text. How many past tenses are there? Which auxiliary verb is sometimes used for emphasis?

B ANALYSE Read the extract in Exercise A again.

Form Complete the table with examples from the text.

Tense	Form	Examples
past simple	-ed, irregular forms (was, had, etc)	I **(1)** _____ up in remote northern Canada … … my life **(2)** _____ completely …
past simple with *did* for emphasis	*did* + infinitive without *to*	I **(3)** _____ to fit in …
past continuous	*was/were* + -ing form	… he **(4)** _____ our language …
past perfect	*had* + past participle	… my family background and community **(5)** _____ me who I was …

WHAT'S RIGHT?

○ When I was young, I went fishing almost every day.

○ When I was young, I was going fishing almost every day.

Function Write the names of the correct tenses to match the explanations.

1 _____: This tense describes a completed event, action or state that took place before another past event, action or state. It is used to talk about things that happened before the main action.

2 _____: This tense describes a completed event, action or state in the past. It is usually the main tense used to talk about the past.

3 _____: This tense describes actions or states in progress at a particular time in the past. It is often used to describe background action (e.g. the weather).

C PRACTISE Complete Akna's blog entry with the correct form of the verbs in brackets.

This **(1)** _____ (*happen*) soon after Jordan and I **(2)** _____ (*move*) here. That day, it **(3)** _____ (*snow*) and the wind **(4)** _____ (*blow*) really hard. I **(5)** _____ (*be*) in Montreal for just two months, and I **(6)** _____ (*miss*) my family really badly. The St. Lawrence River **(7)** _____ (*freeze*) over a month before, and I **(8)** _____ (*decide*) to go ice fishing. Some of the local men **(9)** _____ (*fish*) out on the ice, and they **(10)** _____ (*look*) a bit strangely at this young Inuit woman with her traditional equipment. Anyway, I **(11)** _____ (*start*) catching fish, and pretty soon people **(12)** _____ (*notice*) that I **(13)** _____ (*catch*) more than the men with their high-tech equipment! People **(14)** _____ (*applaud*) every time I caught a fish and soon everyone **(15)** _____ (*laugh*) and congratulating me! It really **(16)** _____ (*help*) me feel just a little more at home!

D NOW YOU DO IT Work in groups. Think of a time when you felt out of place or that you didn't fit in. Describe what happened. Did you all have similar experiences?

We read different texts for different purposes and in different ways. Before you read a text, think about why you are going to read it. What kind of information does it contain? What do you hope to learn from it? Why did the author write it?

A Work in pairs. Look at the purposes for reading. For each one, think of types of texts you might read for that purpose. Write as many as you can (both electronic and print).

1 for pleasure *a novel, a story, a poem*
2 to find out about a product you are interested in _____
3 to find out news or opinions _____
4 to learn information for school or work _____
5 to find information you need in order to do something _____

B Look at the text below. Decide what type of text it is. Why might someone choose to read a text like this? Choose from the answers below.

1 Text type: _____
2 Possible reasons for reading the text:
  a) to keep up to date with current developments
  b) to prepare for a meeting at work
  c) to decide whether to watch something
  d) to compare your opinion with someone else's
  e) to decide whether to travel to a place
  f) to research becoming an English teacher

New **country,** new **language,** ... new **identity?**

[1] Take four recent immigrants in an English-speaking country and place them with host families for a month. Ask the families to teach them English and film the results. That's the idea behind *Lost in Translation*, the new show from ABTV, which you sense is going to be a hit. In the first episode broadcast last night, we met a young woman, Amaal, 22, from Somalia, who was staying with the Wilson family. Mr Wilson, a businessman, decided to take Amaal with him to work. The resulting clash of cultures, though predictable, made for fascinating viewing. Back in Somalia, Amaal lived a nomadic life where she tended goats, sheep and cattle, and where she knew everyone around her. Though Mr Wilson did try, in his clumsy way, to teach her, and though Amaal is clearly a very intelligent, sensible young woman, she struggled to make sense of much of what goes on in the anonymous business world. Fortunately, her common sense and ready sense of humour got her through.

[2] The most interesting, and unexpected, aspect of the show, though, was the insight we gain into learning a foreign language. In a mix of English and Somali, Amaal explained that she feels like a different person when she speaks in English. It seems that using another language makes it easier for her to talk about certain things. For example, dating and relationships can be sensitive subjects in her country, parts of which are very conservative. As a result, she finds it easier to talk about relationships between men and women in English. Also, her country has been affected by war. Amaal, who is clearly a very sensitive person, can talk about that more easily in English. It appears to give her some distance from a difficult topic.

[3] However, Amaal also talked about some aspects of speaking English that make her uncomfortable. She worries that as she learns more and more about the world beyond Somalia, she may lose contact with her background. She finds herself being defensive about her identity as a Somali and Somali traditions as she encounters the English-speaking world of business, travel, and culture.

[4] The show is available on demand, so if you missed it, make sure you watch this fascinating insight into language and identity.

C Read the text on page 12 and choose the correct answers.

1 Why was there a 'clash of cultures'?
   a) Amaal wasn't interested in Mr Wilson's business.
   b) The Western workplace was new to Amaal.
   c) Mr Wilson didn't understand anything about farming.

2 What effect did Amaal's sense of humour have at work?
   a) It helped her learn English more quickly.
   b) It helped her deal with a difficult situation.
   c) It made people laugh at her mistakes.

3 Why does Amaal find it easier to talk about relationships in English?
   a) The subject is more sensitive in her own country and language.
   b) English-speaking people know more about that kind of thing.
   c) Mr Wilson teaches her the right vocabulary to use.

4 Why does Amaal find it easier to talk about her country's past in English?
   a) In a foreign language, the topic is less emotional.
   b) English has more ways of talking about war than Somali.
   c) She doesn't like speaking Somali when she is so far from home.

D VOCABULARY: *SENSE*

Underline words and phrases in the text that include or are derived from the word *sense*. Complete the sentences (1–7). Use the definitions in brackets to help you.

1 I couldn't _____ what she was saying to me. (*understand*)
2 We can usually _____ when a family member has a problem. (*feel*)
3 You have to have a _____ to work in this crazy place! (*ability to see the funny side*)
4 My sister is very _____ and cares about other people's feelings. (*understanding of others' emotions*)
5 Try to think before you act and be a little more _____ next time. (*reasonable, practical*)
6 Religion can be a _____ topic of conversation in my country. (*needing to be dealt with carefully*)
7 He's very intelligent, but he doesn't have much _____! (*ability to use good judgment*)

E VOCABULARY: *SENSE*

Work in groups. Discuss the questions.

1 Is your sense of identity connected to your language? Is your identity in your first language the same as your identity when you speak English?
2 What topics do you think are sensitive in the classroom? Should there be classroom discussions of sensitive issues, or is it more sensible for schools to avoid those topics?
3 Which do you think is most important in life – a sense of humour, a sense of responsibility, common sense or a sense of loyalty?

PRONUNCIATION: emphatic *do/did* for contrast

A 1.04 Listen to the conversations. For each of B's responses, notice that the words in italics are stressed.

A: Do you think it's important for friends to share the same values and goals in life?
B: No, but I *do* think it's important to share the same sense of humour.
A: You went to Somalia last year, didn't you?
B: No. I *did* go to Africa, but I didn't go to Somalia.

B 1.05 Work in pairs. Read the conversation. Which two words should be stressed? Underline them, then listen and check. Practise the conversation together.

A: I don't have a big social group, but I do have a few close friends.
B: Did you meet your friends at school?
A: No. I did make some friends there, but we've lost touch now.

A LANGUAGE IN CONTEXT Read the magazine excerpt. Which person remembers a family member's annoying habit? What was it?

FAMILY IDENTITY

Family memories are one of the things that help a family bond as a unit and create a sense of family identity. Even things that used to annoy us sometimes become favourite memories!

Kieran:

My dad always used to throw a cricket ball for me so I could practise my batting. He would never say he was too tired, even after working all day. He was sensitive and really understood how I felt. I try to remember that now when my little boy wants me to play with him!

Louise:

My little sister was always sneaking into my room and trying on my clothes. I used to get annoyed with her because she would leave my nice clothes all over the floor! Now we're the same size, and we're always borrowing each other's clothes!

B ANALYSE Read the excerpt in Exercise A again.

Form Complete the table with examples from the text.

Form	Examples
a *would* (*always/never*) + infinitive without *to*	**(1)** _____
b (*always/never*) *used to* + infinitive without *to*	**(2)** _____
c *be + always + -ing* form (present or past continuous)	**(3)** _____ **(4)** _____

Function Match the structure (a–c) to the rule (1–2).

1 These two structures are used to talk about habits or customs which are only in the past. ☐ ☐
2 This structure is used to talk about present or past habits and customs. ☐

NOTICE!
Find and underline all the examples of ***always*** and ***never*** in the text. Which structures are they used with?

C PRACTISE Complete the family story with one of the structures used to talk about habits. There may be more than one correct answer.

My brother is six years younger than me, and when he was young, he **(1)** _____ (*ask*) me to read him stories. He **(2)** _____ always _____ (*make*) me read the same story about four times, and he **(3)** _____ never _____ (*get*) bored! He **(4)** _____ (*carry*) his favourite book around with him. I **(5)** _____ (*hide*) it so he couldn't find me and make me read it to him! And then he **(6)** _____ (*cry*) and I **(7)** _____ (*feel*) bad. Now I'm always **(8)** _____ (*ask*) him if he wants me to read him a story! It's a family joke.

WHAT'S RIGHT?
○ I was always getting ill on holiday.
○ I always was getting ill on holiday.

D ⟨⟨🔊⟩ NOW YOU DO IT Work in groups. Think of a past habit of yours, or of someone in your family, and tell your group about it. Ask each other questions about the effects of these habits. Afterwards, report back to the class on what you discussed.

I remember that my cousin Laura always used to …
I used to think it was … but now I think …

A Read the contributions to the question-and-answer page. What do you think 'peer pressure' means?

Gina: I live in a small town, and I feel that there's so much pressure on everyone to fit in and have the same identity. Everyone seems to do the same things and go to the same places. People are always criticising what other people do. It's hard because I feel like an outsider, both at work and socially. I feel as if my interests are different to everyone else's, and it's only my online life that keeps me sane! Have other people experienced something similar or is it just me?

Maura: I feel sorry for you, Gina, but remember that it's not true of all small towns. I live in a small town where people are very happy to let you be yourself. Maybe it's more to do with your country or culture, rather than the size of the town. Here, the only place where peer pressure is a problem is in secondary school.

Len: Peer pressure can certainly be a problem at work. I work in finance, and there's so much pressure to wear the right clothes, drive the right car, you know, keep up the high-flyer image. People are always going on about that kind of thing. It doesn't make any sense to me.

GaryG: It's important to remember that peer pressure can also have positive effects. When all my friends were doing well at school, the pressure forced me to work hard too. The same thing is true at work. I know everyone else is working hard so I don't want to let them down. Being yourself doesn't mean you shouldn't think about other people!

Aran: I'm from Thailand, and I'm interested in hearing from people in other countries. Does peer pressure exist in every culture? There is definitely peer pressure in my country, but sometimes it can be positive, like when there's pressure to work hard or do well at school.

B Work in groups. Read Aran's comment again. Make a list of examples of peer pressure within your social or professional group. Discuss whether each example has positive or negative effects.

C With your group, use your list to write an answer to Aran. Include the following information.
- information about your social or political group – country, city, age, occupation(s)
- examples of peer pressure
- whether you think peer pressure is positive or negative and why

D 'Post' your answer on the wall in the classroom. Read the other answers to see if other groups have similar ideas to yours.

HOW TO SAY IT

In my social group, there's a lot of pressure to ..., and I think that's ...

People in my town/college/office are always saying that ...

In my last school/job, people were always ... They would ...

LifeSkills

UNDERSTANDING STEREOTYPES

- Be aware of different kinds of stereotypes.
- Consider the stereotypes you hold and what they are based on.
- Think about the negative impact of certain stereotypes.

A Work in pairs. Read the joke in the first paragraph of the article. What positive and negative stereotypes does the joke imply about each of the nationalities?

B In your opinion, are national stereotypes based on actual characteristics? Read the article to find out whether the study supports your opinion or not.

SCIENCE GETS THE LAST LAUGH ON ETHNIC JOKES

'HEAVEN IS WHERE THE POLICE ARE ENGLISH, the cooks are French, the mechanics are German, the romantic poets are Italian, and everything is organised by the Swiss. Hell is where the police are German, the cooks are English, the mechanics are French, the romantic poets are Swiss, and everything is organised by the Italians.'

Obviously, the national stereotypes in this old joke are generalisations, but such stereotypes are often said 'to exist for a reason.' Is there actually a sliver of truth in them? Not likely, an international research team now says.

The study, which compares 'typical' personalities in many cultures with the personalities of real individuals from those cultures, appears in Friday's issue of the journal *Science*, published by AAAS, the non-profit science society.

Generalisations about cultures or nationalities can be a source of identity, pride … and bad jokes. But they can also cause a great deal of harm. Both history and current events are full of examples in which unfavourable stereotypes contribute to prejudice, discrimination, persecution or even genocide.

'National and cultural stereotypes do play an important role in how people perceive themselves and others, and being aware that these are not trustworthy is a useful thing,' said the author of the study, Robert McCrae of the National Institute on Aging.

The new findings also call into question other stereotypes, such as age stereotypes, according to McCrae.

The researchers tested the possibility that cultural stereotypes might be based, at least partly, on real experiences that people have interacting with each other. If this were true, then such stereotypes would reflect the average personality of real members of that culture.

But McCrae and his colleagues studied real and perceived personalities in roughly 50 countries, and found this wasn't the case.

'These are, in fact, unfounded stereotypes. They don't come from looking around you and doing your own averaging of people's personality traits,' McCrae said.

NBCNEWS.COM

Self and Society
Work and Career
Study and Learning

C 🗣 **Work in groups. Make a list of stereotypes about your region, country or culture. Then discuss the questions.**

1 Are most of the things on your list positive or negative? Are they true? How do they make you feel?
2 Which of these things do you think cause cultural stereotyping?
   • people from your country living in other countries
   • impressions tourists get when they visit your country
   • the media
   • jokes and other forms of oral stereotyping
3 How can people avoid believing stereotypes about other countries?

HOW TO SAY IT

People are always saying …
The media is always showing …
People assume that …
Teenagers are seen as …
People tend to think that teenagers …

D 🗣 **Work in pairs. Look at the people in the diagram. For each one, write as many stereotypes as you can. Then compare your diagram with another pair.**

People say that teenagers are lazy and sleep too much.

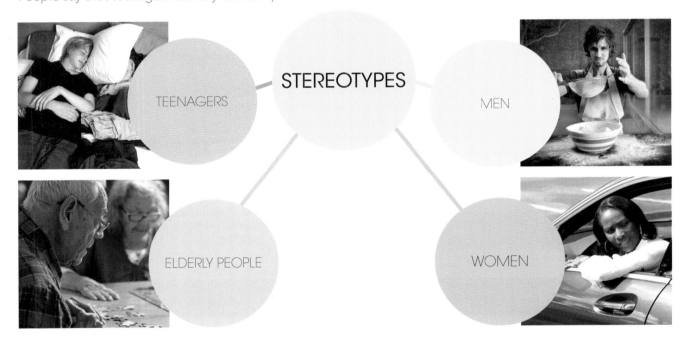

TEENAGERS   STEREOTYPES   MEN

ELDERLY PEOPLE   WOMEN

E 🗣 **Work in pairs. For each set of people in Exercise D, decide what the consequences of the negative stereotypes you have identified might be.**

Someone might not give a hard-working teenager a job because of the stereotype that teenagers are lazy.

F 🗣 **Work in groups. Discuss the questions.**

1 Do you feel you now have a better understanding of stereotypes? In what ways?
2 Will you be more able to recognise stereotypes in the future when they refer to you?

REFLECT … How can the skill of understanding stereotypes be useful to you in **Work & Career** and **Study & Learning**?

RESEARCH …

Find out about a person who has been stereotyped and the negative impact this has had on them. In your next lesson, tell the class about the person you read about.

Language wrap-up

A Complete the conversation with the words from the box. One of the options can be used more than once. (6 points)

> family   identity   life   sense   social

Alicia: Do you think your **(1)** _____ background has made you who you are?

James: Well, yes, I suppose it's given me a strong sense of **(2)** _____. And we all learn values from our parents, don't we?

Alicia: Hmm, it's not always easy to make **(3)** _____ of your own past. I'm not sure how much my family made me who I am today. I have very different **(4)** _____ goals from my parents. I think my sense of identity is really connected to my **(5)** _____ group.

James: Maybe, but I'm sure your parents influenced you, too. They taught you common **(6)** _____, didn't they?

B Choose the correct options to complete the conversation. (6 points)

Alicia: Yes, of course! But things like social **(1)** level / status are very important to my parents and not as important to me. The people in my social **(2)** crowd / group come from all kinds of backgrounds.

James: But your parents have influenced you in different ways. You and your dad have exactly the same sense of **(3)** funny / humour. And you and your mum are both very **(4)** sensitive / sensible when people are unhappy or upset.

Alicia: That's true. My mum and I can both **(5)** know / sense what the other person is feeling.

James: On the other hand, she's very **(6)** sensible / thinking, but you're …

Alicia: Hey!

> **10–12 correct:** I can talk about personal identity and use words and phrases with *sense*.
> **0–9 correct:** Look again at the vocabulary sections on pages 10 and 13.   **SCORE:**   /12

Choose the correct options to complete the text. (12 points)

When I was a child, my dad **(1)** had done / was always doing silly things. For example, sometimes, we **(2)** had waited / would be waiting in a queue or something and he **(3)** used to / was used to try to stand on his head. Things like that. He did it even after I **(4)** had asked / would ask him to just behave like a normal, sensible dad. He never **(5)** used to / would listen and I **(6)** found / was finding it very embarrassing. My uncle (my dad's brother) **(7)** used to tell / had told my dad to act his age. I remember he **(8)** would say / was saying, 'Act your age, not your shoe size!' My dad **(9)** had tried / did try, but soon, he **(10)** was forgetting / would forget and do something silly. Well, now I'm grown up, and so is my dad. Now I **(11)** would always ask / am always asking him to do some of the things that **(12)** used to embarrass / were embarrassing me. But my dad is 90 years old, and he doesn't have as much energy now. It's funny how we don't appreciate things until they are gone!

> **10–12 correct:** I can use past tenses and expressions describing habits in the past.
> **0–9 correct:** Look again at the grammar sections on pages 11 and 14.   **SCORE:**   /12

A Read the article. In your own words, explain what advice the writer gives.

How to survive
CULTURE SHOCK

Are you thinking of moving to another country, either to work or to study? If you are, there's a chance you'll face a number of challenges. You might find it hard to make sense of your new country or you may feel that people are always stereotyping you and not seeing the real you. What can you do about it?

Well, first of all, lighten up and don't be so sensitive! You may encounter stereotypes, but now's your chance to prove them wrong! And no one expects you to understand your new environment straight away. People are generally happy to give you time to work things out. Ask questions and don't be afraid to make mistakes. People usually enjoy explaining their culture to people from other countries.

Secondly, if you find that people expect certain things from you because of their stereotypes, don't see it as a problem. See it as your chance to show them that you're an individual. Try to explain, in a sensitive way, why their view of people from your country is wrong or incomplete.

Above all, you have to be open to new experiences and not worry about losing your identity. Instead, you need to be ready to accept your new identity. Welcome to your new life!

B Look back at the article and choose *T* (true) or *F* (false). The writer ...

1 uses a question to engage the reader.	T / F
2 uses a conversational, chatty style.	T / F
3 mentions a few potential problems and then gives solutions to those problems.	T / F

C You are going to write an article giving advice to people who are going abroad to study or work. First, make notes in your notebook.

1 Make a note of two or three problems someone who has recently arrived in a new country might face.

2 For each problem you have identified, make notes on what advice you could give.

D Now use your notes to write your article. Write approximately 200 words.

HOW ARE YOU DOING?

○ I have tried to engage the reader in the article.
○ I have used a conversational, chatty style.
○ I have given clear advice on the problems.

UNIT 2   GLOBAL VIEWS

IN THIS UNIT YOU

- ⚙ learn language to talk about globalisation and taking social action
- ⚙ listen to a discussion about globalisation
- ⚙ write a formal email to organise a meeting
- ⚙ read about shopping locally
- ⚙ talk about the advantages and disadvantages of social media
- ⚙ learn about effective internet search terms
- ▶ watch a video about the advantages of eating locally-produced food

LISTENING
discourse markers

When you listen to native speakers, do you sometimes hear words or phrases that don't seem to have much meaning? Why do you think people use them?

WRITING
a formal email

When do you need to write a formal email? How is a formal email different from an informal email?

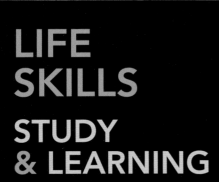

LIFE SKILLS
STUDY & LEARNING

understanding internet search terms
The internet provides massive amounts of information on almost every topic. What are some effective ways you have found to search for information on the internet?

A 🗣 **Work in pairs. Look at the photos and discuss the questions.**

1 Which, if any, of these aspects of globalisation affect your country? In what ways?
2 What are the positive and negative features of each of these aspects of globalisation?
   a) in general   b) specifically for your country

1 trade

2 human migration

3 communication

B 🗣 **Work in groups. What other aspects of globalisation can you think of? Do you think they have mostly positive or mostly negative consequences? Why?**

LISTENING: understanding discourse markers

⚙ Discourse markers or 'fillers', such as *like, you know* or *well* are often used in informal speech. Such words and phrases can have several meanings, but when used as fillers, they don't mean very much at all. Fillers are often used to give the speaker time to think about what they want to say.

A 🎧 **1.06** Listen to the five people discussing globalisation. Write the missing discourse markers.

Speaker 1 _____, it's easier for countries to export goods …

Speaker 2 … companies increase their profits by, _____, setting up factories in poorer countries …

Speaker 3 _____, you see the same fast-food restaurants … wherever you go.

Speaker 4 I _____ think it's sad that regional cultures are disappearing …

Speaker 5 and … _____ … that helps everyone.

B Listen again and match the speakers (1–5) to their opinions of globalisation (a–e).

Speaker 1	**a)**	it benefits economies
Speaker 2	**b)**	it destroys local cultures
Speaker 3	**c)**	it harms local businesses
Speaker 4	**d)**	it improves communication
Speaker 5	**e)**	it creates inequality

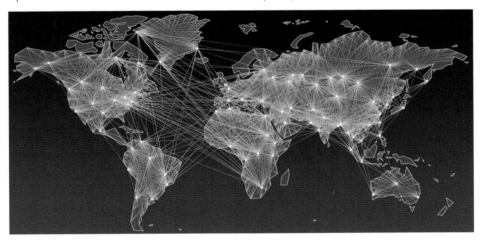

C VOCABULARY: GLOBALISATION
Choose the definitions that match the words or phrases in bold.

1 'There's been huge **economic growth** in recent decades.'
   a) increase in size of the economy   **b)** decrease in size of the economy

2 'Companies increase their **profits** by setting up factories in poorer countries.'
   a) financial gain   **b)** financial loss

3 '**Multinational** companies are completely taking over.'
   a) in one country   **b)** in many countries

4 '**Regional** cultures are disappearing.'
   a) local   **b)** international

5 'The same music and films **dominate** popular culture everywhere.'
   a) destroy   **b)** control

6 'The internet **facilitates** information sharing.'
   a) makes easier   **b)** encourages

D VOCABULARY: GLOBALISATION
Work in pairs. Do you agree with each of the statements in Exercise C? Explain why.

GRAMMAR: verbs with stative and dynamic uses

A LANGUAGE IN CONTEXT Read the text. What positive aspects of multinational corporations are mentioned?

MULTINATIONAL SPREAD

Walk around almost any city in the world and you see signs advertising multinational corporations. These companies are having a major effect on emerging economies around the world. They often have branches in many countries and can offer varied job opportunities, especially for young people. A recent study showed that more young people than ever are thinking of applying for jobs with such companies. However, some people think that large companies take money out of the country. They would prefer local companies to do well. Whatever the pros and cons are, it looks as if multinational corporations are here to stay.

> **NOTICE!**
> Underline the verbs in the text that are in the simple form. Then circle the same verbs that are used in the continuous form. How does the form of the verb change the meaning?

B ANALYSE Read the text in Exercise A again.

Form & Function Read the information and complete the table with examples from the text.

> Some verbs are rarely used in continuous forms. They are called stative verbs because they usually refer to states or conditions that continue over a period of time, e.g. *know, prefer* or *agree*. However, some stative verbs commonly have both stative and dynamic uses with different meanings.

	Verbs with stative and dynamic uses	
	Stative use (simple verb form)	**Dynamic use (continuous verb form)**
be	*Multinationals are huge companies.* (permanent state, general truth)	*You're not being serious!* (acting or behaving)
have	**(1)** _____ (possession, characteristics)	**(2)** _____ (causing, experiencing)
see	**(3)** _____ (notice, observe, understand)	*Janie has been seeing Tom for two years now.* (meet or date)
think	**(4)** _____ (have an opinion)	**(5)** _____ (the process of thought)

C PRACTISE Choose the correct options to complete the sentences. Discuss your choices in pairs.

1 I think / am thinking of applying for a job with a large company.
2 We don't have / are not having an office in Australia.
3 Stop behaving like that! You are / are being ridiculous!
4 Yes, I see / am seeing your point of view.
5 What do you think / are you thinking of multinational corporations?
6 There are / are being fewer jobs for young people these days.
7 I saw Jim and Davina having dinner together. Do they see / Are they seeing each other?

> **WHAT'S RIGHT?**
> ○ She is being an intern at a multinational company.
> ○ She's an intern at a multinational company.

D NOW YOU DO IT Work in pairs. Choose a roleplay card. Plan three ways to convince your partner of your opinion. Use some of these verbs: *be, have, look, see, think.* Then debate with your partner.

> **Student A**
> You agree with the spread of multinational corporations.

> **Student B**
> You disagree with the spread of multinational corporations.

SPEAKING: talking about social media

A Read the definition of social media. What social media do you use?

Web terms: Your questions answered

Q: What is social media?

A: The term *social media* refers to websites and networks that help us communicate with each other. It includes websites where we post comments, share photos or videos or interact with friends and large groups of people. Social media is contributing to globalisation by connecting everyone around the world.

B 🎧 **1.07** Listen to three people giving their opinions about social media. Complete the table with the information.

Speaker	Social media used	Advantage / Disadvantage
1		
2		
3		

C Think about one form of social media you use. Make brief notes to complete the table.

Social media	
How often you use it	
Advantages	
Disadvantages	
Effect on communication	

D 🗣 Independent Speaking Work in pairs to do the task below. Then change roles. When you have finished, tell the class what you learnt about your partner.

Student A
Tell your partner about the type of social media you have chosen.

Student B
As you listen, take notes in your notebook.

PRONUNCIATION: voiced and voiceless consonant sounds

A 🎧 **1.08** Listen to each pair of words. 1) Put your hand on your throat and say the first word of each pair. You should feel a vibration. 2) Put the palm of your hand a few centimetres in front of your mouth and say the second word in each pair. You should feel a puff of air after the first letter.

a) vast   fast   c) base   pace   e) goal   coal
b) do   too   d) drain   train

B 🎧 **1.09** Listen to five sentences. Choose the word you hear in Exercise A.

C 🗣 Work in pairs. Take turns saying one word from each pair in Exercise A. Your partner will try to identify which word you are saying.

GRAMMAR: repeated and double comparatives

A LANGUAGE IN CONTEXT Read the opinions. Which person do you agree with more?

'Communication <u>has got faster and faster</u>, and all forms of social media are becoming more and more popular. People around the world feel closer to each other and understand each other better. The more we understand each other, the more peaceful the world will be.'
Kate, Windsor, UK

'We live in a global village, and we have friends all over the world. But the faster communication becomes, the less interesting our messages become. We send more and more messages about unimportant things. Sometimes slower is better.'
Luca, Modena, Italy

NOTICE!
Look at the underlined phrase. Why do you think *faster* is repeated?

B ANALYSE Read the opinions in Exercise A again.

Form & Function Complete the table with examples from the text.

Form	Function	Examples
comparative + *and* + comparative *more and more* + multisyllable adjective *less and less* + multisyllable adjective	**Repeated comparatives** used to emphasise something that is changing	**(1)** Communication has got _____ and _____ **(2)** … social media are becoming _____ and _____.
the + *more* (+ noun) + verb phrase, *the* + comparative + verb phrase *the* + comparative + *the* + noun + verb phrase	**Double comparatives** used to describe how two things are changing at the same time, or how one thing changes as a result of a change in something else	**(3)** … better. _____ we understand …, _____ the world will be. **(4)** But _____ communication becomes, _____ our messages become.

More and *less* can be used with nouns: *The more work I get, the less time I have.*
We send more and more instant messages these days.
More and *less* can also be used on their own: *The more I see, the less I understand.*
If we use a comparative adjective with a noun, we add *the* before the noun:
The better the teacher, the quicker you learn.
Some expressions can leave out the verb: *The sooner the better.* (NOT: *The sooner it is, the better it is.*)

WHAT'S RIGHT?
○ Social media is getting more and more powerful.
○ Social media is getting more powerful and more powerful.

C PRACTISE Complete the sentences with the words in brackets. Use either a repeated or a double comparative.

1 People are becoming _____ towards people in other countries. (*sympathetic*)
2 The world is becoming _____ with each new form of media that appears. (*small*)
3 _____ I use Twitter, the _____ I am in its possibilities. (*more, interested*)
4 _____ I read his blog, _____ I find it. (*more, funny*)
5 _____ you use social media, _____ it becomes. (*more, confusing*)
6 _____ broadband becomes, _____ it is to transmit information. (*fast, easy*)

D **NOW YOU DO IT** Complete the sentences with your own ideas and then compare your answers in pairs.

1 The more I _____, _____.
2 The less we _____, _____.
3 I believe the world is becoming _____ and _____.

A Work in pairs. How do you prefer to shop: in a small local shop, in a large department store or online? Tell your partner and explain why. Then read the magazine article and find out if any your ideas are mentioned.

GOING LOCAL

[1]It's Saturday morning and the farmer's market in Notting Hill, London, is already busy with shoppers looking for locally-grown fresh fruit and vegetables, as well as locally produced eggs, cheese and bread. 'I'm here because I want to **support** local farmers, and I feel that I'm buying real food that has a connection to the place I live in,' says Emma Simpson. 'It's also just nice to meet the farmers and producers – you get a real sense of community.'

[2]Markets like this are becoming increasingly popular in towns and cities in the UK as consumers move away from food produced and packaged by large multinational companies. '"Fresh food" in supermarkets is rarely fresh,' says Tom Nichols, who **campaigns** for local farmers and growers. 'It's usually been packed and refrigerated several days or weeks before it reaches the shop. It often uses additives to extend shelf life and also consumes more energy as it is transported over long distances.'

[3]Small Business Saturday is an initiative that helps to **promote** local businesses. It takes place on the first shopping Saturday in December and is intended to encourage shoppers to do their shopping at small independent shops. 'It helps to **boost** our business at the start of the Christmas shopping season,' says Anne Newton. 'The Small Business Saturday campaign definitely **generates** more interest in shopping locally.'

[4]Large supermarkets often have lower prices and are able to provide a greater choice, especially of larger consumer items such as furniture or household appliances, but most of the money spent there goes to owners and suppliers in other countries. Small businesses can't compete with their prices and still make a profit, which is why the campaign to go local is so important.

'We **value** the experience of going into these small shops, talking to the owners and finding out about how things are made,' says Jack Wilson. 'That's something you won't find in big department stores or online.' And for lots of people, it's this experience that makes it worth paying a little more for certain items.

[5]**Participating** in the 'go local' movement doesn't mean completely ignoring the advantages of large stores or of online shopping, but it does mean thinking about ways to spend your money that can help **sustain** the local economy in the face of increasing globalisation of the manufacturing and food industries.

B Work in pairs and answer the questions.

1 Find at least six reasons for shopping locally that are mentioned in the article.
2 Find two reasons for shopping in a large supermarket or department store.
3 Is the writer of this article for or against 'going local'? How do you know?

C VOCABULARY: VERBS FOR TAKING SOCIAL ACTION

Match the words in bold in the article to the synonyms (1–8). Use the infinitive form.

1 help _____
2 appreciate _____
3 create _____
4 fight _____
5 take part _____
6 keep alive _____
7 encourage _____
8 increase _____

D VOCABULARY: VERBS FOR TAKING SOCIAL ACTION

Work in pairs. Choose the correct options to complete the sentences. Then discuss the questions.

1 How do your shopping habits sustain / promote local businesses?
2 How do shop owners in your town or city try to value / generate business?
3 What could shoppers do to generate / support small shops in your neighbourhood?
4 What do you campaign / value about the experience of shopping in small shops?

WRITING: a formal email

We can use different levels of formality in English to suggest particular meanings. More formal language can be used to be respectful to people we don't know very well, or who are more senior to us or if want to appear more serious. We can use less formal language if we want to seem friendlier or if we know the person we are talking to well.

A Work in pairs. In which situations would you need to send a formal email? Brainstorm ideas and tell the class.

B Read the emails about arranging a global citizenship meeting. Which email is more formal? Which language helps you identify it?

Hi Kathy,

Thanks so much for volunteering to help organise the meeting about global citizenship.
Can you contact our guest speaker, Andrew Scott, with more information? He's been to lots of places and seen global citizenship projects in action. Ask him:
– date: 28th or 31st March – which does he prefer?
– venue: Beckett Auditorium
His email address is: andrew01@netglobe.com
Oh, and see if he has any photos of places he's visited recently. It would be great if he could base the talk on real examples. The more examples we can give people, the better.

Thanks a lot!

Jerry

Dear Mr Scott,

My name is Kathy Allen. Jerry Greenlow has asked me to write to you about the global citizenship meeting. Thank you for agreeing to be our guest speaker. We're all looking forward to meeting you and hearing about your experiences.

The meeting will take place on campus at the Beckett Auditorium. There are two possible dates: 28th or 31st March. Could you please let us know which one you would prefer? The sooner you can do that, the sooner we can finalise the other details. We would also appreciate it if you could bring any photos you have from recent trips. Examples will really help people understand what it means to be a global citizen.

Please contact me if you have any questions.

Regards,

Kathy Allen

C Work in pairs. Are the expressions formal or informal? Tick the correct column and discuss your answers.

		Formal	Informal
1	Dear Mr Scott,	☐	☐
2	Hi Andy!	☐	☐
3	Thanks very much.	☐	☐
4	Thanks a lot!	☐	☐
5	With love,	☐	☐
6	Sincerely,	☐	☐

To do

Email guest speaker (Carol Sinclair) for global citizenship meeting.

Details: Victory Hotel, either 5th September @ 6pm or 19th September @ 8pm.

Ask if she needs any equipment for the talk.

D You have agreed to help organise a meeting. Write an email based on the note on the right.

LifeSkills

UNDERSTANDING INTERNET SEARCH TERMS

- Determine what information you need to find.
- Choose effective search terms.
- Evaluate search results and refine your search if necessary.

A Read the essay topic and underline the key words. Make notes on what kind of information you will need to include in the essay.

> Choose two international fast-food chains that have branches in India.
> Describe the impact they have had on the local economy and discuss whether these effects have been mainly positive or negative.

B 🗣 Work in pairs. Discuss the internet search terms. How effective are they? What results do you think you would get?

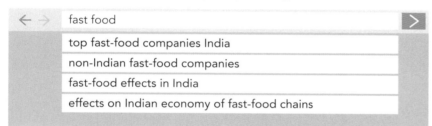

← →	fast food	>
	top fast-food companies India	
	non-Indian fast-food companies	
	fast-food effects in India	
	effects on Indian economy of fast-food chains	

HOW TO SAY IT 🗣

The problem with this search term is that it's too specific / not specific enough / too general.

This search term would probably return results that ...

C 🗣 Work in pairs. Many search engines allow you to refine your search in various ways. Discuss what each of these five searches means.

- fast-food restaurants in India
- India AND food AND industry
- McDonald's OR KFC India
- India culture -celebrity
- India * industry

D 🗣 Work in groups. Think of the last time you used a search engine.
1. Did you find the information you wanted?
2. Is there anything that you would do differently next time you do an internet search? What? Why? Share your ideas.

E Work in pairs. A search engine can give a wide variety of results in response to a keyword search. Discuss which ones below might be useful for the essay in Exercise A, and why.

← →　india globalisation　　　　　　　　　　　　　 >

India globalisation
Influence of globalisation on developing countries
www.globalmonitor.com/globalization/developing-countries.html
India has benefited from globalisation, but … There have been a number of negative effects on local culture …

American fast food? No thanks!
www.blogmasterglobal.com/vijay
It's time we got foreign influences out of India … We need to protect our culture. In my experience, we've been affected by foreign investment …

IBC NEWS Fire strikes fast-food outlet, Delhi, India
indiabc.com/headlines/delhi-fire.html
A fire broke out in a BestBurger restaurant in the early hours yesterday morning … The police have described the damage as 'devastating' …

India fast-food industry statistics
www.india-food.in/statistics/
This page contains various statistics related to the fast-food industry in India … Local companies … International companies … Public opinion …

F Work in groups. Complete the Internet Research Plan for the task below.

You are going to study the effect of globalisation on your local economy. Your tutor has asked your group to prepare a short presentation for the next lesson. You have been asked to include some specific statistics, as well as broad concepts.

Internet Research Plan
Topic to be researched: _____
Information we want to find: _____
Key phrases we might use in searches: _____
Search terms to try: _____　　_____　　_____

G Tell the class about your Internet Research Plan. Listen to the other plans and take notes about good ideas you would like to add to your plan.

H Work in groups. Discuss the questions.
1 Do you feel you now have a better understanding of internet search terms? Give examples of things you have learnt.
2 Will you apply what you have learnt when you are using the internet for research? Why or why not?

RESEARCH …

Make notes for an internet research plan on the essay topic below.

What effect has globalisation had on work and employment in your country? Give examples from two different industries and explain how jobs and working conditions have been affected.

 REFLECT … How can the skill of understanding internet search terms be useful to you in **Work & Career** and **Self & Society**?

Language wrap-up

1 VOCABULARY

Complete the paragraph with the words from the box. (12 points)

> boost campaign dominated economic growth facilitate generating
> multinational profits promote regional support value

Globalisation has had a great impact on the **(1)** _____ of emerging economies.
Many **(2)** _____ companies have set up factories and offices around the world
that create employment and **(3)** _____ cheaper production, while at the same
time **(4)** _____ huge **(5)** _____ for themselves. Many countries have
benefited dramatically from this process. Some experts, however, are worried that the
global economy will become **(6)** _____ by a few powerful companies and that
(7) _____ cultures and traditional skills will disappear.
In contrast with the trend toward increasing globalisation, some communities are seeing
more people who **(8)** _____ the experience of shopping locally. People are going
to local farmers' markets to **(9)** _____ local growers and producers. Small Business
Saturday in December is also part of a growing **(10)** _____ to **(11)** _____ local
businesses and **(12)** _____ profits for local shops.

> **10–12 correct:** I can talk about globalisation and social action.
> **0–9 correct:** Look again at the vocabulary sections on pages 22, 26 and 27. **SCORE:**   /12

2 GRAMMAR

Choose the correct options to complete the conversation. (12 points)

Vicky: I've been reading a lot recently about the effects of globalisation on the world
economy.

Alex: Really? **(1)** Do you think / Are you thinking it's a good thing, or not?

Vicky: That's difficult to say. There are many advantages. For example, companies now
(2) have / are having factories all over the world, so economies are more closely
connected. **(3)** More connected / The more connected economies become, the
more we depend on each other. On the other hand, there are disadvantages,
too. These days, many countries **(4)** have / are having financial problems caused
by economic issues in other countries around the world. It's becoming **(5)** more
and more / the more and more difficult to avoid a global economic crisis in a
globalised world.

Alex: I **(6)** see / am seeing what you mean. But the internet makes it
(7) easier and easier / more and more easy to share information. **(8)** More /
The more we communicate, **(9)** better / the better we will understand each other.

Vicky: That's true. Now, it **(10)** is / is being **(11)** more common and more common /
more and more common to have friends and colleagues all over the world.

Alex: I **(12)** think / am thinking of going to the café. Why don't we go together and talk
about it a bit more?

Vicky: Good idea!

> **10–12 correct:** I can use verbs with stative and dynamic uses and repeated and double
> comparatives.
> **0–9 correct:** Look again at the grammar sections on pages 23 and 25. **SCORE:**   /12

A 🔊 **1.10** 🎙 Listen to someone describing the photo. Take notes on the main points the speaker makes. Use the following headings. Then compare your notes in pairs.

Where it is _____
A description of the people _____
_____
What they are doing _____
_____
Anything unusual or interesting _____

B Listen again and tick the points the speaker mentions.

The speaker …
- ☐ describes the background
- ☐ describes the foreground
- ☐ describes the person who took the photo
- ☐ describes the people and what they are doing
- ☐ describes the general setting and context
- ☐ makes an inference about where the people come from
- ☐ makes an inference about the relationship between the people

C 🎙 Look at the photo below. Prepare to describe it. Make notes with your own ideas under the following headings. Then compare your ideas in pairs.

- Where was it taken?
- Who are they?
- What are they doing?
- Are they doing anything unusual or interesting?

D 🎙 Work in groups. Present your description.

HOW ARE YOU DOING?
- ⚪ I described all the details in the photo.
- ⚪ I spoke clearly.
- ⚪ I varied the tone of my voice.

UNIT 3 FAME AND FORTUNE

IN THIS UNIT YOU

- ⚙ learn language to talk about fame
- ⚙ read about the drawbacks of wanting to be famous
- ⚙ talk about the advantages and disadvantages of being famous
- ⚙ listen to a gossip columnist's opinions about different levels of fame
- ⚙ write a blog post about someone you admire
- ⚙ learn about evaluating arguments
- ▶ watch a video about an actor working in Los Angeles

READING
for different purposes
Why do you think we read different types of texts in different ways?

SPEAKING
clarifying misunderstandings
What kinds of phrases can you use to explain or clarify what you are saying when someone misunderstands you?

LIFE SKILLS

WORK & CAREER

evaluating arguments The word *argument* has two meanings. It can be a disagreement or it can be ideas and evidence that someone presents to convince other people to agree. Think of a time when you argued for or against something. Were you able to convince other people to agree with you?

A Work in pairs. Who do you think are five of the most famous people in the world? Try to think of a variety of famous people, not just entertainers. Use the photos to help you. Share your ideas with the class.

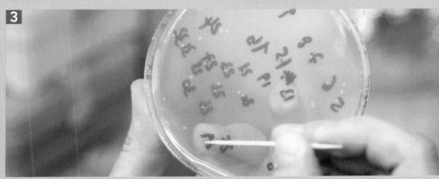

B Work in groups. Do you think the famous people you chose in Exercise A are different or special compared to ordinary people? If so, how?

A LANGUAGE IN CONTEXT Read the magazine article. Was each person's experience of fame positive or negative? Why?

The artist *Andy Warhol* once said that everyone would be famous for 15 minutes. Here we look at two people who have had their 15 minutes of fame and what the experience meant to them.

STEVE JENNINGS was just 17 when he appeared as Des in the popular TV series *Angels* back in the 90s. He became famous overnight, but Steve said no one had told him what to expect and how to deal with it. Although he enjoyed aspects of his celebrity, he admitted that he would do things differently if he became famous now, and confessed that he had had to get help to deal with the pressures of fame.

And then there's **TOM REYNOLDS** from San Diego, who unexpectedly inherited a fortune from an uncle he never knew and became famous when the news was widely publicised by reporters. Within a short time, Tom had spent the whole of his inheritance and ended up living on the streets. He commented that people in a similar situation should get advice on handling and investing their money. But he also suggested that lots of people might not admit that they need help.

B ANALYSE Read the article in Exercise A again.

Form Answer the questions. Then complete the table with the correct verb or modal forms.

1   In reported speech, what usually happens to the verb which comes after the reporting verb? Does the tense change?
2   Now look at the reporting verbs you underlined in the article. Does the verb that follows the reporting verb always change form in reported speech?

> **NOTICE!**
> Find and underline five reporting verbs in the text. Can you think of any more examples?

No tense change	Examples
past perfect → past perfect	Direct: *'I hadn't thought about what fame would really be like.'* Reported: *He admitted that he* **(3)** _____ *about what fame would really be like.*
Modal change	**Examples**
can → could may → might must → had to will → would	Direct: *'I may never work in television again.'* Reported: *He suggested (that) he* **(4)** _____ *never work in television again.*
No modal change	**Examples**
could – could should – should might – might would – would	Direct: *'Would you do things differently?'* Reported: *She asked if he* **(5)** _____ *do things differently.*

> **WHAT'S RIGHT?**
> ○ He said he had to give an interview yesterday.
> ○ He said he must give an interview yesterday.

C PRACTISE Rewrite the direct quotes in reported speech with the reporting verbs in brackets.

1   Andrew: 'I would like to see Lily Allen in concert.' (*said*)

   _____

2   *Entertainment Weekly*: 'Pharrel Williams may perform at the new stadium.' (*reported*)

   _____

3   Clare: 'Will I see some celebrities during my holiday in Los Angeles?' (*asked*)

   _____

4   Security guard: 'You have to leave your cameras at the door.' (*told us*)

   _____

5   Dylan: 'I had never used Twitter before went to university.' (*said*)

   _____

D 🗣 **NOW YOU DO IT** Work in pairs. Complete the statements about the disadvantages of fame and then tell your partner what you think. Afterwards, report your partner's opinions to another pair.

Celebrities have to / don't have to …
Famous people can/can't …

If I were famous, I would/wouldn't …
It would/wouldn't be difficult to …

LISTENING: to a gossip columnist

A 🗣 Work in pairs and discuss the questions.

1 Does being a *celebrity* mean the same as being *famous*?
2 Do you think all famous people are celebrities?

B 🗣 Work in pairs. Look at these photos of famous people. Say if you know each person and what you know about them. Which people are celebrities?

C 👂 **1.11** 🗣 Listen and then discuss the questions as a class.

1 According to the gossip columnist, what is the difference between A-, B- and C-list celebrities?
2 Look at the people in Exercise B that you considered to be celebrities. In your opinion, what categories do they belong to?
3 Think of some famous people in your country. According to the definitions of A-, B- and C-list celebrities, which category would each person be in?

D VOCABULARY: WAYS TO BECOME FAMOUS
Listen again. Complete the phrases with the words from the box. Then add any other ways to become famous you can think of.

break	cause	come up with	discover	inherit	run	write

1 _____ a world record
2 _____ a global company
3 _____ a fortune
4 _____ a best-selling novel
5 _____ a cure for a disease
6 _____ a scandal
7 _____ a new invention/idea

E 🗣 **VOCABULARY: WAYS TO BECOME FAMOUS**
Work in pairs. Think of three people who became famous for one of the reasons in Exercise D. Do you think they are celebrities? If so, are they A-, B- or C-listers? Why? Write sentences about them as in the example below.

British athlete Kelly Holmes became famous for being the first British woman to win two gold medals in the same Olympic Games when she won the 800-metre and 1500-metre races in Greece in 2004. She is now in her 40s and is actively involved in promoting athletics to people of all ages. I think she would be considered a B-list celebrity because she's probably only well-known in the UK.

F 🗣 Work with another pair. Talk about your ideas.
We said Kelly Holmes became famous because she won two gold medals at the 2004 Olympic Games.

When you've identified why you're reading something, the next step is to identify how to read it effectively. Different texts require different reading techniques.

A Match the text types (a–j) to the ways you normally read each one (1–4).

a) newspaper articles ☐   f) textbooks ☐
b) novels/stories ☐   g) internet articles ☐
c) reference books ☐   h) telephone directories ☐
d) magazine articles ☐   i) poetry or lyrics ☐
e) advertisements ☐   j) text messages ☐

1 **Skimming:** Looking quickly at an article or a book to get a general idea of what it is about. This includes looking at visuals, headings and subheadings.
2 **Scanning:** Looking for specific information in a text, such as headings and key words.
3 **Reading in detail:** Reading a text carefully in order to learn concepts and details. This often involves marking important information or taking notes.
4 **General reading:** Reading a text completely, but without concentrating on learning specific information.

B Read the first question below and write the best strategy (1–4) from Exercise A to use to answer it. Then read the text in that way to find the answer. Do questions 2–5 in the same way.

1 What is the text about? ☐ _____
2 What careers did children want to have 25 years ago? What careers do they want to have now? ☐ _____
3 What has caused the changes in children's career ambitions, and how does the author feel about these changes? ☐ _____
4 According to the author, what has made people believe that it's easy to become famous and wealthy? ☐ _____
5 According to the author, why do fame and fortune sometimes have negative effects on people? ☐ _____

www.family.values.com

WHEN I GROW UP ... TEACHER OR ROCK STAR?

[1] 'What do you want to be when you grow up?' For generations, children have been asked this question, but it seems their answers are changing. A recent study has revealed a dramatic and rather worrying shift in children's **ambitions**.

[2] Twenty-five years ago, the most common **aspiration** of the average British child was to be a teacher, followed by a career in finance and then medicine. Today's younger generation, on the other hand, say they want to be a sports star, a singer or an actor: all careers associated with great wealth and, perhaps more significantly, fame.

[3] We now live in a culture that worships celebrities, so perhaps it is not surprising that so many children grow up with a desire to be famous. Some would argue that this is a positive thing; that it is good to aim high and that there is no harm in dreaming. However, others feel that this trend will ultimately lead to dissatisfaction.

[4] This cult of celebrity has been intensified by an increasing number of TV talent competitions through which winners can acquire wealth and fame in a very short time. This quick route to fame and fortune creates unrealistic expectations and the belief that a celebrity lifestyle is easy to achieve. For the majority who inevitably will not reach their goal, failure can lead to intense feelings of disappointment and even low **self-esteem**. In addition, individuals can waste years of their lives pursuing their dream, missing out on opportunities for education and training that would make them employable in the real world.

[5] Even for the lucky few who do **make it big**, fame and fortune do not always have a positive impact on their lives. Many careers **in the spotlight** are brief – an athlete's physical peak lasts only a few years, and a lot of musicians turn out to be one-hit-wonders. The careers of reality-show celebrities are likely to be even shorter. When the sole focus of their lives suddenly disappears and their earnings **dwindle**, these former stars can suffer feelings of **worthlessness** and a lack of purpose. It can also be difficult for them to adapt to normal life again. Many **washed-up** celebrities end up competing in 'celebrity' reality shows, desperate to be famous again.

[6] It is worrying that so many young people these days value fame above more realistic aspirations, not only because so few of them will achieve it, but because fame can be a **traumatic** experience for those who actually succeed and become celebrities. Unfortunately, these changing aspirations could have a very negative impact on the happiness of a generation.

C VOCABULARY: GUESSING MEANING FROM CONTEXT

Read the text again. Choose the correct options to complete the sentences.

1 **Ambition** and **aspiration** have similar / different meanings.
2 **Self-esteem** refers to the state of a person's mind / body.
3 **Make it big**, means successful / unsuccessful.
4 **In the spotlight** relates to fame / happiness.
5 **Dwindle** refers to an increase / a decrease.
6 **Worthlessness** has a positive / negative meaning.
7 **Washed-up** has a positive / negative meaning.
8 **Traumatic** has a positive / negative meaning.

D ⧉ VOCABULARY: GUESSING MEANING FROM CONTEXT

Complete the questions with the correct form of a word or phrase from Exercise C. Then discuss the questions in pairs.

1 Do you agree with the author that children having _____ to become rich and famous is a negative thing? Why or why not?
2 Do you think personal problems are more or less _____ for people who are _____?
3 If you were a celebrity, what would you do when your fame started to _____?

WRITING: a website post

A Look at the photo. What do you know, or what can you guess, about Dany Cotton? Read the website post and check your ideas. Why is she the writer's hero?

● ● ●   www.family.values.com

My personal HERO

Written by Elaine from Birmingham Updated on 16 May 11.32.09 pm

Why do so many people look up to 'celebrities' who have achieved nothing more than earning a fortune for appearing on a reality TV show or creating a media scandal? Why are these people considered so important in our culture? Today I want to talk about someone who has really made a difference – a real hero.

Danielle (Dany) Cotton joined the London Fire Brigade in 1988, when she was only 18 years old. She became Assistant Commissioner of the Brigade in 2012 and is the highest-ranking female firefighter in the fire service. Rising to the top in a 'man's profession' was not easy. In one interview, Dany talked about some of the misconceptions that people have and the questions they ask her. She said that she had been asked, for example, if female firefighters had different, less difficult training than men, and whether there are things that male firefighters do that women are not expected to do. The answer to both questions is 'No'. Dany Cotton has had to work even harder than her male colleagues to prove her worth in the dangerous, demanding job of fighting fires, and she has excelled. She is a hero to many people whose lives she has saved, and she should be a hero to any young person who has aspirations of doing something extraordinary in life.

B Think of someone you admire and write a website post about him or her.

C ⧉ Work in pairs. Tell your partner why you admire the person.

PRONUNCIATION: silent letters – consonants

A ⧉ 1.12 Listen to the words. What happens to the underlined consonant sound in each one when it is pronounced? Listen again and check your ideas.

b: num*b*, de*b*t, dou*b*t   k: *k*nown, *k*not   g: forei*g*n, si*g*n
p: *p*sychology   h: r*h*yme, *h*ours, w*h*en   l: cou*l*d, shou*l*d

B ⧉ 1.13 ⧉ Listen and underline the silent consonant sound in each word. Then work in pairs and practise saying the words in Exercises A and B.

> comb   designer   ghost   honest   knee   knife   knock   resign

A LANGUAGE IN CONTEXT Read the article. How does Ilham Anas feel about looking like a famous person?

NOTICE!
Underline five examples of reported speech in the text. Which tense is used after the reporting verb?

US News Bulletin January · Volume 4

Take a look at the two pictures. Can you tell which one is Barack Obama and which is a lookalike? No, we couldn't either, but the man in the left-hand picture isn't President Obama! His name is Ilham Anas, an Indonesian photographer who suddenly became a celebrity in Jakarta when Mr Obama was first elected in 2008.

At first, when Mr Anas's relatives pointed out his similarity to the president, he said he couldn't see a strong likeness. Then colleagues asked him to pose for photographs with an American flag, wearing a suit and tie, and suddenly everything changed. Before long, the pictures were all over the internet and Mr Anas was receiving calls from TV channels and an advertising agency. His life hasn't been the same since. He has appeared on a national talk show and in a TV advert, among other things.

Surprisingly, Mr Anas revealed that he is a shy person who doesn't like being in the spotlight. However, he explained that he sees looking like Mr Obama as a blessing. He said that he'll keep taking all the opportunities that come along as long as they do not conflict with his personal values. Of course, the excitement of the presidential election has worn off now, and Mr Anas told journalists that he isn't getting much 'Obama work' anymore and is returning to a more normal life. There may be less demand for Barack Obama lookalikes, but while Mr Obama is President of the United States, we're certain that Mr Anas's life won't be completely normal.

B ANALYSE Read the article in Exercise A again.

Form Read the information and complete the table with examples from the text. Then answer questions 6 and 7 below.

> When we report speech, we generally shift the verb tense back into the past. This is called 'back-shifting'. Sometimes this is optional.

Back-shifting is *optional* when reporting ...	Direct speech	Reported speech – back-shifting	Reported speech – no back-shifting
... a general truth.	'I am a shy person.'	He revealed that he was a shy person.	He revealed that he is a shy person.
... something that is true at the moment of reporting.	'I'm not getting much "Obama work" anymore.'	He told reporters (1) _____	He told reporters (2) _____
... future possibilities or plans.	'I'll keep taking all the opportunities that come along.'	He said (3) _____	He said (4) _____
Back-shifting is *necessary* when reporting something that is no longer true.	'I can't see a strong likeness.'	At first, he said (5) _____	

6 Do people always use back-shifting when they report what people said?

7 Look at the pairs of sentences below. For each pair, which is correct: a, b or both?

i a) He said he doesn't like being in the spotlight.
  b) He said he didn't like being in the spotlight.

ii a) At first, he claimed he can't see a strong likeness.
   b) At first, he claimed he couldn't see a strong likeness.

WHAT'S RIGHT?
○ He said he will never get used to being famous, but he seems to like it now.
○ He said he would never get used to being famous, but he seems to like it now.

C PRACTISE Rewrite the direct speech as reported speech with and without back-shifting. In one example, only back-shifting is possible.

1 **John:** 'They are holding an Oscars party.'
   John announced _____. John announced _____.

2 **Nadia (yesterday):** 'I'm really excited about the concert this evening.'
   Nadia told us _____. Nadia told us _____.

3 **Lecturer:** 'Technological advances will change the way we watch films.'
   The lecturer declared _____. The lecturer declared _____.

4 **Julia:** 'You don't have to be 18 to get a backstage pass.'
   Julia stated _____. Julia stated _____.

D NOW YOU DO IT Work in pairs. Choose a roleplay card. Do the roleplay, take notes and then swap roles. Afterwards, work with a new partner. Report on what you asked your partner in the roleplay and what their answers were.

Student A

You are a reporter. Student B is a lookalike of a famous person. Prepare four or five questions to ask them about their experience as a lookalike. Take notes.

Student B

You are a lookalike of a famous person. Student A is a reporter who is going to interview you. To prepare, think about what it's like to be a lookalike.

SPEAKING: clarifying misunderstandings

When you feel you haven't explained something clearly enough, there are phrases you can use to clarify what you mean.

A Work in pairs. Look at the photo and the quote. Discuss what you think are the disadvantages of being famous.

'The image is one thing and the human being is another. It's very hard to live up to an image, put it that way.' – Elvis Presley

B 1.14 Listen to six short conversations about the disadvantages of fame. Complete the phrases the speakers use to clarify what they mean.

1 Well, what I _____ was …
2 What I'm trying to _____ is …
3 Maybe I'm not _____ myself clear.
4 Maybe I should _____ that.
5 _____, that's not what I meant.
6 _____ it that way.

C Complete each sentence with an appropriate phrase from Exercise B. There may be more than one correct answer.

1 I didn't mean that fame had brought Elvis Presley a huge amount of unhappiness. _____ that it didn't bring him the happiness he thought it would.

2 _____. I didn't mean all celebrities have problems. I just meant that a lot of them seem to.

3 I'm not saying the media was responsible for Michael Jackson's difficulties, but I don't think they made his life easy; _____.

4 _____. It's not that actors who cause scandals are less talented. It's just that they become more well known for their scandals than for their acting.

D Work in pairs. Discuss your opinions about fame. Rephrase to clarify what you mean where appropriate.

A: I think it would be really difficult being famous.
B: Really? I think it would be fun!
A: Maybe I should rephrase that. I'm not saying that it wouldn't be fun sometimes. What I meant was that certain things, like going out in public, would be difficult.

LifeSkills

EVALUATING ARGUMENTS

- Identify claims made and evidence for those claims.
- Understand strong and weak points.
- Evaluate the argument based on the strength of the points.

A Read the definition of *argument*. Then read the proposal to change the content of a large city newspaper in the USA. Read the sentences in bold again. Underline the ones which are claims and circle the ones which provide evidence to support the claims.

- a claim (a statement that may or may not be true)
- evidence (provable factual information to support the claim)

> **argument (n.)** /ˈɑː(r)gjʊmənt/ **[COUNTABLE/ UNCOUNTABLE]**
>
> a reason or reasons used to persuade other people to support an idea. An argument usually includes an introduction to the situation or problem, one or more claims and evidence. It also often includes personal opinion.

To:	Editorial board
From:	Tanya Stevens
RE:	Proposal to reduce extent of print edition
Date:	February 12 2015

As you are aware, newspaper sales started to drop in the 1960s when TV became widely available and more recently, sales have dropped further due to the availability of news and other information on the internet. **(1) According to a Pew Research Center survey, the number of people who read a newspaper daily dropped from 41% in 2002 to 23% in 2012.** Consequently, the newspaper industry has to make adjustments if it is to survive.

One approach is to cut costs, and **(2) the best way to do this is to decrease the size of the newspaper.** Therefore, I propose that we cut one of the less important sections of the paper. **(3) Newspaper readers in the 21st century are a smaller and more specific group than a decade ago.** They tend to be older, college educated and interested in international and national affairs. **(4) A recent survey by the Newspaper Association of America revealed that 87% of readers read the front page and main news, 85% read the local news, and 54% read the international and national news. In contrast, only 45% read the lifestyle and entertainment section.**

It makes sense to offer only the most popular sections of our newspaper. We could consider cutting sections like travel, or science and technology, but I think that those sections are too small to have an impact on our costs. Based on the data, I propose that we cut our Lifestyle and Entertainment section. I appreciate that this change will not be easy. However, as in any type of evolution, those who do not adapt cannot survive. **(5) If we start targeting our newspaper at the 21st century reader, it will not only survive, but it will also grow.**

B ♫ **1.15** Listen to an excerpt from the Editorial board meeting. What action do they decide to take?

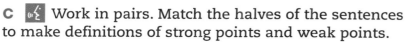

C Work in pairs. Match the halves of the sentences to make definitions of strong points and weak points.

1 A strong point …
2 A weak point …

a) states a personal opinion or makes a claim not based on evidence.
b) makes a claim based on evidence from a reliable source.

D Work in pairs. Discuss the claims in the table below and label each one S (strong) or W (weak).

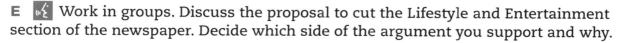

Against cutting the L&E section	For cutting the L&E section
1 ☐ We get dozens of letters to the editor each week with comments about articles in the L&E section. In fact, last week we got 50 letters related to that section.	1 ☐ Newspaper readers in the 21st century are a smaller and more specific group than a decade ago.
2 ☐ If L&E disappears, we're going to get lots of complaints.	2 ☐ What these 21st century readers want is news; the news sections are read by many more people than sections such as lifestyle and entertainment.
3 ☐ People in our community want a newspaper that offers a variety of content.	3 ☐ A recent survey by the Newspaper Association of America revealed that 87% of readers read the front page and main news, and an average of 69.5% read international or local news. In contrast, an average of only 45% read the lifestyle section.
4 ☐ Also, several national surveys have shown that when young people *do* read the newspaper, they tend to read the L&E sections.	4 ☐ I believe that if we start targeting our newspaper at the 21st century reader, it will not only survive, but it will also grow.
5 ☐ If we cut that section, we'll lose any young readers that we have!	5 ☐ Yes, but we get hundreds of letters about the news stories and editorials, far more than we get for L&E.
	6 ☐ People want to read real news.

E Work in groups. Discuss the proposal to cut the Lifestyle and Entertainment section of the newspaper. Decide which side of the argument you support and why.

F Work in groups. Discuss the questions.

1 Do you feel that you are now able to recognise strong and weak arguments? Why or why not?
2 Do you think the side with the most points is usually the strongest? Explain your answer.

HOW TO SAY IT

Tanya Stevens claimed that … / said she thought that …
I think this is a good/bad argument because …
This point is weak/strong because …
I agree / don't agree with Tanya Stevens's claim that …
I think it would be a better idea to …

RESEARCH …

Compare a print newspaper to its online version. Consider these questions and make notes in order to report back to the class.

1 If you do not have a subscription to an online paper, are you able to access all sections?
2 How does the price of an online subscription compare with the print version?
3 Do both versions of the newspaper have the same content and layout?

REFLECT … How can the skill of evaluating arguments be useful to you in the areas of **Study & Learning** and **Self & Society**?

Language wrap-up

1 VOCABULARY

A Complete the sentences with the correct form of a verb from the box. (7 points)

break   cause   come up with   discover   inherit   run   write

1   Madonna **(1)** _____ a scandal in 2009 when she adopted a child from Malawi.
    She is a singer, but she has also **(2)** _____ a best-selling children's book.
2   Allegra Versace **(3)** _____ her fortune after her uncle was killed in 1997. She now
    (4) _____ a fashion company.
3   Scientists in this country **(5)** _____ the gene that causes certain types of cancer.
4   Usain Bolt **(6)** _____ the world record for the 100-metre sprint in the 2012 Olympics.
5   This man is famous for **(7)** _____ a new machine that made cartoon characters look more realistic.

B Complete the sentences with a word or phrase from the box. Change
the form if necessary. (5 points)

ambition   dwindle   in the spotlight   make it big   washed-up

1   For every person who **(1)** _____, there are thousands of others who don't
    succeed in becoming famous.
2   If your **(2)** _____ is to become a famous singer, actor or sports star, you have to be
    prepared to work very hard.
3   Celebrities should be prepared for the time when their fame **(3)** _____ and they
    are no longer **(4)** _____.
4   Many **(5)** _____ celebrities will do anything to become famous again.

10–12 correct: I can talk about fame and ways to become famous.
0–9 correct: Look again at the vocabulary sections on pages 35, 36 and 37.   **SCORE:**   /12

2 GRAMMAR

Rewrite the direct speech as reported speech in two different ways. Use
the verbs in brackets. (10 points)

1   The manager: 'You have to wear a tie if you want to get into the club.' (*said*)
    _____
    _____

2   Rachel: 'You have to be very self-confident to be an actor.' (*commented*)
    _____
    _____

3   Vicky: 'Will the film industry change a lot in the near future?' (*asked*)
    _____
    _____

4   Anton: 'I've seen lots of celebrities around here.' (*revealed*)
    _____
    _____

5   Sonia: 'I can help you find an agent.' (*told me*)
    _____
    _____

8–10 correct: I can use reported speech with modals and optional back-shifting.
0–7 correct: Look again at the grammar sections on pages 34 and 38.   **SCORE:**   /10

WRITING WORKSHOP

Writing a short essay

A Read the essay and choose T (true) or F (false).

In general, are celebrities a positive or negative influence on others?

It is true that some celebrities are not a positive influence on young people. They constantly cause scandals or get into trouble. However, many celebrities use their position in the spotlight to do good things, and they have a very positive influence on society.

One important thing celebrities do is donate money, time and their names to good causes. When there is a disaster such as a hurricane or an earthquake, many celebrities help raise money. For example, when model Gisele Bündchen said that she would donate $1.5 million to the Red Cross after a hurricane in Haiti, that inspired the public to donate too. Another generous celebrity is the singer Bono, who gives benefit concerts and meets with world leaders to raise money and promote programmes to help poor children around the world.

Apart from supporting good causes, celebrities can also be good role models for young people. When celebrities have qualities such as compassion, honesty and tolerance, they can influence teenagers and younger children to develop those qualities too. There are definitely many celebrities who use their fame in positive ways.

1 The writer thinks that many celebrities have a positive influence on society.	T / F
2 People tend to give money to charity if a celebrity donates money.	T / F
3 Bono gives many benefit concerts in support of environmental charities.	T / F

B Look at the essay again. Choose the correct options to complete the statements.

1   The purpose of the first paragraph is to …
   a) present the writer's general opinion.   **b)** give reasons for the opinion.   **c)** explain who the writer is.

2   In paragraph 2, the author gives … examples of charitable celebrities to support his point.
   a) two   **b)** three   **c)** four

3   In paragraph 3, the author gives … examples of positive qualities to support his point.
   a) two   **b)** three   **c)** four

4   The last sentence of the essay …
   a) gives an example.
   b) gives a reason for the writer's opinion.
   c) restates the writer's general opinion.

C Plan a short essay giving your opinion about the question in Exercise A. If you agree with the writer of the sample essay, give different reasons in your essay. Write notes for your essay.

Introductory topic sentence: _____
Reasons for your opinion (at least two): _____
Supporting details or examples (at least one or two): _____
_____
Concluding sentence: _____

HOW ARE YOU DOING?

○ My opening paragraph states my general opinion.

○ I have given enough reasons to support my opinion.

○ My paragraphs include a topic sentence summarising the main point of the paragraph.

D Use your notes to write your essay. Write approximately 200 words.

UNIT 4 UPS AND DOWNS

IN THIS UNIT YOU

- learn language to talk about mood and life satisfaction
- listen to a lecture about wealth and happiness
- write a thank-you note
- read about research on happiness
- talk about having a positive attitude
- learn about being a positive team member
- ▶ watch a video about the concept of Gross National Happiness

LISTENING
discourse markers
What are some phrases you might hear that signal a change of topic or the conclusion of a topic?

WRITING
a thank-you note
In what situations do you need to write a thank-you note? Would different situations require a different style? Why?

LIFE SKILLS
WORK & CAREER

being a positive team member When you are working as part of a team, it is important to be positive. What are some characteristics of a positive team member?

A 🗣 Do you agree with these definitions of happiness? Explain why or why not.

1 Happiness is having good friends you can talk to.

2 Happiness is feeling you've done your best.

3 Happiness is helping other people.

4 Happiness is feeling peaceful and safe.

5 Happiness is having enough money to buy whatever you want.

6 Happiness is being independent.

B 🗣 Work in pairs. First, complete the definition in your own words. Then explain your definition to your partner.

Happiness is …

Discourse markers often act as signposts, giving a listener clues about what they might hear next. They might introduce additional points, contrasting ideas or a conclusion. The correct use of discourse markers in both writing and speaking is one of the things that examiners often look for in academic and proficiency exams.

A 🎧 **1.16** Listen to the introduction to a lecture. What is the lecture going to be about?

B 🎧 **1.17** Listen to the full lecture. As you listen, write one word to complete each of the phrases below. Then write each phrase in the correct place in the table.

_____ general   _____ addition
_____ the other hand   _____ a result

Phrases used to talk generally	Phrases used to introduce a contrasting point	Phrases used to introduce a result	Phrases used to introduce an additional point
(1) _____	(2) _____	(3) _____	(4) _____
On the whole	That said	As a consequence	What's more
To a great extent	Nevertheless	Consequently	Furthermore

C 🗣 Listen to the lecture again and answer the questions. Discuss your answers in pairs.

1 What did the first study find out?
2 How did the second study contradict the first study?
3 What is the difference between satisfaction and happiness?
4 Why do you think wealthier people enjoy everyday pleasures less?

D VOCABULARY: LIFE SATISFACTION
Complete the tables with the correct form of each word.

Adjective	Noun		Verb	Noun
happy	_____		_____	appreciation
wealthy	_____		enjoy	_____
_____	pleasure		_____	satisfaction
_____	contentment			

E 🗣 VOCABULARY: LIFE SATISFACTION
Work in pairs. Complete the sentences with the correct form of the word in brackets. Then discuss them with your partner.

1 I feel _____ (satisfaction) with my life when I …
2 People usually _____ (appreciation) happiness more when they …
3 I think people are generally more _____ (contentment) when they …
4 Material _____ (wealthy) can sometimes cause unhappiness because …
5 _____ (enjoy) of life depends on … as well as …

GRAMMAR: noun clauses as objects

A 🎧 **1.18 LANGUAGE IN CONTEXT** Read the poster. Then listen to the conversation. According to Michelle, how does laughter therapy work?

Clara: Look at this! Laughter therapy!

Michelle: Yeah, I've read about that. Apparently, laughing can help people feel happier and less stressed, so now they're using it as a therapy!

Clara: That sounds really interesting. Do you know what it involves?

Michelle: I'm not exactly sure, but I think they explain how laughter could help you deal with a problem. I think you learn techniques to see the positive side of a situation.

Clara: That sounds useful! I wonder when they're holding the workshop. Does it say where we can get more information?

Michelle: I'm sure there's more information on the website. I think we need to register online, and we might need to explain why we want to attend.

Clara: So, do you want to try it?

JOIN OUR ONE-DAY
LAUGHTER THERAPY
[WORKSHOP]

LAUGHTER CAN CHANGE YOUR LIFE!
Venue: Main Hall
Time: 9am–5pm
Limited to 40 participants.
http://laughtertherapy.campusworkshops.net

REGISTER TODAY!

NOTICE!
Underline all the examples of **what**, **where**, **when**, **why** and **how** in the conversation. What do you notice about the word order in the clauses that follow each one?

B ANALYSE Read the conversation in Exercise A again.

Form Complete the table with examples from the text.

Noun clauses can begin with	Examples
_____ (= the thing(s))	*Do you know* **(1)** _____ *it involves?*
_____ (= the way)	*They explain* **(2)** _____ *laughter could help you deal with a situation.*
_____ (= the time)	*I wonder* **(3)** _____ *they're holding the workshop.*
_____ (= the place)	*Does it say* **(4)** _____ *we can get more information?*
_____ (= the reason)	*We might need to explain* **(5)** _____ *we want to attend.*

C PRACTISE Complete the sentences with *what, where, when, why* or *how*.

1 I think you'll be interested in _____ they have to say about happiness.
2 I don't understand _____ laughter therapy works.
3 The presenters will demonstrate _____ laughter can help you be positive.
4 I sometimes wonder _____ people at work are so stressed.
5 They told us _____ the workshop will take place, but now I've forgotten the room number.
6 Do you know _____ the next workshop will be held? Is it next month?

D 🎤 **NOW YOU DO IT** Work in pairs. Complete the sentences in your own words. Then compare with your partner. How similar or different are your ideas?

I'd like to learn about what …
I'm happier if I know why …
I often wonder how …
I'm happiest in places where …

WHAT'S RIGHT?
◯ I agree with what you said.
◯ I agree with what did you say.

A Read the article. Find two ways to be happier, according to the research mentioned.

HAPPINESS

WHAT IS HAPPINESS?

[1] Is it being **in a good mood**? Is it a state of contentment, or is it a feeling of excitement or pleasure? It seems that happiness is all of these things. Psychologists have defined it as a '**state of well-being**' – a combination of life satisfaction and experiencing more positive than negative **emotions**.

WHAT MAKES US HAPPY?

[2] Happiness is a very subjective state and can mean different things to different people. However, researchers have identified some basic components of happiness.

[3] One component is our physical condition, such as our level of income and state of health. There is no doubt that financial stress and illness can have a negative impact on our level of happiness. But wealth on its own isn't enough; you can be very wealthy and also very unhappy.

[4] Another component is genetic; it seems that some of us may be born to be cheerful. Some of our character traits are inherited and may include a tendency to either be more **optimistic** or to get **depressed** more easily.

[5] By far, the greatest influence on our happiness is our choice about how we feel and think. We can make a decision to be optimistic about life, or choose to focus on the negative side and be more **pessimistic**. Some recent research has found that practising positive emotions such as gratitude, joy, hope and kindness can have a positive effect on our general state of well-being. In other words, we can control how happy we are.

HOW CAN WE MEASURE HAPPINESS?

[6] One simple method is just to ask people how they are feeling. A recent research project used a mobile phone app to track how happy people were. From time to time, the app sent a message asking the person to report how happy he or she was feeling, as well as what activity the person was doing. The study found that people who are less **focused** on what they're doing tend to feel less happy. When they get **distracted**, they start to worry or think about negative things, which makes them unhappy.

WHY DO SCIENTISTS RESEARCH HAPPINESS?

[7] Researchers believe that researching happiness is very useful. The more we understand about the causes of happiness, the more we can learn about developing social or psychological traits that contribute to our general state of well-being and help us lead fuller lives.

B Read the statements and choose T (true), F (false) or NM (not mentioned).

1	It is impossible to measure happiness.	T / F / NM
2	Scientists disagree about the causes of happiness.	T / F / NM
3	Our personality influences our level of happiness.	T / F / NM
4	It is possible to learn how to be happier.	T / F / NM
5	Asking people about their state of mind is unreliable.	T / F / NM
6	Lack of concentration can cause negative emotions.	T / F / NM

C VOCABULARY: MOOD

Match the words in bold in the text to the definitions (a–h).

a) having a generally positive attitude _____
b) preoccupied, thinking about sth. else _____
c) feeling of general happiness _____
d) having a generally negative attitude _____
e) feelings _____
f) unhappy _____
g) concentrating on what you're doing _____
h) cheerful _____

D 🔊 VOCABULARY: MOOD

Work in pairs and answer the questions.

1 How are you feeling at the moment?
2 Do you consider yourself to be generally optimistic or pessimistic? Why?
3 Do you ever get depressed? If so, what do you do?

GRAMMAR: review of conditional forms

A 🔊 1.19 LANGUAGE IN CONTEXT

Listen to the conversation. What advice does Tom's uncle give him?

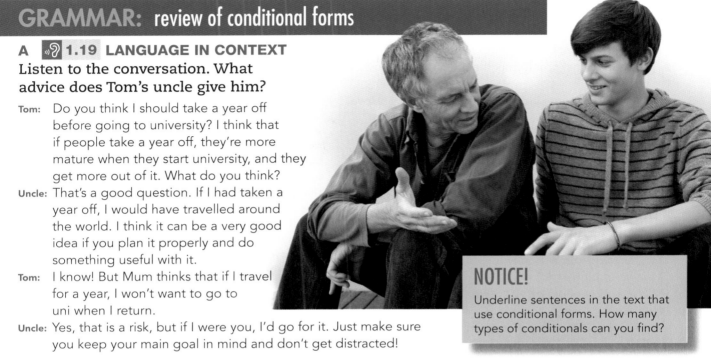

Tom: Do you think I should take a year off before going to university? I think that if people take a year off, they're more mature when they start university, and they get more out of it. What do you think?

Uncle: That's a good question. If I had taken a year off, I would have travelled around the world. I think it can be a very good idea if you plan it properly and do something useful with it.

Tom: I know! But Mum thinks that if I travel for a year, I won't want to go to uni when I return.

Uncle: Yes, that is a risk, but if I were you, I'd go for it. Just make sure you keep your main goal in mind and don't get distracted!

NOTICE!
Underline sentences in the text that use conditional forms. How many types of conditionals can you find?

B ANALYSE Read the conversation in Exercise A again.

Form & Function Complete the table with examples from the text.

Type of conditional	Form	Function and Examples
third	If + past perfect, would(n't) have + past participle	To talk about unreal situations in the past. (1) _____
second	If + past simple, would(n't) + base form	To talk about things the speaker feels are unreal or unlikely in the present or future. (2) _____
first	If + present simple, will (won't) + base form	To talk about things that the speaker thinks are likely or possible in the future. (3) _____
zero	If + present simple, present simple	To talk about things that are generally true. (4) _____ (5) _____

C PRACTISE Match the beginnings (1–4) to the endings (a–d) to make sentences.

1 You would have studied harder
2 You'll always succeed
3 People are generally friendly
4 You would have more friends

a) if you were more outgoing.
b) if you'd had more time.
c) if you're polite to them.
d) if you work hard enough.

WHAT'S RIGHT?
○ If you had said you were ill, I would have called a doctor.
○ If you would have said you were ill, I had called a doctor.

D 🔊 NOW YOU DO IT Work in pairs. Complete the sentences and tell your partner.

Ask questions to get more information. Find three things you have in common.

If I had studied …, I would have …   *If I hadn't …, I wouldn't have …*   *If I were richer, I would …*

WRITING: a thank-you note

Writing a thank-you note for a present or a favour is an important way to make people feel appreciated. In a thank-you note, make sure you say what you are thanking the person for, and explain what effect it has had, if relevant.

A Read the thank-you note and answer the questions.

1 Identify two things the writer is saying thank you for.
2 What positive changes does the writer report since the event?
3 Is this a formal or informal thank-you note? How can you tell?
4 What three words in the note increase the positive tone?
a) i_____
b) f_____
c) b_____

B Choose one of these situations and write a thank-you note. Write your note using the prompts to help you.

> You received some money for your birthday from your aunt.
> You attended a job interview with a computer company.
> You received a leaving present from your colleagues when you left your job.
> You had dinner at your tutor's home.

Dear Lucinda,

Thank you so much for your inspiring workshop at our annual professional development day last week. It was fascinating to hear your advice on maintaining a positive attitude in the workplace. We have tried out some of your ideas and it has already had a beneficial effect on our office environment. We're all smiling more than we used to, thanks to you! And thank you so much for explaining how our work environment affects our mood. If you hadn't, we wouldn't have thought of changing things. It's a much more attractive and pleasant place to work now. We are planning to use many of your ideas in our office over the coming months.
We hope to attend one of your workshops again very soon.
Many thanks again from all of us here.
Yours sincerely,
Kate Dansworth
Human Resources Manager

Starting expression:
I am writing to thank you for …
I would like to express my gratitude/appreciation for …
Thank you for your wonderful hospitality/generosity/kindness.
Your present was so thoughtful/inspiring/helpful.
Beneficial effect (if any): _____
Ending expression: _____

C Work in pairs. Read each other's notes and then suggest ways to improve them.

PRONUNCIATION: reduced forms of *would you* and *did you*

A 🔊 1.20 Listen to the questions. How are *would you* and *did you* pronounced?

1 a) What would you do?   b) What did you do?
2 a) Why would you go?   b) Why did you go?
3 a) When would you leave?   b) When did you leave?
4 a) How would you find out?   b) How did you find out?

B 🔊 1.21 Listen and choose which question you hear from each pair in Exercise A.

C Work in pairs. Say one question from each pair in Exercise A. Your partner will identify which one they hear.

SPEAKING: talking about having a positive attitude

A  Work in groups. Discuss what you think each of these sayings means. Does each one express a positive or negative attitude?

EVERY CLOUD HAS A SILVER LINING

THINK OF the glass as HALF FULL, NOT HALF empty.

→ Always expect ← ★ THE WORST ★ = and then = • YOU'RE NEVER • disappointed.

B 🎧 **1.22** Listen to the person talking about a workshop he attended. Tick the things that helped him.

- ☐ talking about a problem
- ☐ thinking positively
- ☐ talking to an expert
- ☐ learning techniques for relaxation
- ☐ remembering a similar experience

C Think of a time when you experienced a difficult situation at work or in a place of study. Complete the notes.

What was the difficult situation?	
How did it make you feel?	
What did you do about it?	
If things had been different, what might have happened?	

D 👥 **Independent Speaking**
Work in pairs. Tell each other about the situation you made notes on in Exercise C. Then ask your partner to tell your problem back to you. Try to offer positive advice and suggestions on what you could have done differently.

HOW TO SAY IT 🗣️

I'd like to tell you about what happened when …
It was difficult for me because …
If I hadn't …, he/she/they wouldn't have …

LifeSkills

BEING A POSITIVE TEAM MEMBER

- Focus on finding solutions rather than blaming people for problems.
- Listen to other team members with a positive attitude.
- Present your point of view in a positive way.

A   Read about the following situation. What is the problem? Underline the issues.

Sportsense is a company which produces sports and fitness equipment. Their latest project, developing a new range of fitness equipment, has run into serious problems. It's very behind schedule, and the costs seem to be increasing. There also seem to be personal problems among some of the team members. If something isn't done very soon, the project may fail.

B   Look at these pairs of sentences. For each pair, write P next to the sentence that focuses on the problems, and S next to the one that focuses on solutions.

1   a)   _____ The project is behind schedule because we had a lot of unexpected problems.
    b)   _____ The project faced some unexpected challenges, but I'd like to make some suggestions.
2   a)   _____ It may be possible to work with the supplier to control the increasing costs.
    b)   _____ Someone chose the wrong supplier, so costs are increasing.
3   a)   _____ Some of the team members don't get on well and there are constant arguments.
    b)   _____ We should arrange team-building exercises to improve relationships within the team.
4   a)   _____ The design is creative, but perhaps we need to simplify it so that we can finish on schedule.
    b)   _____ If the design hadn't been so complicated, we would have finished this project by now.

C Work in groups. Each person chooses one of the following roles. Prepare for a meeting to discuss the project. Make notes of positive ways to present your problems, along with possible solutions.

Project Leader

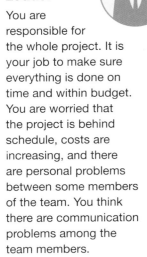

You are responsible for the whole project. It is your job to make sure everything is done on time and within budget. You are worried that the project is behind schedule, costs are increasing, and there are personal problems between some members of the team. You think there are communication problems among the team members.

Research and Development Manager

You are responsible for designing the equipment. It is your job to make sure that it is safe and develops fitness. You have fallen behind schedule because there aren't enough people working in your department. You feel that the marketing department hasn't given you a clear idea of what they want and that they should have done more market research.

Logistics Manager

You are responsible for supplies. It is your job to make sure everyone has the materials they need at the right cost. You feel that the design department is being too ambitious and should try to cut costs. You also think that everyone needs to stick to the schedule more because delays increase costs.

Sales and Marketing Manager

You are responsible for selling the equipment. It is your job to make sure the company sells as many pieces of equipment as possible. You feel that the current designs won't appeal to enough people. You would like to have new designs as soon as possible so that you can do more market research.

HOW TO SAY IT

That's a good suggestion, and we could ...
That's a good point. I'd like to add that ...
I take your point. From my point of view, ...
Thanks for bringing that up.

D Roleplay the meeting. Listen to others carefully and make positive comments when appropriate. Finish your meeting by agreeing on a list of three or four action points (things to do next).

E Report your ideas to the class. Explain how you are now planning to deal with the problems.

F Discuss the questions.

1 Do you feel you now have a better understanding of what it means to be a positive team member? In what ways?
2 Which aspects of being a positive team member come naturally to you? Which aspects do you think you need to work on?

REFLECT ... How can the skill of being a positive team member be useful to you in **Study & Learning** and **Self & Society**?

RESEARCH ...

What else makes someone a good member of a team? Go online and look at a few websites that discuss this idea. Make a note of what you discover and report back to the class. Do all the websites you have looked at agree?

Language wrap-up

1 VOCABULARY

Complete the paragraph with the words from the box. (12 points)

appreciate content depressed distracted emotions enjoyment
mood optimistic pessimistic pleasures wealth well-being

Do you sometimes feel sad or **(1)** _____? Do you often experience negative
(2) _____? Do you have a generally **(3)** _____ outlook on life? If you
answered yes, then this workshop is for you. Thought Power is a new technique that
helps put you in a good **(4)** _____ and recover your **(5)** _____ of life.
Happiness doesn't depend on material **(6)** _____. We can all become more
(7) _____ with our lives by focusing on the positive and not being **(8)** _____
by negative thoughts. Learn to be more **(9)** _____ and improve your state of
(10) _____. It's easy to **(11)** _____ the simple everyday **(12)** _____ of life
by using this simple technique. Try it and see!

10–12 correct: I can use words for describing life satisfaction and mood.
0–9 correct: Look again at the vocabulary sections on pages 46, 48 and 49. **SCORE:**   /12

2 GRAMMAR

A Complete the second sentence so that it has a similar meaning to the first. Use noun clauses as objects and the words in brackets. (4 points)

1 I went to a laughter workshop last year. (*when*)
   I want to tell you about _____.
2 Something happened at work the other day. (*what*)
   Did I tell you about _____?
3 You aren't happy. (*why*)
   I don't understand _____.
4 Stress can affect our state of well-being in many ways. (*how*)
   The instructor explained _____.

B Choose the correct options to complete the text. (8 points)

'Did you hear about Megan? I saw her by chance. I was in a shop, and if I **(1)** had / hadn't
turned round when I did, I **(2)** won't / wouldn't have seen her. She told me that she's
looking for a new job. She got fired because she was an hour late one morning! Just
imagine that! If she **(3)** were / would be more punctual, she **(4)** would / wouldn't still have
her job. I don't understand it!
Well, she was really depressed, so I encouraged her to be more optimistic. If you
(5) have / will have a positive attitude, it usually **(6)** helps / will help you find a solution
to a problem. She seemed happy to hear that. Anyway, if I **(7)** will have / have time this
weekend, I **(8)** will invite / invited her for dinner. I'm sure with a little support, she'll be
able to find something else very soon.'

10–12 correct: I can use noun clauses as objects and use a variety of conditional structures.
0–9 correct: Look again at the grammar sections on pages 47 and 49. **SCORE:**   /12

SPEAKING WORKSHOP

Expressing personal preference

A  »)) **1.23** Read the question and listen to one man's response. Make notes about the two main points the speaker makes and an example for each. Compare your notes in pairs.

> Some people think that money is the key to happiness. Others think that family and friends are more important. What do you think? Explain why and give an example to support your answer.

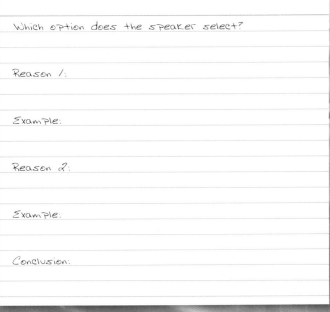

```
Which option does the speaker select?


Reason 1:


Example:


Reason 2:


Example:


Conclusion:
```

B Listen again and match the two parts to make phrases.

1	Although	a)	of all
2	There are	b)	give you an example
3	First	c)	what I've been saying
4	Let me	d)	two main reasons
5	To sum up	e)	many people believe that …

C Read the question. Prepare your response. Complete the notes. Use the expressions in Exercise B.

```
Which option do you select?
Reason 1:
Example:
Reason 2:
Example:
Conclusion:
```

> Some people think that happiness is a matter of good luck. Others think it is something you can create and control. What do you think? Explain why.

D «{ Work in pairs. Speak to your partner. Make sure you cover all the points in your outline.

HOW ARE YOU DOING?

○ I stated my opinion clearly.

○ I supported my opinion with at least two reasons and examples.

○ I used a variety of discourse markers.

UNIT 5 SOMETHING IN THE WATER

READING
inferring opinion
What do you think the expression 'read between the lines' means?

SPEAKING
suggesting alternatives
When was the last time you helped someone make a decision? What kinds of phrases can you use to suggest alternatives?

LIFE SKILLS

SELF & SOCIETY

developing empathy When you see someone less fortunate than yourself, how do you feel? Why might imagining how someone feels in a situation be important?

SPEAKING: suggesting alternatives

When you want to help someone make a decision about something or offer them advice, you can use certain phrases to suggest different alternatives to them.

A Look at these photos from advertising campaigns for different charities. Match them to the texts A–C. Say what environmental issue each advertisement aims to address.

A

YOU WOULDN'T GIVE THIS WATER TO A CHILD TO DRINK

But millions of people worldwide have to ... Please give generously to support Pure Water Action and help prevent the spread of diseases caused by water pollution.

B

THIS LAND HAS FED SAID'S FAMILY FOR GENERATIONS

With your help, it still can. A donation to Food for Thought of just £2 per month could help prevent famine in Africa.

C

Humans can't survive without water. Or with too much. To help fund research into the effects of climate change, call 0300 300300 and give what you can.

B ♪ 1.27 Listen to the discussion about helping one of the charities in Exercise A. Tick the phrases used for suggesting alternatives.

- ☐ What if we do ... instead?
- ☐ There's always ...
- ☐ What about ... ?
- ☐ We could try ...
- ☐ I'd suggest ...
- ☐ Another option/idea would be to ...
- ☐ Have you considered giving ... a try?

C  Work in pairs and follow the instructions. Then report to the class.

- Choose one of the charities in Exercise A that you'd like to support.
- Discuss things you could do to help support it.
- Suggest different alternatives as necessary.
- Give reasons for your choice.

LifeSkills

DEVELOPING EMPATHY

- Think of an experience that you have had that is similar to another person's situation.
- Compare the difficulty of your experience with that of the other person.
- Imagine how you would feel in the other person's situation.

A 🗣 **Work in pairs.**

1 Make a list of the different ways you use water every day.
2 Estimate your water usage per day in litres. The following information might help.

Compare your water usage with your classmates'.

taking a shower = approx. 25 litres per minute
taking a bath = approx. 150 litres per bath
brushing teeth = 6 litres per minute
flushing the toilet = approx. 6 litres per flush
washing clothes = 50 litres per load
cooking and drinking = approx. 5 litres per day

B 🗣 **Work in groups and discuss what kinds of water problems you've experienced in your home or community. Say how you, and others, felt.**

empathy /ˈempəθi/ **noun [U]** the ability to understand how someone feels because you can imagine what it's like to be them. When you empathise with someone, it makes it easier for you to communicate with them, even if their experience of something is very different from yours.

HOW TO SAY IT 🗣

Last spring/summer, etc we had a drought/flood, and …

One winter our pipes froze, so …

It's not easy being without water because …

C Read the information about Shartati and her family. Work in pairs to estimate how much water you think she and her family use per day. Use the notes in Exercise A for comparison.

This is Shartati and one of her daughters. She has five children ranging in age from six months to nine years old. They live in a village in northern Ethiopia. Shartati's husband is a farmer.

D **1.28** Listen to Shartati talking about her daily routine. How accurate were your guesses about her family's water usage?

E Work in groups. Discuss the questions.

1 Think about the water problems you discussed in Exercise B. How serious are or were your problems compared with Shartati's difficulties in getting water?
2 Look back at the water usage you calculated in Exercise A. What things would you need to give up if you were able to use only the amount of water that Shartati's family uses?
3 With your answers to 1 and 2 in mind, imagine yourself in Shartati's situation. How would you feel?

F Work in groups. Discuss the questions.

1 Do you find it easy to empathise with people you don't know? Why or why not?
2 Did the process you followed in Exercise E help you empathise with Shartati? Why or why not?
3 How might the world be different if people took more time to empathise with others?

REFLECT ... How can showing empathy be useful to you in **Study & Learning** and **Work & Career**?

RESEARCH ...
Find out about a water issue in an area of your country, or in another country, and prepare a short report on it. Make suggestions for how to deal with it. Present your report to the class and discuss your suggestions.

Language wrap-up

1 VOCABULARY

A Complete the text with the correct form of phrases from the box. (5 points)

to be as much about … as …   to make … worth …   to market as …
to put … up against …   to range from … to …

The most refreshing and convenient water money can buy, delivered to your door!
When we **(1)** _____ Water 2U _____ our competitors, nine times
out of ten people preferred our water. That's because we **(2)** _____ quality
_____ service. Is it expensive? It depends on your perspective. Our prices
(3) _____ $15 _____ $25 per bottle, but we think the quality and service
(4) _____ our water _____ the price! We don't **(5)** _____ our water
_____ anything it's not. If you don't like it, we'll give you your money back!

B Choose the correct options to complete the text. (5 points)

When a tsunami hit Indonesia in 2004, many villages in coastal areas were washed away by the
(1) floods / drought. But the disaster had other consequences: **(2)** water poverty / diseases spread
rapidly due to poor levels of **(3)** water pollution / hygiene and a lack of medical supplies. It was also
difficult to find safe drinking water because of **(4)** climate change / water pollution. Disasters like
this can also cause **(5)** famine / water poverty because of the loss of animals and crops.

8–10 correct: I can use marketing vocabulary and words to describe environmental issues.
0–7 correct: Look again at the vocabulary sections on pages 59 and 62.   **SCORE:**   /10

2 GRAMMAR

A Rewrite the sentences in the passive. (5 points)

1 'Climate change has affected the environment.'
   'The environment _____.'
2 'The water company cut off our water supply last week.'
   'Our water supply _____.'
3 'Before we bought the house, a flood had damaged the cellar.'
   'Before we bought the house, the cellar _____.'
4 'They're charging me £5 for this bottled water!'
   'I _____.'
5 'They limit water usage in some areas.'
   'Water usage _____.'

B Complete the sentences with a suitable expression of purpose.
There may be more than one correct answer. (5 points)

1 I use tap water _____ cooking, but not drinking.
2 Turn off the tap when you brush your teeth, so _____ avoid wasting water.
3 Take an umbrella _____ you don't get wet!
4 _____ not to have a big water bill, water your lawn only once a week.
5 We use rainwater _____ clean the patio.

8–10 correct: I can use the passive and expressions of purpose.
0–7 correct: Look again at the grammar sections on pages 58 and 61.   **SCORE:**   /10

A Read the writing assignment and a student's answer. Do you think they have answered the question? Why or why not?

> The table below shows the consumption of bottled water in the USA over a ten-year period. Write a report of approximately 200 words. Summarise the information, reporting the main features and making comparisons where relevant.

US bottled water market

	Per capita consumption	
Year	Gallons per capita	Annual % Change
1	21.6	
2	23.2	7.5%
3	25.4	9.7%
4	27.6	8.4%
5	29.0	5.3%
6	28.5	-1.8%
7	27.6	-3.2%
8	28.3	2.7%
9	29.2	3.1%
10	30.8	5.3%
11	32.0	4.0%

Adapted from data at: http://www.beveragemarketing.com/news-detail.asp?id=300

The table shows changes in the annual **per capita** consumption of bottled water over a ten-year period in the USA. We can clearly see that consumption **rose sharply** between **Year 1 and Year 5**, but that it fell in **Years 6 and 7**. It started to rise again in Year 8 and it **rose steadily** from Years 8 to 11. By the end of the period, Americans were consuming **over 10 gallons more** bottled water per person per year than they had in the first year.

In Year 1, an average of 21.6 gallons of bottled water per person was consumed. The figure rose each year over five years, with the **sharpest rise** in Year 3 (9.7%). Consumption continued to rise over the next two years. However, in Years 6 and 7, it **dropped dramatically**, with a **decrease** of 1.8% and 3.2% **respectively**. In Year 8, consumption began to rise again, but it rose much more slowly in the last four years than it had in the first four.

Overall, we can clearly see that the consumption of bottled water in the USA increased **over a decade**, although **the rate of change** was much lower at the end of the decade than at the beginning.

Their source: Beverage Marketing Corporation

B Look back at the model answer and discuss the questions as a class.

1   Look at the bold phrases. What do they mean? Discuss any you are not sure about.
2   Look at the structure of the text. What kind of information does the first paragraph give? How is it different from the information in the second paragraph? What is the purpose of the third paragraph?

C Write a report based on the data in the table below. Identify the main features and any comparisons you can make.

Global bottled water market

Year 2 Rank	Countries	Millions of Gallons		% change
		Year 1	Year 2	
1	USA	8,255.0	9,107.3	2.0%
2	China	4,163.3	7,686.4	13.0%
3	Mexico	5,359.9	7,520.7	7.0%
4	Brazil	3.301.6	4,500.9	6.4%
5	Indonesia	2,155.9	3,760.6	11.8%
6	Thailand	1,426.2	3,118.8	16.9%
7	Italy	3,115.5	3,034.7	-0.5%
8	Germany	2,808.9	2,954.2	1.0%
9	France	2,285.3	2,291.0	0.0%
10	Spain	1,524.0	1,514.6	-0.1%
	Top 10 subtotal	34,395.6	45,489.3	5.8%
	All others	12,606.8	15,880.7	4.7%

Adapted from data at: http://www.bottledwater.org/files/2011BWstats.pdf   Their source: Beverage Marketing Corporation

D Write your report, using the model in Exercise A and your notes from Exercise C. Try to include some of the phrases in bold in the model. Write approximately 200 words.

HOW ARE YOU DOING?

○ My first paragraph gives general information about what the table shows.
○ My second paragraph gives statistics to support the information in the first paragraph.
○ My third paragraph gives a summary of the main trends shown in the table.

UNIT 6 LIVING TRADITIONS

IN THIS UNIT YOU

- ⚙ learn language to talk about traditions and personal rituals
- ⚙ listen to interviews with members of the public expressing opinions on traditions
- ⚙ write a blog post about a family tradition
- ⚙ read about a tradition involving an animal
- ⚙ talk about personal rituals
- ⚙ learn about managing distractions
- ▶ watch a video about everyday rituals

WRITING
avoiding run-on sentences

What do we use commas for? Make a list of as many uses as you can think of.

LISTENING
for main ideas

In which situations might it be important to understand the main ideas without worrying too much about the details?

LIFE SKILLS

STUDY & LEARNING

managing distractions How easily are you distracted when you are trying to work or study?

- ● I find it hard to concentrate, and I get distracted by texts, Twitter, etc.
- ○ Sometimes I get distracted, but mostly I can concentrate enough to get things done.
- ○ I'm never distracted from the work I need to do.

A 🗣 Work in pairs. These people are wearing traditional dress from their countries. Match the photos to the countries and describe each kind of traditional dress.

Albania ☐   Ecuador ☐   Kenya ☐   Morocco ☐   Norway ☐   Wales ☐

B 🗣 Discuss the questions.

1   Describe traditional dress from your country. Are there different costumes for different occasions?
2   What other traditions (festivals, events, family traditions, etc) are there in your region/country?
    Do you think they are relevant to the modern world? Explain why or why not.

GRAMMAR: *be used to / get used to*

A 🎧 **1.29 LANGUAGE IN CONTEXT Listen to the conversation. What traditions are mentioned?**

Tao: So, Daniel, I'm coming to the UK this year to study. Are there any traditions or customs I should know about? I'll be arriving at the end of October.

Daniel: Well, one tradition that's quite popular is Halloween on the 31st of October. People, especially children, dress as scary characters and have fancy-dress parties. They might also go trick or treating. That's where kids in costumes knock on your door and you're expected to give them sweets.

Tao: I'm used to parties, but I'm not used to dressing in fancy-dress costumes, so that'll be interesting! Anything else?

Daniel: November the 5th is Bonfire Night. People often make a large fire, called a bonfire, and set off fireworks. Sometimes, they burn a Guy on top of the bonfire.

Tao: What's a Guy?

Daniel: Ha! It's a figure made of old clothes stuffed with newspaper. It represents a man called Guy Fawkes, who tried to blow up parliament. In fact, Bonfire Night is traditionally called Guy Fawkes Night.

Tao: I don't think I'll ever get used to some aspects of life in the UK, and I'm sure I'll never get used to the British sense of humour, either!

Daniel: You'll have to get used to a lot more than that in my country!

B ANALYSE Read the conversation in Exercise A again.

Form Complete the table with examples from the text.

Form	Examples
be + used to + -ing / noun	(1) _____ (2) _____
get + used to + -ing / noun	(3) _____ (4) _____ (5) _____

> **NOTICE!**
> Find and underline examples of **used to** in the conversation. What part of speech follows each one?

Function Choose the correct options to complete the rules.

1 We use be / get *used to* to talk about things we are / are not already familiar with.
2 We use be / get *used to* to talk about the process of becoming familiar with something.

C PRACTISE Complete the sentences with the correct form of *be used to* or *get used to*. Use negative forms where appropriate.

1 I can't _____ living here. The customs are just so different.
2 It's traditional to look after old people in my country, so people _____ it.
3 I _____ eating with chopsticks when I lived in Vietnam for a year.
4 If you _____ spicy food, you might find some of our dishes too hot!
5 Did you _____ speaking English all the time while you were there?
6 Don't worry about the local traditions – you _____ them in no time!

D 🗣 NOW YOU DO IT Work in pairs. Think of a time when you were in a new situation (e.g. a new school, a new neighbourhood, etc). Ask and answer the questions.

1 What things did you have to get used to in your new situation?
2 Are you completely used to them now?
3 Did it take you long to get used to them?
4 What helped you get used to them?
5 Was there anything you couldn't get used to?

> **WHAT'S RIGHT?**
> ○ I'm used to cooking dinner for everyone.
> ○ I'm used to cook dinner for everyone.

LISTENING: for main ideas

If you know what the topic is before listening, try to predict some of the things the people will talk about and the vocabulary they will use. While listening, pay attention to clues such as verbs of attitude (*love, dislike,* etc), adjectives (*wonderful, horrible,* etc), signal words and phrases (*because,* etc), and tone of voice.

A Read the description in an online programme guide. Answer the questions below.

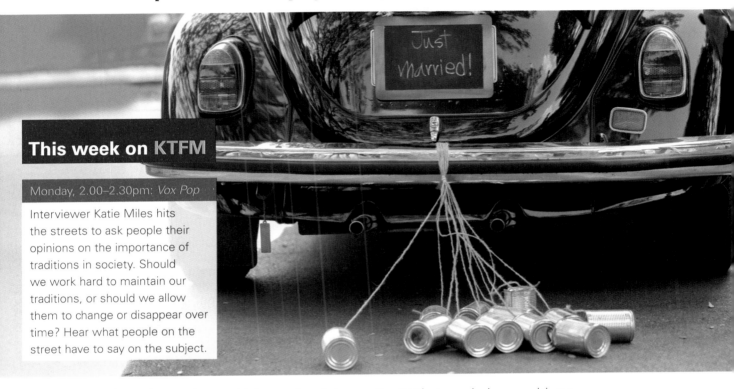

This week on KTFM

Monday, 2.00–2.30pm: *Vox Pop*

Interviewer Katie Miles hits the streets to ask people their opinions on the importance of traditions in society. Should we work hard to maintain our traditions, or should we allow them to change or disappear over time? Hear what people on the street have to say on the subject.

1 What specific traditions do you think people might mention? What vocabulary would you expect to hear related to those traditions?
2 What reasons might people give for maintaining traditions?
3 What reasons might they give for not maintaining traditions?

B 🎧 **1.30** Listen to the interviews. For each interviewee, tick the box if the person thinks it's important for traditions to be maintained and put an X if they do not. Then underline the sentence that best states the main idea.

Interviewee 1 ☐
a) Most young people don't know about traditions.
b) Old people want to keep traditions.
c) Traditions are not relevant to young people.

Interviewee 2 ☐
a) Traditions are important to society.
b) Each generation changes traditions in some way.
c) Graduation ceremonies are different each year.

Interviewee 3 ☐
a) Traditions are important and should not be lost.
b) Young people don't like the city history festival.
c) Some young people are interested in traditions.

Interviewee 4 ☐
a) Many young people find traditions boring.
b) Traditions support family and society identity.
c) A traditional wedding is best.

C Listen again. Make a note of the reasons the interviewees give for their opinions.

Interviewee 1:

Interviewee 2:

Interviewee 3:

Interviewee 4:

D 🗣 Work in groups. Say which of the opinions expressed you agree with and why.

A 🗣 **Look at the photo and discuss what you think it shows. Then read the paragraph and check your ideas.**

ST ANDREWS *Tradition*

St Andrews University has a number of traditions to get used to. There's Rory McLion, mascot of the University Charities Campaign, and there's the red academic gowns. And there's the PH. The letters appear in the pavement outside part of the university, and students avoid walking on them because anyone who does so is said to fail their degree! And then there's the academic family. One thing you'll need to do when you come to St Andrews is find yourself a mum and dad. You're going to need them for Raisin Weekend!

B 🗣 **What traditions are described? What do you think the effect of these traditions is?**

Raisin Weekend

[1] Before you arrive at St Andrews, you need to arm yourself with knowledge of the traditions. Most people know that you're just a fresher and that it takes time to get used to some of them, but the more prepared you are, the better. One of the things you might have heard about is the academic family. This is a great way of forming relationships between students with different levels of experience. Higher-ranking students (mostly third- or fourth-year students) adopt freshers as their 'kids'. When you're adopted, your academic mother and father will help you during your time at university in all kinds of ways. Remember that you can ask someone to be your mother, but you must wait for someone to ask to be your father. It may only be symbolic, but many members of the same academic family become great friends.

[2] And you'll need your academic mother and father for Raisin Weekend, which is an initiation into the life of the university. On Raisin Sunday, your academic mother will invite you for a party in the morning, and your father will host a party in the evening. One part of the ritual is that you're expected to give your mother a present (traditionally a pound of raisins).

[3] The next morning, Raisin Monday, your father will give you a 'raisin receipt' for the present, which you have to carry with you all day. The catch is that the 'receipt' could be written on anything, from a ladder to a donkey! Then, all the students put on fancy-dress costumes and get together in part of the university for the Foam Fight – a massive fight involving shaving foam!

[4] Welcome to St Andrews University!

C VOCABULARY: INSTITUTIONAL TRADITIONS
Match the words (1–6) to the definitions (a–f).

1	initiation (*n.*)	a)	a first-year student at a university or college
2	symbolic (*adj.*)	b)	1. a formal ceremony; 2. something that you do regularly and always in the same way
3	high-ranking (*adj.*)	c)	an animal, person or object used as a symbol of a team or organisation
4	fresher (*n.*)	d)	a process or ceremony in which someone becomes a member of a group
5	ritual (*n.*)	e)	in a position of importance in an organisation
6	mascot (*n.*)	f)	representing sth. important

D 🗣 **VOCABULARY: INSTITUTIONAL TRADITIONS**
Work in groups. Discuss the questions.

1 Are there any rituals or traditions at your school or college?
2 Why do you think some organisations have initiation rituals?
3 What other examples of mascots can you think of? Do you know of any other mascot traditions?

GRAMMAR: verb + object + infinitive

A))) **1.31 LANGUAGE IN CONTEXT**

Listen to the conversation. How does the woman's new job compare to a traditional job?

Keira: So, how are you enjoying your new job?

Lorena: Oh, it was a bit strange at first, but I'm getting used to it! They <u>allow</u> people to arrive at any time they want, and they don't ask us to work exactly eight hours. I actually end up working more hours because there's no specific time that I have to leave! They say they don't force people to work if they aren't feeling creative. They even ask us not to work at our desks all day. They encourage us to move around, talk to people and work in different places. If someone needs you to do something, they text you. It's nice, I suppose, just not what I'm used to.

> **NOTICE!**
> Find and underline in the text verbs that are followed by an object of that verb and then an infinitive. Where do **not** and **don't** go in these types of structures?

B **ANALYSE** Read the conversation in Exercise A again.

Form **Complete the table with examples from the text.**

Verb + noun + infinitive	Negative verb + noun + infinitive	Verb + noun + *not* + infinitive	Verbs
They allow (1) _____ at any time they want.	They don't ask (2) _____ exactly eight hours.	They even ask (3) _____ at our desks all day.	advise, allow, ask, encourage, expect, force, get, invite, need, order, permit, persuade, tell, want, warn, would like

Function **Which statements are true?**

The structure verb + subject + infinitive is used to report …

- ☐ advice
- ☐ encouragement
- ☐ requests
- ☐ commands
- ☐ warnings
- ☐ emotions

> **WHAT'S RIGHT?**
> ○ They tell us don't work at our desks all day.
> ○ They tell us not to work at our desks all day.

C **PRACTISE** Rewrite the sentences with the verbs in brackets.

1 In the army, people have to show respect for higher-ranking members.
The army _____. (*force*)

2 Many universities tell freshers that it is a good idea to join an organisation.
Many universities _____. (*encourage*)

3 Doctors say that people shouldn't look at a computer screen for too long.
Doctors _____. (*warn*)

4 I have to ask someone for help with this project.
I _____. (*need*)

5 At some universities, freshers don't have permission to live off campus.
Some universities _____. (*allow*)

6 Our boss says it isn't a good idea to eat lunch at our desks.
Our boss _____. (*advise*)

D **NOW YOU DO IT** Work in pairs. Discuss the advantages of these traditional and non-traditional ways of working. Can you think of any others? Choose the ways of working that you think suit, or would suit, you best.

Traditional
working in an office
working office hours

Non-traditional
working from home
setting your own schedule

A 🎧 **1.32** Listen to the words ending in *-tion* and *-sion*. Where does the stress fall in each one?

tradition   initiation   institution   permission   distraction   graduation

B 🎧 **1.33** 🗣 Listen to the text. Then work in pairs and take turns reading it. Pay particular attention to words ending in *-tion* and *-sion*.

There's an initiation ritual at our institution which is a very old tradition. All the freshers have to take a test while the established students try to distract them by making lots of noise. You have to try and ignore all the confusion and the distractions, and it takes all your powers of concentration! It's a fun occasion and a real celebration!

SPEAKING: talking about personal rituals

A 🗣 Say whether you think most people follow rituals in their daily lives. Then read the paragraph to see if it supports your opinion.

When you think of rituals, you probably think of traditions at weddings or activities at club initiations. But there is another type of common ritual – personal rituals. For example, an athlete may do things in a certain order on the day of a game, or a singer may always greet an audience in the same way. Personal rituals can be very simple; for example, maybe you always sit in a favourite chair to have your morning coffee, or perhaps you write down the things you have to do every day and cross them off your list as you do them. Other rituals are a little more unusual or even obsessive. There are people who can't sleep if they haven't put away everything in their bedroom or cleaned out their email inbox. Other people count exactly how many times they chew their food before swallowing. Whether they are simple or complex, personal rituals are a part of everyone's life.

B   VOCABULARY: PHRASAL VERBS FOR PERSONAL RITUALS
Complete the sentences with the correct forms of the verbs.
One of the words can be used more than once.

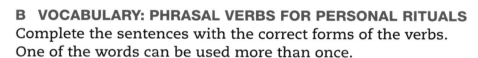

clean   cross   go   line   put   work   write

1   I always _____ on my clothes in the same order every day – socks first!
2   To get organised, I _____ a to-do list; then I _____ things off my list when I have done them.
3   I don't make a list, but every morning I mentally _____ over the things I have to do.
4   I _____ through my wardrobe at the weekend and _____ out what I'm going to wear for the whole week.
5   Every spring, I _____ out all my cupboards and organise the house from top to bottom.
6   Before an exam, I always _____ all my pens up in a certain order on the desk.

C 🎧 **1.34 VOCABULARY: PHRASAL VERBS FOR PERSONAL RITUALS**
Listen to three people talking about their personal rituals. What rituals do they mention?

D 🗣 Think about your personal rituals. Make notes about the things you do. Include reasons why you do them.

E 👥 Independent Speaking Work in pairs. Tell your partner about your rituals.

WRITING: avoiding run-on sentences

An independent clause is a simple sentence (e.g. it has a **subject** and a **verb**). It expresses a complete idea and makes sense on its own. A common error in writing is to connect two independent clauses with a comma, e.g.
The people were wearing traditional costumes, they were celebrating a national festival.
These are called 'run-on sentences'. It is important to check your work and correct any run-on sentences. There is more than one way to do this:

Separate independent clauses with a full stop:
The people were wearing traditional costumes. They were celebrating a national festival.

Add a suitable conjunction:
The people were wearing traditional costumes **because / as** they were celebrating a national festival.

A Read the sentences. Tick the ones that are correct. Correct the run-on sentences.

1 I look forward to having breakfast with my family and going over our plans for the day. ☐
2 Some of our family traditions are normal, some of our traditions might seem strange to other people. ☐
3 Some families are used to doing things in a certain way, they don't like to change. ☐
4 When it's a holiday, we all get together and have a big family meal. ☐
5 One tradition in my family is Sunday dinner, we all relax and talk about our week. ☐
6 Every summer we have a family sports event, in which we all compete against each other! ☐

B Read the blog. Underline any run-on sentences. Then work with a partner and suggest ways to correct them.

> I think family traditions are really important! One in our family is the summer picnic, we organise one every year. Everyone makes sure they have the day off work and the whole family helps prepare. Mum tells everyone to get things ready, she's the one in charge! Everyone has a job and there's lots of activity and noise. Even the little ones have things to do, they love getting involved. Other people think maybe it's someone's birthday or a special occasion, but it never is. It's just our family day, it's very special to all of us because it means we're making time for each other. And the things that happen at the picnic usually keep us laughing for the rest of the summer!
>
> What about you? Do you have any family traditions? Are they important to you? Let us know!

Share Comment . Next post

C 🎧 Work in pairs. Talk about your family traditions. Explain where they come from and what they mean to you.

D Write a comment on the blog describing your family tradition(s). Check your work for run-on sentences. Ask a partner to read your comment and point out any run-on sentences you have missed.

LifeSkills

MANAGING DISTRACTIONS

- Recognise your main distractions.
- Find out ways to change habits and choose ones that work for you.
- Make a plan for managing distractions.

A Read the webpage and take the quiz about electronic distractions.

HOME · COURSES · FACULTY · GR. PRO

STUDENT SUPPORT SERVICES
EFFECTIVE STUDYING

Many students are able to remain completely focused while they are studying, but most of us allow ourselves to be distracted from a task at least some of the time. Our brain seems to let us know when we need a break, so we stop what we're doing to make a phone call, talk to someone in person, eat something, have a coffee or something else. This has always been the case, but in the 21st century there are more potential distractions than ever before. We are constantly bombarded with emails, text messages, tweets, instant messages and other electronic distractions. An important part of being an effective student is to learn to manage those distractions to get the best out of the time you spend studying. Complete our quiz to get an idea of where you might have problems dealing with distractions.

Tick the statements that are true for you. Then estimate how much time you spend every day doing each activity you ticked.

When I am studying/ working ...	YES	NO	MINUTES/ HOURS PER DAY
I check my personal email.	●	●	
I answer my mobile phone.	●	●	
I answer text/instant messages.	●	●	
I chat online.	●	●	
I use social networking sites.	●	●	
I read messages on Twitter, etc.	●	●	
I surf the internet.	●	●	

B Work in pairs. Compare your answers to the quiz. Which of you is more easily distracted? Then discuss the questions.

1 What are your three main electronic distractions? How much time do you spend doing each one every day?
2 What effect do these distractions have on your life? Do they make you less effective when studying?

C Read the rest of the webpage. Discuss the suggestions the writer makes. Make a list of your ideas and then compare it with another pair.

Most people have personal rituals associated with their study habits. For example, some people can't even think about starting to study if their desk isn't organised. Others are used to studying with music on, and they say it helps them stay relaxed while they work. Others always end their day by answering email. These are the normal types of routines that make us feel comfortable. The problem is when rituals or routines become distractions. For example, studies show that most people check their email at least once every 15 minutes. This type of constant distraction disrupts concentration and can make a task longer and more difficult. For many people, email has become more of a bad habit than a useful tool.

If you allow yourself to become distracted too easily, you will have to work to break the habit. Click here to read our top suggestions.

D Help each other make a plan for managing the three main distractions you identified in Exercise B. Write down the changes you plan to make for each distraction. Use suggestions from Exercise C and your own ideas.

A: I always answer text messages immediately, even if they're not urgent. I'm constantly interrupting what I'm doing to go through my messages. I feel nervous if I don't check them.
B: Well, why don't you check them once an hour? You can answer any that are important and answer the rest after work.
A: Yeah, I'm going to force myself not to check them every ten minutes!

E Work in groups. Discuss the questions.

1 What have you learnt about distractions and how to avoid them?
2 How will you manage distractions in the future?

HOW TO SAY IT

You need to get used to …
I would advise you to …
Don't you get tired of …?
It might be a good idea to …
Get someone to help you …

RESEARCH …

Research techniques to help you avoid distractions (e.g. the Pomodoro Technique). Choose one technique and in the next lesson, be ready to explain how this technique works. Consider using it, or the ideas behind it, the next time you study.

REFLECT … How can the skill of managing distractions be useful to you in **Work & Career** and **Self & Society**?

Language wrap-up

1 VOCABULARY

Complete the text with the correct forms of the words from the box. (10 points)

cross off   fresher   go over   initiation   line up
mascot   ritual   symbolic   work out   write down

To: j.patterson@ug.mac.wd

From: kylie@mastermail.mac.wd

Subject: Hello

I can't believe it – I'm actually going to be a University of Georgia student! On Saturday I went to a party for new students. It was a sort of combination welcome party and **(1)** _____, and all the **(2)** _____ had to wear costumes. Wearing a silly costume is a University of Georgia **(3)** _____ and it's **(4)** _____ of our low status, but it's fun too! I went dressed as a chicken because that's the university **(5)** _____! The party was good because I've been quite nervous about starting classes next week. I've **(6)** _____ everything I have to do before next week, and the lists are all over my room. Every day I **(7)** _____ the things I've done, but the lists never seem to get smaller! I've walked around the campus to **(8)** _____ the fastest ways to get from one class to another, and I've **(9)** _____ my timetable mentally lots of times to memorise it. I've bought all my books and have them **(10)** _____ on my desk.

8–10 correct: I can describe institutional traditions and use phrasal verbs for personal rituals.
0–7 correct: Look again at the vocabulary sections on pages 72 and 74.   **SCORE:**   /10

2 GRAMMAR

Choose the correct options to complete the email. (12 points)

To: kylie@mastermail.mac.wd

From: j.patterson@ug.mac.wd

Subject: Re: Hey

Hey Kylie, I'm arriving in Georgia on Thursday to move into my halls before classes start. I just can't **(1)** be / get used to the idea that I'm finally going to be living away from home! Did your parents manage to persuade **(2)** to live / you to live at home? My parents want me **(3)** stay / to stay in halls for at least a year. Anyway … you sound a little nervous. I was too, but my brother told me **(4)** not to / don't worry. He's in his third year here, so he's **(5)** use / used to the place. I think I'm going to need **(6)** he / him to show me around! He said that the first week is pretty light. They don't **(7)** expect / expect you to do lots of homework, and they just allow you **(8)** settle / to settle in. They encourage freshers **(9)** to go / going out and **(10)** be / get used to the campus and the city. I was going to do six classes, but my brother warned me not **(11)** take / to take so many in my first term, so I'm doing the normal five classes. Anyway, once I'm settled, I'll invite **(12)** to stay / you to stay! See you soon!

10–12 correct: I can use *be/get used to* and verbs followed by object + infinitive.
0–9 correct: Look again at the grammar sections on pages 70 and 73.   **SCORE:**   /12

SPEAKING WORKSHOP   Comparing photos

A 🎧 **1.35** Listen to someone comparing these two photos and answering the question below. Make a note of the speaker's main points. Compare your notes in pairs.

Why might these traditions be important to these people?

B Listen again and complete the phrases the speaker uses to compare the photos.

1 _____ photos show …
2 _____ the first photo is of a traditional meal, …
3 One thing the photos have _____ …
4 In the first one it's a family, _____ in the second …
5 The photos are _____ because …
6 _____ the first photo, the second photo shows …

C 🗣 You are going to compare the photos to answer the question from Exercise A. Complete the table with your own ideas. Then work in pairs and compare your answers.

What do the photos have in common?	How are the photos different from each other?
They both show traditional activities.	*A is a family meal, while B is a traditional dance.*
These traditions might be important to these people because _____ _____	

D 🗣 Work in groups and discuss the question in Exercise A.

HOW ARE YOU DOING?
◯ I used good phrases to say what the photos have in common.
◯ I used good phrases to say how the photos differ.
◯ I answered the additional question after comparing the photos.

UNIT 7 DESIGNED TO PLEASE

IN THIS UNIT YOU

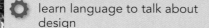

- learn language to talk about design
- read about 3D printing in design
- talk about interior design
- listen to a conversation about celebrity designers
- write a biography about a designer
- learn about showing initiative
- ▶ watch a video about supermarket design

READING
inferring factual information
Why is it important to be able to infer facts when you are reading? Give an example from something you have read recently.

SPEAKING
distancing language
Give some examples of situations when you would need to make a very polite request. What kind of language would you use?

LIFE SKILLS
WORK & CAREER

showing initiative Employers often look for employees who can show initiative at work. What is initiative? What are some different ways to show initiative? Why is it sometimes difficult to show initiative at work?

3 Nathan's boss hasn't arrived at work yet and he can't get in touch with her. Nathan knows that his boss has an important meeting that morning so he decides to contact the other people who are coming to the meeting and rearrange it for an hour later.

Did Nathan show initiative? ☐ yes ☐ no
If not, what could he have done differently?

_____

_____

_____

_____

4 Justin works in a café. He notices that the place is very quiet on weekday mornings. He finds himself standing around a lot at those times. He gets bored until the manager gives him a task to do.

Did Justin show initiative? ☐ yes ☐ no
If not, what could he have done differently?

_____

_____

_____

C 🔊 **2.05** Listen to this man describing his situation at work. What is he worried about?

D 👥 Work in pairs. Make an action plan for the man. Decide what he should do over the next few weeks.

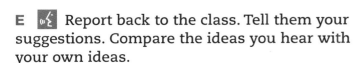

volunteer to attend the conference

E 👥 Report back to the class. Tell them your suggestions. Compare the ideas you hear with your own ideas.

F 👥 Work in groups. Discuss the questions.

1 Do you think you would find it easy to show initiative? Why or why not?
2 Are there any possible risks of showing initiative? What are they, and what could you do about them?

HOW TO SAY IT 👥

He should put himself forward for …
If he volunteered to …, then he could …
One thing he might consider is …
He could show initiative by …
His boss would be impressed if …

 REFLECT … How can the skill of showing initiative be useful to you in **Study & Learning** and **Self & Society**?

 RESEARCH …

Find out about performance reviews. What are they and how do people feel about them? What kind of questions do you need to be prepared for?

Language wrap-up

1 VOCABULARY

Complete the paragraph with words from the box. (12 points)

> affordable   bring   catch   come up   innovative   manufacture
> miniature   personalised   take   template   top quality   unique

Myamazingdesign.com is an **(1)** _____ new website for anyone who has ever dreamt of being a fashion designer. Simply **(2)** _____ with a **(3)** _____ idea for a new fashion trend in clothing or accessories and send your design to us. The design can be **(4)** _____ with your name or logo. We will **(5)** _____ a **(6)** _____ 3D model of your design and send you the model as well as a digital **(7)** _____ that can be used to create a full-size model. All the designs will be shown to the very best **(8)** _____ designers in the field. The low cost makes it an **(9)** _____ way to find out if your designs are going to **(10)** _____ off. Who knows? Maybe your idea will **(11)** _____ on and you'll **(12)** _____ out your own fashion range. . Your career in fashion design starts here!

> **10–12 correct:** I can use words and phrasal verbs connected to design.
> **0–9 correct:** Look again at the vocabulary sections on pages 82 and 84.   **SCORE:**   /12

2 GRAMMAR

Read the paragraph. Correct the mistakes with apostrophes and write the verbs in the correct tense (past perfect or past perfect continuous). Write your answers on the lines below. (12 points)

Stella McCartney is a British fashion designer, as famous for her innovative designs as for her **(1)** fathers' celebrity status. Daughter of the former **(2)** Beatles's singer and bass player, Paul McCartney, her childhood was spent travelling around the world with her **(3)** parents's band *Wings*. By the time she was a teenager, Stella **(4)** _____ (already design) her first jacket. Before bringing out her own fashion label in 2001, she **(5)** _____ (work) for famous designers in Paris and Milan for over two years. By 2003, she **(6)** _____ (open) 53 shops worldwide and **(7)** _____ (launch) her own perfume. Influenced by her **(8)** mother campaign against animal cruelty, Stella refuses to use animal fur or leather in her fashions. Many people admire **(9)** Stellas brand name, which promotes ethical and sustainable fashion. She **(10)** _____ (create) fashionable and ethical clothing for many years before she was appointed designer of the British **(11)** athlete's uniforms in the London Olympics in 2012. It was the first time a fashion designer **(12)** _____ (be) responsible for the design of the British Olympic and Paralympic Team uniforms.

(1) _____   (5) _____   (9) _____

(2) _____   (6) _____   (10) _____

(3) _____   (7) _____   (11) _____

(4) _____   (8) _____   (12) _____

> **10–12 correct:** I can use possessive apostrophes, the past perfect and the past perfect continuous.
> **0–9 correct:** Look again at the grammar sections on pages 83 and 85.   **SCORE:**   /12

WRITING WORKSHOP
Writing a review

A First, look at the photos and read the review. Which place is being reviewed?

Jeff Conley

 5 reviews

 2 helpful
votes

I stayed at the Da Vinci Hotel in London for three days last April because I wanted to visit some popular art exhibitions in the city. The hotel's exterior has the appearance of an old-fashioned 18th century town house, but inside it is full of surprises. Each room is designed in the style of a different artist so that whichever room you choose to stay in, you will have a unique experience. I chose the Van Gogh Room, which was decorated to look like one of Van Gogh's most famous paintings, Bedroom in Arles. This was done so effectively that I felt as if I had travelled back in time to when he painted it in 1888. The room was simply furnished and the dominant colours were yellow and bright blue, reminding me of the sunflowers and the sky of the south of France. It was delightful to be surrounded by furnishings of such unique character and atmosphere.

I also enjoyed eating in the hotel's restaurant, which offered an innovative fusion of Italian and Japanese cuisine. It was disappointing to find that breakfast was not included in the price; however, the service was friendly. The hotel is conveniently located near museums and art galleries. The main disadvantage was the traffic noise because my room overlooked a busy street, but this is difficult to avoid in central London.

B Complete the phrases with words from the text in Exercise A.

Expressing approval

You will have a _____ experience.

It was _____ to be surrounded by …

I also _____ eating in …

Expressing disapproval

It was _____ to find that …

The main _____ was …

C Choose a hotel from the photos on page 87 or one that you have stayed in. Make some notes under the following headings: *room*, *location*, *food*, *service*.

D Write your review. Remember to include some positive and some negative points. Write approximately 200 words.

HOW ARE YOU DOING?

○ I used phrases to express my opinion.

○ I described several aspects of the hotel, including the design.

○ I balanced positive and negative comments.

UNIT 8   A FAIR DEAL?

IN THIS UNIT YOU

- learn language to talk about social problems and solutions
- listen to a lecture about fair trade
- write about international aid
- read about celebrities involved in humanitarian work
- talk about social problems
- learn about rights and responsibilities
- ▶ watch a video about a scheme for lending money to small businesses in the developing world

LISTENING
for main ideas
What kinds of phrases help you identify the main ideas in a lecture or a talk?

WRITING
sentence variety
Why is it important to use a variety of grammatical structures in your writing?

LIFE SKILLS
SELF

understanding rights and responsibilities
We all have rights and responsibilities as citizens, parents, children, students and workers. Why is it important to be aware of these rights and responsibilities?

A 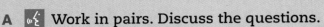 Work in pairs. Discuss the questions.

1 What does the infographic show? What information does it give us?
2 What other types of social inequality exist? Use the photos to help you.

Global Wealth Distribution

RICHEST

Each horizontal band
represents an equal fifth
of the world's people

POOREST

World population	World income
■ Richest 20%	82.7%
■ Second 20%	11.7%
■ Third 20%	2.3%
■ Fourth 20%	1.9%
■ Poorest 20%	1.4%

http://businessideaslab.com/wp-content/uploads/2013/08/wealth_distribution_in_the_world.png

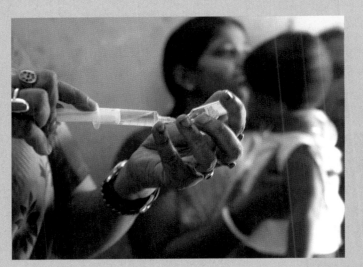

B 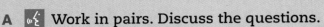 Work in groups. Discuss the questions.

1 Do any types of social inequality exist in your country? If so, what are they?
2 What are some ways we can try to reduce social inequality?

GRAMMAR: *would rather* and *would prefer*

A ♪ **2.06 LANGUAGE IN CONTEXT Listen to the conversation. Is Pete in favour of donating to charities? Why or why not?**

Pete: I think we should get more involved in campaigning for social justice and equality.

Josh: Do you mean by donating money to charity?

Pete: No, not really. I'd rather we didn't just donate money. I'd rather we took some positive action ourselves instead. You know, like collecting clothing for the homeless, or starting a food bank.

Josh: So does that mean you'd rather not work through a charity?

Pete: Yes, I think I'd prefer not to do that. I'd rather get directly involved and start our own campaign.

Josh: Yes, I'd prefer to do that too. I think most people would prefer charities to organise campaigns, but it would be really worthwhile to start our own!

> **NOTICE!**
> Find and underline examples of **prefer** and **rather** in the text. What kind of verb forms follow each one?

B ANALYSE Read the conversation in Exercise A again.

Form & Function Complete the table with examples from the text.

Function	Form	Examples
express the subject's preference about their own actions	*would rather (not)* + infinitive without *to*	(1) _____
		(2) _____
	would prefer (not) + infinitive with *to*	(3) _____
		(4) _____
express a preference about the actions of the subject and someone else, or someone else alone	*would rather* + subject + (negative) verb in past tense	(5) _____
		(6) _____
	would prefer + object + (*not*) + infinitive	(7) _____

C PRACTISE Choose the correct options to complete the sentences.

1 I'd rather start / to start my own campaign.
2 I'd prefer get / to get involved directly.
3 They'd prefer us donate / to donate money to a charity.
4 We'd rather they didn't organise / not organised the campaign.
5 You'd prefer not to work / not work for a charity, wouldn't you?
6 I'd rather didn't raise / not raise money on my own.

> **WHAT'S RIGHT?**
> ○ I'd rather start a food bank.
> ○ I'd rather to start a food bank.

D 🗣 **NOW YOU DO IT Work in pairs. Imagine you are planning a charity event. Discuss what kind of event would be most effective and easy to organise. Say which one(s) you would prefer to do and why.**

- fashion show • charity run • cake sale • jumble sale • volleyball

READING: biographical profiles

A Read the profiles on page 95 and then answer the questions.

1 Who works to help people who have had to leave their home country? _____
2 Who works to help promote education? _____
3 Who also works to protect animals? _____

B 🗣 **Work in pairs. Look at the details below. Which biography are they mentioned in? Write A (Angelina), S (Shakira), B (both) or N (neither). Discuss the evidence for your choices.**

date and place of birth ___	causes they support ___	awards/recognition they received ___
occupation ___	charities they are involved with ___	reason why they became ___
what they studied ___	how they raise money ___	interested in humanitarian issues ___
how they became famous ___		

ANGELINA JOLIE

Angelina Jolie was born on 4th June, 1975 in Los Angeles, California. Her parents were both actors and she began acting at a young age, studying at the Lee Strasberg Theater Institute at just 11 years old. She later studied film at New York University. At 16, she took up a career in modelling. She started acting in films in the 1990s and in 1999 won an Oscar for Best Supporting Actress in the film, *Girl Interrupted*. She has since become one of Hollywood's top names, having starred in over 30 films.

Off-screen, Angelina Jolie devotes considerable time and money to **humanitarian** causes. One of her main interests is helping internationally displaced people. She began visiting **refugees** in camps around the world to draw attention to their needs. In 2011, she was appointed as a Goodwill **Ambassador** for the United Nations High Commissioner for Refugees (UNHCR). She has also received the Global Humanitarian Action Award from the United Nations Association of the USA for her activism on behalf of refugee rights. In addition to forming the Jolie-Pitt **Foundation**, whose aim is to help eradicate **poverty** and conserve wildlife, she regularly donates money to organisations such as Doctors Without Borders and travels the world, drawing attention to global issues.

SHAKIRA

Born on 2nd February, 1977, in Barranquilla, Colombia, Shakira wrote her first song at the age of eight and is now a hugely successful pop singer and dancer. Her music is a blend of Latin, rock and Arabic music styles. Her hit album, *Pies Descalzos*, meaning 'bare feet', sold more than three million copies. By 2012, her worldwide album sales had reached more than $70 million. She is the highest-selling Colombian artist of all time.

In addition to her busy music career, Shakira is known for **philanthropic** work in her native Colombia. As a young girl, she often saw street children who slept in the park every night and she promised to do something to help them one day. After achieving her phenomenal musical success, she created the Fundación Pies Descalzos (Barefoot Foundation) to fight against social **injustice**. The aim of the foundation is to help **underprivileged** children escape a life of poverty. Since 2003, it has opened six schools in Colombia providing education, nutrition and counselling to more than 4000 children and their families. Although it is based in Colombia, the Barefoot Foundation is planning to expand to other countries and has started projects in South Africa and Haiti. Shakira is also a UNICEF Goodwill Ambassador and was named a member of President Obama's Advisory Commission on Educational Excellence for Hispanics in 2011.

C VOCABULARY: SOCIAL ISSUES

Match the words (1–8) to the definitions (a–h).

1 humanitarian (*adj./n.*)
2 refugee (*n.*)
3 ambassador (*n.*)
4 foundation (*n.*)
5 philanthropic (*adj.*)
6 poverty (*n.*)
7 underprivileged (*adj.*)
8 injustice (*n.*)

a) a situation that is not fair or equal
b) the state of not having enough money to pay for basic needs
c) someone who leaves their home country because it is not safe there
d) helping people, especially by giving money to those who need it
e) not having as many advantages as other people
f) an organisation that provides money for research or charity work
g) concerned with helping people who are suffering
h) someone who represents an organisation

D VOCABULARY: SOCIAL ISSUES

Discuss the questions in pairs.

1 Which humanitarian causes do you feel are most important in the world today? Why?
2 What do you think is the role of a Goodwill Ambassador for an organisation like the UN?
3 What do you think is the best way to help refugees? What about people who live in poverty?
4 What kind of social injustice is most serious in your country, in your opinion?

A lecture usually consists of a series of main ideas, each followed by further details and examples. Often, key phrases tell you whether you are hearing the next main idea (*The next point I'd like to discuss is ...*, etc) or further details and examples (*such as ...; for example ...*).

A 🎧 **2.07** You are going to listen to a lecture. Look at the photos and say what you think the speaker is going to talk about. Then listen to the introduction to the lecture and check your ideas.

B 🎧 **2.08** 🗣 Listen to the rest of the lecture. As you listen, choose the option that best expresses each main idea. Compare your answers in pairs.

Purpose:
a) to give producers a fair price
b) to make sure that the producers make more money than the company selling the product

History:
a) Fair trade started with the selling of handmade objects in the 1960s, including things such as jewellery and fabrics.
b) There has been a change from an emphasis on handmade objects to an emphasis on agricultural products.

Labelling:
a) Labels allow fair-trade products to be identified more clearly in supermarkets.
b) Coffee is one of the products that often carries a fair-trade label on the packaging.

Criticism:
a) A number of economists think that coffee producers find it hard to make a living.
b) Several economists say that by paying higher prices, fair trade could make things worse.

C Listen to the lecture again and choose T (true) or F (false).

1	Changing fashions impacted on the kind of fair trade products produced.	T / F
2	Most fair trade these days involves agricultural products.	T / F
3	Fair-trade labels help consumers make their decision.	T / F
4	Anyone can decide to put a fair-trade label on a product.	T / F
5	Few people have benefited from fair trade.	T / F
6	Fair-trade products are usually cheaper than other products.	T / F

PRONUNCIATION: the contracted form of *would*

A 🎧 **2.09** Listen to the sentences. Notice that the contracted form of *would*, (*'d* /d/ or /əd/), is used in the second sentence.

1 a) I would prefer them to give money to local people.
  b) I'd prefer them to give money to local people.
2 a) I would give money to this organisation.
  b) I'd give money to this organisation.
3 a) It would be better to provide medical equipment.
  b) It'd be better to provide medical equipment.

B 🗣 Practise saying one sentence from each pair in Exercise A. Your partner will identify whether you are saying sentence a or b.

A 🎧 **2.10** Listen to the young man taking part in a debate. Tick the points that he makes to support his argument.

'A fair society helps its poorer members.'

1 ☐ Everyone should have enough to eat.
2 ☐ We may know some poor people personally.
3 ☐ We should give children a good chance in life.

B VOCABULARY: SOCIAL JUSTICE

Replace each phrase in italics with a word or phrase from the box.

> benefits (n.)   can't afford (phr.)   have a responsibility (phr.)
> have the right (phr.)   live on (phr. v.)   unemployed (adj.)

1 Some people *manage to survive on* very little money every day.
   _____

2 They *don't have enough money* to buy food for their families.
   _____

3 The government should provide *money for the poor* so that no one goes hungry.
   _____

4 We should all *be allowed* to have enough food.
   _____

5 Anyone can lose their job and be *out of work*.
   _____

6 We all *have an obligation* to help the next generation.
   _____

C VOCABULARY: SOCIAL JUSTICE

Complete the sentences with words and phrases from Exercise B.

1 We should all _____ to freedom and a good standard of living.
2 Many people who are _____ would prefer to work.
3 Unfortunately, life is expensive and we _____ to care for weaker members of society.
4 I'm shocked that some people _____ almost no money.
5 The _____ people get when they are out of work can make life a little easier.
6 Do you agree we _____ to help other people if we can?

D 🗣 Work in pairs. Read the statement below. Student A is *for* the statement. Student B is *against* the statement. Think of three reasons to support your opinion and make notes.

> 'People who are unemployed should get financial support from the government.'

_____
_____
_____
_____
_____
_____
_____

E 👥 Independent Speaking Explain your opinion to your partner. After you have both spoken, say whether your partner has convinced you to reconsider your opinion. Which arguments convinced you?

A 🎧 **2.11 LANGUAGE IN CONTEXT** Listen to the conversation. According to Ranjit and Akhil, why is it difficult for young people to get jobs?

Ranjit: Unemployment is a real problem for young people these days. What's really difficult for them is getting their first job, because employers always look for candidates with work experience.

Akhil: That's right. And if you don't have experience, you can't get a job in the first place! It's really unfair. What students need is good work experience while they're at school so they have a better chance of getting a job after they leave.

Ranjit: That's a good point. How students prepare for work is so important. Who gets the best job very often depends on already having the right skills and experience.

Akhil: Yes, I agree. And where you get your first job can influence your whole future career.

B ANALYSE Read the conversation in Exercise A again.

Form & Function Complete the table with examples from the text. Underline the verb in the noun clause and circle the verb in the main clause.

We can use a noun clause at the beginning of a sentence to highlight information that we think is important.

NOTICE!
Find and underline examples of **what**, **how**, **who** and **where** in the conversation. What kind of clause does each word introduce?

Form	Examples
noun clause about a subject: *What/Who* + base form + noun/adjective	**(1)** *What* _____ *their first job* … *Who* <u>gets</u> *the best job very often* (depends) *on* …
noun clause about an object: *What/How/Who/Where* + noun + base form	*What students* <u>need</u> (is) *good work experience* … **(2)** *How* _____ *so important.* **(3)** … *where* _____ *influence your whole future career.*

C PRACTISE Rewrite the sentences beginning with the noun clause.

1 need / young people / are / what / more training opportunities

_____

2 your job application / you write / is / very important / how

_____

3 you / a big difference / makes / who / interviews

_____

4 your self-confidence / you / where / work / affect / can

_____

5 can create / a good impression / what / a positive attitude / is

_____

WHAT'S RIGHT?
○ What young people need is ….
○ What do young people need is ….

D 🗣 **NOW YOU DO IT** Work in pairs. What would you do to help reduce youth unemployment in your country or city? Discuss ideas and decide on three or four action points. Write them down along with your reasons for choosing them, then share them with the class.

What I would do first is …
What's really important is …

WRITING: sentence variety

⚙ You can often choose different grammatical structures to express an idea. Using a wider range of grammatical structures will make your writing more interesting.

A Read the extract. What problems does the writer suggest are sometimes caused by international aid?

☐☐ Giving aid to countries that are facing economic problems seems like a good idea. ☐ It helps people in a time of crisis. ☐ It's important to continue to support very poor people in the world. However, there are also some dangers associated with giving aid.

☐☐ If an aid organisation provides money and food, it can create dependence that is harmful for the local economy. ☐☐ Importing cheap food can also hurt local producers who cannot compete and therefore lose their income.

☐☐ What world aid organisations need to do is provide training that will enable countries to develop their own economies. ☐ When a country has all its aid supplied in the form of money or food, it can easily become dependent. ☐ Providing medical care and education is a much better way of helping other countries. ☐ If all countries have access to good healthcare and education, they can develop the ability to become independent participants in the global market.

B Read the extract again. Find examples of the following grammatical structures. Underline each one and label it with the correct number(s).

1 subject + verb + object sentence structure
2 noun clause as subject
3 gerund as subject
4 *It's* + adjective + infinitive
5 conditional
6 relative clause
7 causative (*have/get something done* or *have someone do / get someone to do something*)

C Rewrite the sentences with the structures from Exercise B.

1 It is not right to provide aid to countries that are at war.
   Providing aid _____.
2 We should provide aid or people will suffer.
   If we _____.
3 We should make people work for the aid they receive.
   What we _____.
4 Giving suffering people money or food is fair.
   It's fair _____.
5 The government should increase the size of aid payments.
   We should get _____.
6 We provide aid to many countries. It has both advantages and disadvantages.
   Aid, which we _____.

D Write two or three paragraphs explaining your opinion of international aid. Use a range of grammatical structures in your sentences.

You might want to write about
• how important you think international aid is and who you think should receive it.
• whether you think international aid should be increased or decreased.

LifeSkills

UNDERSTANDING RIGHTS AND RESPONSIBILITIES

- Understand what rights and responsibilities are.
- Decide what rights and responsibilities are valid in a given environment or situation.
- Be aware of rights and responsibilities in different contexts.

A Read the definitions of *right* and *responsibility*. As a class, discuss what is meant by 'rights' and 'responsibilities'.

Eleanor Roosevelt with the Universal Declaration of Human Rights

right (*n.*): something that you are morally or legally allowed to do or have
Many new laws have been introduced to protect workers' rights.
Examples of workers' rights include fair pay, equal pay for equal work and the right to work in a safe environment.
Common terms include: human rights, women's rights, workers' rights, children's rights, equal rights

responsibility (to/towards) (*n.*): a moral or legal duty to behave in a particular way
What is the individual's responsibility to others in modern society?
Examples of responsibilities include the responsibility to follow the law, to be tolerant and to respect the rights of others in society.
Common terms include: individual responsibility, social responsibility, collective responsibility

B Work in pairs. Discuss the statements. Decide whether each one is a right or a responsibility. Some statements may be both. Which ones do you agree with? Give reasons.

Parents have the right / responsibility to:

		Right or responsibility?	Agree	Disagree
1	provide food and shelter for their child	☐	☐	☐
2	be a good role model for their child	☐	☐	☐
3	send their child to school	☐	☐	☐
4	help choose their child's school / school subjects	☐	☐	☐
5	teach their child at home	☐	☐	☐
6	discipline their child	☐	☐	☐
7	choose their child's husband or wife	☐	☐	☐
8	provide financial support for their child after the age of 18	☐	☐	☐
9	_____			
10	_____			

Children have the right / responsibility to:

		Right or responsibility?	Agree	Disagree
1	study hard and get good results in school	☐	☐	☐
2	help choose their school / school subjects	☐	☐	☐
3	work part-time after school or at weekends	☐	☐	☐
4	get help and support from their parents when they are in trouble	☐	☐	☐
5	help their parents with cooking and household chores	☐	☐	☐
6	take care of younger siblings	☐	☐	☐
7	take care of their parents when they are old or ill	☐	☐	☐
8	get financial support from their parents after the age of 18	☐	☐	☐
9	_____			
10	_____			

C Work in pairs to add two more rights or responsibilities that 1) parents 2) children have. Then compare your ideas with another pair.

A: *I think parents have the right to …*
B: *I don't agree. Parents should never …*

D Work in pairs. Consider your society as a whole. Make lists of the rights and responsibilities you believe citizens of your country have. Think about the areas below.

Citizenship

Citizens in my country have a right to …	Citizens in my country have a responsibility to …

E Share your lists with the rest of the class. Did anyone come up with any rights or responsibilities that weren't on your lists?

F Work in groups. Discuss the questions.

1 Do you feel you now have a better understanding of rights and responsibilities in general?
2 What have you learnt about your own rights and responsibilities?

REFLECT … How can awareness of rights and responsibilities be useful to you in **Study & Learning** and **Work & Career**?

RESEARCH …

Go online and find a website that gives advice about citizens' rights and responsibilities in the USA, the UK or another English-speaking country. Which of these rights and responsibilities do you think are international and apply in all countries, and which might be different elsewhere?

Language wrap-up

1 VOCABULARY

Complete the paragraph with words and phrases from the box. (12 points)

afford   Ambassadors   foundations   humanitarian   injustice   live on
poverty   refugees   responsibility   right   underprivileged   unemployed

Too many people in the world today are facing (1) _____ and hunger. There are
too many (2) _____, who have been forced to leave their homes by war or
natural disasters. Everyone has a (3) _____ to basic necessities such as food,
water and shelter, but many people cannot (4) _____ them. There are too many
(5) _____ children who lack access to education and healthcare. How can we help
people who have lost their homes and are now (6) _____ without enough money
to (7) _____? Charities and aid organisations believe it is our (8) _____
to help fight against social (9) _____, and some celebrities use their fame to
support (10) _____ causes; some have started their own aid (11) _____
and others have been appointed as Goodwill (12) _____ for organisations like
UNICEF and the United Nations.

10–12 correct: I can talk about social issues and social justice.
0–9 correct: Look again at the vocabulary sections on pages 94, 95 and 97.   **SCORE:**   /12

2 GRAMMAR

A   Choose the correct options to complete the sentences. (6 points)

1   We would prefer / would rather discuss the best way to raise money for charity.
2   I'd prefer charities provide / to provide more health education.
3   They'd rather us not send / we didn't send financial aid.
4   I'd rather to start / start a programme to provide job training.
5   We'd prefer to organise / organise our own charity foundation.
6   I'd prefer them / they to support local organisations.

B   Rewrite the sentences using a noun clause as a subject. (6 points)

1   The world needs more tolerance and understanding.
   What _____.
2   Global trade issues cause some countries to be poorer than others.
   Why _____.
3   Most help is needed in schools and hospitals.
   Where _____.
4   The international community decides which countries receive the most aid.
   Who _____.
5   The worst time to think about training is just after you've lost your job.
   When _____.
6   We need to focus on getting help to people who need it most.
   What _____.

10–12 correct: I can use *would rather* and *would prefer*. I can use noun clauses as subjects.
0–9 correct: Look again at the grammar sections on pages 94 and 98.   **SCORE:**   /12

SPEAKING WORKSHOP   Proposing a solution

A 🔊 **2.12** Read the problem. Then listen to someone proposing some solutions. Complete the notes. What solutions are proposed?

The problem in my city is that rents are much too high. They just aren't affordable. For many people, rent takes up over 50% of their income. Landlords raise the rent every year and there's nothing tenants can do about it. If rents continue to rise, I'll have to leave the city and I'll lose my job. Soon, only rich people will be able to live here. It isn't fair. I think the local authorities should do something about it.

Karina Green, 32, mother of two children

KEEP COSTS LOW

Solution 1:

Solution 2:

B Listen again. Tick the things below that the speaker does.

- ☐ restates the problem in her own words.
- ☐ suggests one solution.
- ☐ suggests two solutions.

- ☐ explains why one solution was better than another.
- ☐ adds details to support each solution.
- ☐ makes a concluding statement.

C Read the problem and make notes for your answer.

University fees set to rise ...

The problem in my country is that university fees are too high. I can't afford to go to university. How can I get a good job if I don't have education and training? I don't think it's fair. Can't the government do something about it?

Solution 1:

Solution 2:

D 🔊 Present your solutions to the class and answer the question in Exercise C.

HOW ARE YOU DOING?

- ◯ I restated the problem in my own words.
- ◯ I suggested two possible solutions with supporting details.
- ◯ I made a concluding statement.

UNIT 9 COMPETITIVE EDGE

IN THIS UNIT YOU

- learn language to talk about competition, personality types and science
- read about the reasons for competitiveness
- talk about different aspects of competition
- listen to experts' opinions about the effects of competition on young people
- write a description of a TV contest
- learn about synthesising information
- ▶ watch a video about a cat show competition

SPEAKING
paraphrasing
In what situations do you need to paraphrase (say in different words) what another person has said or written?

READING
understanding text organisation
Do you often read factual texts? If so, for what reasons? What types of information do writers of factual texts tend to include?

LIFE SKILLS

STUDY & LEARNING

synthesising information How is the skill of synthesising information (using information from different sources) related to the skill of paraphrasing (writing or saying something in your own words)?

A 🗣️ Work in groups. Look at the photos of competitions in different places around the world. Number them in order of how strange you think they are from 1 (strangest) to 6 (least strange). Then discuss the questions.

1 Did most people in the group have similar choices for the strangest and least strange competitions?
2 Do you know of any other unusual competitions? If so, do they take place in your country or other countries?

☐ extreme ironing

Challenge: to iron a shirt while doing an extreme sport
Winner: most creative; best ironing skills

☐ air guitar world championships

Challenge: to pretend to play an electric guitar
Winner: best technical accuracy and artistic form

☐ beard and moustache competitions

Challenge: to grow facial hair
Winner: most creative style

☐ limbo skating

Challenge: to roller skate under low objects
Winner: the skater who clears the lowest object

☐ mobile-phone throwing world championships

Challenge: to throw a mobile phone
Winner: furthest throw

☐ wing suit flying

Challenge: to wear a flying suit and jump off a high point
Winner: the jumper who lands first

B 🗣️ Work in groups. Come up with an idea for a new and unusual competition. Explain it to the class. Take a class vote on the best idea for a competition.

GRAMMAR: gerunds after prepositions

A LANGUAGE IN CONTEXT Read the text. Do you know people who fit each of the four personality types?

A, B, C or D?

[1] Do you get excited about having new challenges? Are you fond of competing in games or competitions? Do you complain about having to queue? Are you easily bored with doing routine activities? Then you are probably a Type A personality.

[2] Do you look forward to going to parties or other social events? Are you good at telling stories or jokes? Are you interested in having a career that involves working with lots of different people? Then you may be a Type B.

[3] Do you care about having all the facts and insist on getting the details right? Do you like to be responsible for organising information or events? Do you worry about making mistakes? You are probably a Type C.

[4] Finally, do you feel happy about doing repetitive activities? Are you capable of following instructions and sticking to routines? Do you object to making changes in the way you do things? Those are traits of a Type D personality.

[5] Of course, the truth is that most people are a combination of two or more personality types, but we may have more traits of one type than of all the others.

B ANALYSE Read the text in Exercise A again.

Form Complete the table with verb and adjective phrases from the text.

Verb + preposition (+ gerund)		Adjective + preposition (+ gerund)	
complain about		excited about	
_____	_____	_____	_____
_____	_____	_____	_____
_____	_____	_____	_____
		_____	

> **NOTICE!**
>
> Find and underline in the text the gerunds that follow prepositions. How do we form gerunds?

C PRACTISE Complete the sentences with the correct preposition and the gerund form of the verbs in brackets.

1 Do you care _____ (use) correct grammar when you speak English, or are you more interested _____ just _____ (communicate)?
2 Do you object _____ (have) to queue for a bus?
3 Are you fond _____ (tell) stories and jokes or are you more interested _____ (listen) to other people talk?
4 Do you get excited _____ (compete) in games or sports?
5 Do you get bored _____ (do) repetitive activities, or do you feel happy _____ (do) routine things?
6 Do you look forward _____ (learn) to do new things, or do you worry _____ (make) mistakes if you have to do something new?
7 Do you enjoy being responsible _____ (organise) things or do you prefer to follow others' instructions?
8 Are you capable _____ (concentrate) on very detailed information for long periods of time?

> **WHAT'S RIGHT?**
> - ◯ I look forward to going out tomorrow.
> - ◯ Sherrie is opposed to see violent films.
> - ◯ We want to go out tomorrow.
> - ◯ I would like to seeing that film.

D NOW YOU DO IT Work in pairs. Ask each other the questions in Exercise C and discuss which dominant personality type you are.

You said that you care about using correct grammar, you don't get excited about competing and you don't get bored with doing repetitive activities. I think you're probably a Type C or D.

LISTENING: to experts' opinions

A  Work in pairs. Look at the title of the presentation and brainstorm some of the things the speakers might mention.

Is competition healthy?

B))) 2.13 Listen to the presentation and check your ideas.

C Listen again and take notes on the main arguments each speaker presents. Compare your answers in pairs and revise your notes if necessary.

D Work in small groups. Say which speaker you most agreed with and why. You can refer to your notes.

E VOCABULARY: SCIENTIFIC NOUNS AND VERBS
Complete the table. Use Nouns and the infinitive of verbs from the presentation. Check your answers in a dictionary.

Verb	Noun	Verb	Noun
test	(1) _____	theorise	(5) _____
(2) _____	study	(6) _____	experiment
research	(3) _____	(7) _____	measurement
prove	(4) _____	(8) _____	conclusion

F VOCABULARY: SCIENTIFIC NOUNS AND VERBS
Complete the sentences with a word from Exercise E in the correct form. There may be more than one correct answer.

1 Psychologists use different methods to _____ theories to find out if they are true.
2 In the field of psychology, _____ are done on the behaviour of both people and animals.
3 I don't think that theory has been _____ yet.
4 After reading this article, I have _____ that a limited amount of competition is good.
5 The desire to play games is one _____ of competitiveness.
6 I want to do some internet _____ on the effects of competition on young adults.
7 I don't think scientists should _____ on animals.
8 His theory is interesting, but I want to see some _____ to support it.

PRONUNCIATION: nouns and verbs with different pronunciation

A))) 2.14 Listen to the words. Underline the stressed syllable in each one. Which syllable is stressed in 1) nouns 2) verbs?

	Noun	Verb
1	record	record
2	present	present
3	produce	produce
4	increase	increase

B))) 2.15 Work in pairs and practise saying the sentences. Then listen and check whether you pronounced them correctly. If not, try again.

1 There is no record of any studies on this topic, so I'm going to research it for my thesis.
2 The research presents two theories about why our brains produce certain chemicals.
3 This machine records data about when there is an increase in the levels of dopamine present in the brain.

SPEAKING: paraphrasing

⚙ To paraphrase something is to express information that you hear or read in your own words. You can do this by changing the vocabulary and sentence structure. Paraphrasing information shows that you have understood it and helps you to avoid plagiarism (copying someone else's work).

A Read the list of paraphrasing techniques. Then read the text and its paraphrased version below. Match the techniques (a–d) to paraphrased sentences (1–4).

a) Change words to different parts of speech, e.g. a noun to a verb. ☐
b) Use synonyms (words that have the same meaning as other words). ☐
c) Change the word order or the sentence structure and add or delete words as necessary. ☐
d) Use different connectors, or break a long sentence into two sentences. ☐

The results of one study suggested that what increased children's sense of self-worth and motivation the most was engaging in group activities, which led the researchers to conclude that more emphasis should be placed on cooperation-based activities.

(1) <u>One study indicated</u> that children experienced (2) <u>an increase</u> in (3) <u>self-esteem</u> and motivation when they did activities in (4) <u>groups. This</u> caused researchers to come to the conclusion that children should engage in more cooperative activities.

B 🔊 Work in pairs. Read the original text and the paraphrased version. Find at least one example of each paraphrasing technique.

Original
If we use our brain for activities such as problem-solving or information recall, it will generate more neurons and axons related to those activities, which improves brain function and causes us to perform better. So the more we do something, the better we get at it, and very often the better we are at something, the more we want to do it. The implication of this may be that the more frequently we play competitive sports and games, the more we want to play them, which may make us more competitive.

Paraphrase
Using our brain for solving problems or recalling information causes it to create more neurons and axons connected with those activities. Our brain functions more effectively, so we improve in these activities. When we are good at something, we often want to do it more often, so it's possible that competing a lot makes us want to compete even more.

C 🔊 2.16 🔊 Work in pairs. Listen to two people discussing a study on peer support among young adults. Paraphrase what each person says. Then compare your ideas with another pair.

D 🔊 Work in pairs. Choose a short text or a paragraph that you have read in this book so far. Paraphrase your text for your partner. If you are not sure about any part of your partner's paraphrase, ask for clarification.

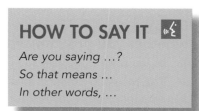

HOW TO SAY IT 🔊

Are you saying …?
So that means …
In other words, …

GRAMMAR: verb + gerund

A 🎧 **2.17 LANGUAGE IN CONTEXT** Listen to the conversation. Does Sandra dislike all reality shows?

Sandra: You know how my brother always laughs at me when I watch reality shows? Well, last night he was watching *Hunting Heroes*!

Rick: Seriously? That has to be the worst reality show in the world! Who would want to <u>watch a load of men</u> hunting wild birds and animals?

Sandra: Yeah, I <u>have trouble</u> understanding why people <u>waste their time</u> watching shows like that.

Rick: <u>I've seen you</u> watching other reality shows though.

Sandra: Yeah. I like some of the competitive ones, like *The Voice* and *Project Runway*. It's interesting to <u>observe the competitors</u> going through the process of learning and building on their talent. You can just <u>feel their confidence</u> increasing every time they pass another round. I could <u>spend my life</u> watching those!

Rick: Not me. I don't like to <u>sit at home</u> watching TV. I <u>have more fun</u> doing outdoor activities.

NOTICE!
Look at the underlined phrases in the conversation. Which verb form follows them?

B ANALYSE Read the conversation in Exercise A again.

Function Choose the correct option to complete the rule.
An object and a gerund often follow verbs of action / perception.

Form Complete the table with words and phrases from the conversation.

Form	Examples
have + object + gerund	objects: *a good time / a hard time / difficulty /* (1) _____ / (2) _____
verb of perception + object + gerund	verbs: *notice / hear / listen to / imagine /* (3) _____ / (4) _____ / (5) _____ / (6) _____
spend/waste + expression of time + gerund	time: *a long time / most of your time / days / years /* (7) _____ / (8) _____
sit/stand/lie + expression of place + gerund	place: *there / at your desk /* (9) _____

C PRACTISE Complete the questions with appropriate verbs in the correct form. There may be more than one correct answer.

1 Do you enjoy _____ around watching TV, or do you prefer being active?
2 In general, how much time do you _____ watching TV a day?
3 What do you _____ the most fun doing? What do you hate to _____ time doing?
4 Do you like _____ people compete on reality shows? If so, which ones?
5 How would you complete this statement? I have a hard time _____ why people watch …
6 On reality shows, you often _____ people behaving badly. Do you think shows like that are a bad influence on society? Why or why not?

WHAT'S RIGHT?
○ He wastes too much time watch TV.
○ He wastes too much time watching TV.

D 🎤 **NOW YOU DO IT** Work in groups. Discuss your answers to the questions in Exercise C.

⚙ Texts have different features and are organised in different ways according to their purpose or function. For example, a factual text, especially if it deals with a scientific topic, usually includes supporting information such as definitions or explanations, descriptions and examples. Recognising these features can help you understand a text better.

A 🗣 **Work in pairs. Read the text and answer the questions.**

1 What is the main idea of the text?
2 What are the two theories in the text? Student A, explain the first theory. Student B, explain the second theory.

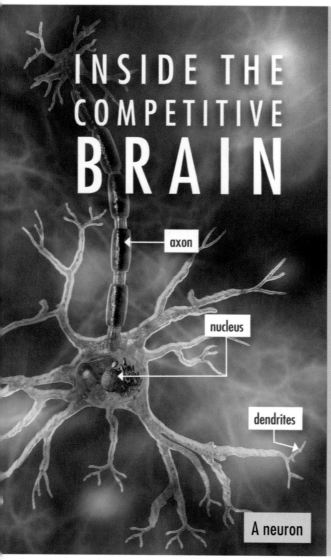

INSIDE THE COMPETITIVE BRAIN

axon

nucleus

dendrites

A neuron

[1] Can we really 'just enjoy the fun of playing the game'? Recent scientific research indicates that the answer may depend on our brain structure and chemistry. There are various theories about how the joy of competing and the will to win may be controlled by nature.

[2] One theory is that our degree of competitiveness is connected to the levels of certain hormones and chemicals in our brain. The male hormone testosterone is actually present in both men and women, and winning causes a rise in testosterone levels, which gives a person a sense of power and success. The desire for this feeling may encourage us to be even more competitive. In contrast, losing appears to cause a drop in testosterone levels, which helps explain the agony of defeat. Winning also stimulates the production of the chemical dopamine, which is a neurotransmitter that produces a feeling of pleasure. The thrill of victory is caused by a combination of increased levels of testosterone and dopamine, and people who have naturally higher levels of these tend to enjoy competing more than those with naturally lower levels.

[3] An alternative theory is that of 'plasticity'. This means that the brain is constantly 'rewiring,' or changing its structure. The nerve cells in the brain are called neurons, and neurons have extensions called dendrites and axons.

These dendrites and axons are responsible for transmitting information to and from other cells in the body. Recent research has indicated that the brain can generate new neurons and axons with use, and this improves brain function. Therefore, if we use our brain for activities such as problem-solving or information recall, it will generate more neurons and axons related to those activities, which improves brain function and causes us to perform better. So the more we do something, the better we get at it, and very often the better we are at something, the more we want to do it. The implication of this may be that the more frequently we play competitive sports and games, the more we want to play them, which may make us more competitive.

[4] These two theories may help to explain why some people are more competitive than others, but can human behaviour ever be attributed just to nature? For example, there may be people with high levels of the brain chemicals associated with competing and winning who don't actually enjoy competitive activities and prefer to channel their energy in other directions. We also all know people who aren't competitive at all who enjoy playing sports even though they seldom win. So the answer to whether we can 'just enjoy the fun of playing the game' appears to be a very unscientific 'it depends'!

B **Look back at the text and underline the following things.**

Paragraph 2

1 a definition of testosterone
2 an explanation of how testosterone is related to winning and losing
3 a description of dopamine
4 an explanation of the effects of testosterone and dopamine

Paragraph 3

5 an explanation of the theory of plasticity
6 a description of neurons
7 an explanation of what dendrites and axons do
8 examples of activities that increase brain function

C **Repeat Question 2 in Exercise A. Did identifying the parts of the text in Exercise B help you understand the text and explain it better the second time? How?**

D VOCABULARY: EXPRESSIONS OF EMOTION

Choose the correct options to answer the questions.

1 These three expressions all have a similar meaning, but they vary in intensity of feeling. Number them in order from the strongest emotion to the weakest.

the joy of ☐   the fun of ☐   the thrill of ☐

2 Which two words are commonly used with 'the agony of'?

defeat ☐   loss ☐   anger ☐   boredom ☐

3 Which two of these three phrases refer to wanting to do something?

a feeling of ☐   the will to ☐   the desire for/to ☐

E 🔊 VOCABULARY: EXPRESSIONS OF EMOTION

Work in groups. Discuss the questions.

1 Do you usually play a game or sport just for the fun of it, or do you have a strong will to win?

2 Does the thrill of victory give you a feeling of power and create a desire for more competition? When you lose, do you suffer from the agony of defeat?

3 Do you generally have a strong desire to compete and be the best? Give examples to support your answer.

WRITING: a description

A Read this description of a reality TV show. Would you like to watch it? Would you like to participate in a reality show? Give reasons for your answers.

THE ISLAND
with Bear Grylls

This reality show tests the survival skills of thirteen men who are left on an uninhabited Pacific island off the coast of Panama. The men have only some very basic tools and a one-day supply of water, so they have to find their own food, water and shelter in order to survive on the island for one month. Most of these men are fit and able, and several of them have some experience of living in extreme conditions, but essentially they are all normal British men used to having the conveniences of modern society. Viewers watch as the men experience the thrill of victory when things go right and the agony of defeat when things go wrong.

The show has been criticised for not being completely real because the producers added extra water to the fresh water on the island and also made sure that there were enough animals on the island to provide sufficient food for the men. However, the show's creator, Bear Grylls, responded that he had a responsibility to make sure that no one actually died, and justified this by adding that the men still had to find the water themselves and hunt the animals for food. Apparently so many men have the desire to test their ability to survive in primitive conditions that over 40,000 have applied to participate in future Bear Grylls' challenges!

B 🔊 Work in small groups. Think of a TV reality show or game show that you all agree is either excellent or terrible. Make notes about what the show involves and why you think it's the best or worst show. With your group, write a description of the show similar to the model in Exercise A.

C 🔊 Choose one member of your group to read your description to the rest of the class. Take a class vote on the best and the worst TV shows based on the descriptions you heard.

LifeSkills

SYNTHESISING INFORMATION

- Gather information from different sources.
- Organise relevant information into categories.
- Combine the information to produce a new idea or a conclusion.

A Read the definition of *synthesising information*. In what situations could synthesising information be useful?

> Synthesising information is the process of combining information and ideas from different sources to create or develop a new idea, focus or perspective, or to reach a conclusion.

B 🎧 Work in groups. Read the instructions on the right and discuss the kinds of information that you need to find out and the types of sources you might use.

Ginkgo biloba – what is it, and does it work?

In teams, prepare a report on what ginkgo biloba is and whether there is any proof that it works. Include information on the following things:

- a description of ginkgo biloba: what it is and what it is used for
- claims made about it by manufacturers of supplements
- statistical or anecdotal evidence to support or refute these claims
- your team's conclusions/opinions based on your findings

C 🎧 Assign one of the texts A–D, below and on page 113, to each group member and follow these steps.

- Read your text in detail and underline the main idea, supporting details and any examples.
- In your notebook, briefly summarise the information that you've underlined in your text.
- Share the information you found out with your group. Decide which information is relevant to your task in Exercise B, and put the relevant information into appropriate categories: description, claims, evidence, conclusions.
- Analyse the information and discuss your conclusions.

A

Ginkgo biloba:
a species of medicinal tree found in China. The leaves contain compounds called flavonoids and terpenoids, which are antioxidants that can help protect the cells of the body. People who want to increase their competitive edge in sports or in their profession often take ginkgo biloba because it is thought to support memory and other brain functions. The substances in ginkgo biloba increase the flow of oxygen to the cells, which can help with blood circulation, boost energy, and produce feelings of physical vitality and mental alertness.

a Ginkgo biloba tree

B

Ⓖ Ginkgo Biloba Capsules

Do you want to perform to the best of your ability? It's a competitive world out there, and whether you are hoping for a promotion at work or competing in a sport, you want to be at your best. Studies have shown that the ancient Chinese tree *Ginkgo biloba* has properties that increase the flow of oxygen to all the cells in the body, including the brain. Benefits of taking gingko biloba supplements may include improvements in memory and other cognitive functions, increased energy and a general feeling of well-being. You will observe your cognitive abilities improving in just a few weeks with ginkgo biloba!

200 capsules 30 ml

£18.95
+ postage and handling

Healthy & Happy SUPPLEMENTS

C

Botany 101, spring term

Nutritional supplements

Review of independent studies to test the effectiveness of ginkgo biloba in increasing cognitive function

Summary	Some data suggests that ginkgo biloba may be effective in increasing mental function and energy levels.
Research	All studies evaluated the effectiveness of taking 30 ml capsules of ginkgo biloba once a day for six months. One third of the participants were older people with memory problems while the others were younger adults who wanted to increase their brain function and energy levels in general.
Results	Three clinical studies in the USA, the UK and Brazil were evaluated. Results were mixed. In one study, 75% of the participants experienced an improvement in memory, and at least a slight increase in energy. In the other two studies, the results were inconclusive; about 20% of the participants experienced some improvement, but the majority showed little to no improvement. In all three studies, researchers observed participants experiencing side effects such as nausea and headaches.
Conclusions	Most of the claims that ginkgo biloba increases brain function are made by manufacturers of supplements, and further studies are needed to prove whether or not ginkgo biloba is actually effective at improving cognitive function and energy levels. There is some evidence that it is; however, there appear to be some negative side effects associated with taking the compound.

D

sallyck: I have a stressful job, and I wanted to increase my energy levels and mental function. I had heard that ginkgo biloba was great for both of those things so I took a supplement for 30 days. My advice? Don't waste your money! The only real effects I had were headaches and nausea, and I didn't feel myself improving in either memory or energy levels. Forget it!

timo34: My grandfather was worried about not being able to remember things, so he started taking ginkgo biloba supplements. After about a month, our family noticed his memory improving, and it also seemed that he had a little more energy. I decided to try ginkgo biloba to see what it would do for me, and I'm glad I did! I have to remember a lot of details in my job, and I think ginkgo biloba has definitely improved my memory.

D 🗣 **With your group, prepare your report. Then present your report to the rest of the class.**

E 🗣 **Discuss the questions.**

1 How can organising information into categories, in this case descriptions, claims, evidence and conclusions, help you synthesise information for a report?
2 Why is it a good idea to use a variety of different sources when writing an analytical report like this one?

HOW TO SAY IT 🗣

In my opinion, this is / isn't relevant, because …

This information can help us prove / conclude …

Although this information suggests …, there is no / some proof here that …

RESEARCH …

Choose another health- or performance-related product that is currently popular. Look up different sources of information on the product. Prepare a report with a short conclusion based on the information you have synthesised. Present your report to the class.

REFLECT … How can the skill of synthesising information be useful to you in **Self & Society** and **Work & Career**?

Language wrap-up

1 VOCABULARY

A Complete the sentences with the phrases from the box. (6 points)

agony of   desire for   feeling of   joy of   thrill of   will to

1 Sitting in the garden gives me a _____ peace.
2 Most athletes have a strong _____ success.
3 Some people enjoy the _____ danger in extreme sports.
4 I don't compete; I run just for the _____ being outdoors.
5 You won't be a champion if you don't have a strong _____ win.
6 It's always difficult to see athletes experiencing the _____ defeat.

B Complete the paragraph with the correct verb or noun form of the words from the box. There may be more than one correct answer. (6 points)

conclude   experiment   measure/measurement   research   test   theory/theorise

We did an **(1)** _____ at university to **(2)** _____ competitiveness in rats. First, we read some **(3)** _____ on the subject, and we decided that our **(4)** _____ was that male rats were more competitive than female rats. We designed a **(5)** _____ in which we put 12 rats (six male and six female) together and put a small amount of food at one end of their cage. We found that the four most competitive rats were two females and two males, so we **(6)** _____ that competiveness, at least in rats, is not based on gender.

10–12 correct: I can use scientific nouns and verbs and expressions of emotion.
0–9 correct: Look again at the vocabulary sections on pages 107, 110 and 111. **SCORE:** /12

2 GRAMMAR

Choose the correct options to complete the text. (12 points)

I think I'm a Type A personality because I love all kinds of competition. For example, I'm not interested **(1)** in / about exercising by myself; I just want to compete! I **(2)** am / have trouble understanding it when I hear people **(3)** to say / saying that they just exercise for the fun **(4)** of / with it. I'm a runner, and I can **(5)** feel / catch my energy **(6)** increases / increasing during a race. I'm capable **(7)** to run / of running much faster when I feel the thrill of competition. I'm pretty competitive at work, too. My colleagues usually spend an hour or more **(8)** to have / having lunch, but I get bored **(9)** with / about sitting **(10)** around / on talking when I could be getting on with my work. I like being responsible **(11)** for / of managing important projects, and I'm looking forward **(12)** to / about being in a top management position some day!

10–12 correct: I can use verb constructions with gerunds.
0–9 correct: Look again at the grammar sections on pages 106 and 109. **SCORE:** /12

WRITING WORKSHOP Writing a discursive essay

A   Read this essay about the use of sports supplements. The writer presents arguments both for and against supplements. Which point of view does she agree with? How do you know?

[1]All sportspeople would like to improve their performance, and there is a whole industry dedicated to helping them do this. Sports supplements are legal, non-prescription products that contain ingredients such as vitamins, minerals, extracts from herbs and other plants, fish oil and caffeine. However, there is some debate about whether they actually do improve performance. In this essay, I intend to discuss the arguments for and against and then conclude with my own opinion.

[2]Proponents of sports supplements say that they cannot harm us and may actually help us. They point out that almost all of the ingredients occur naturally in our bodies or in the foods that we eat. Furthermore, they argue that these supplements really do help us to achieve better results because they contain ingredients that can benefit performance. For example, protein can help to build muscle, or a stimulant such as caffeine can provide extra energy.

[3]However, sceptics list a number of arguments against sports supplements. Firstly, not much medical research has been done, so it is unclear whether they actually work. Secondly, some doctors claim that there are health risks associated with taking supplements. For instance, people often take high doses, which can cause negative side effects. Finally, there is little regulation of the industry, and the supplements often contain too little of the active ingredients to produce the effects that are advertised.

[4]In conclusion, every sportsperson wants to be healthier, fitter and stronger. However, in my opinion, there is no real evidence so far to suggest that sports supplements are effective. I believe the best way for a sportsperson to reach their maximum potential is through training and eating a healthy diet.

B   Look back at the essay and answer these questions.

1   In which paragraph does the writer define sports supplements?
2   The topic sentence of paragraph 2 states that proponents say that supplements 'cannot harm us and may actually help us'. How do the next two sentences support those points?
3   The topic sentence of paragraph 3 says that sceptics list a number of points against supplements. What points does the writer include?
4   Which point of view does the writer agree with? Does she list the points that support her opinion first or second?

C   You are going to write a short essay about the following topic. Read the topic and then use the format below to make notes to help you plan your essay.

A great deal of research is currently being done on how nutrition affects memory and learning. There are some indications that nutrients like fish oil or the substances found in plants like gingko biloba or spirulina improve brain function because they increase circulation of blood to the brain, and therefore they may help stimulate the production of new brain cells. As a result, a number of non-prescription 'brain supplements' are now available to the public. What arguments might there be for or against taking one of these supplements?

Paragraph 1: Topic of essay + explanation or definition
Paragraph 2: First point of view + points supporting it
Paragraph 3: Opposite point of view + points supporting it
Paragraph 4: Summary of your point of view

HOW ARE YOU DOING?

○ I have included a correct greeting and closing.
○ I have stated my reason for writing in my opening paragraph.
○ I have included several points to support my proposal.

UNIT 10 RISKY BUSINESS

LISTENING
rapid speech
Why is it more difficult to understand what someone is saying when they speak quickly in English?

WRITING
requesting action
In what circumstances might you write a letter requesting action? Would you use a formal or informal style? Why?

LIFE SKILLS

SELF & SOCIETY

managing stress Which of these statements describes how you feel about stress at work/school/college?

- ● Stress affects me badly. I get anxious and can't concentrate.
- ● I don't mind a little stress, but too much pressure gets me down.
- ● Stress is just another name for excitement! I love working

GRAMMAR: past modals of deduction

A 🎧 **2.18 LANGUAGE IN CONTEXT** Listen to the conversation. Who are the people talking about. Why do you think he did what he did?

Lili: I've just been reading about Felix Baumgartner; you know, the guy who did that amazing skydive, from 24 miles up. He reached over 800 miles per hour. That's faster than the speed of sound! You **may have** seen the video of it.

Vanessa: Yeah, I know who you mean. He **must have** been terrified. I mean, he **can't have** been sure he'd survive diving from that height.

Lili: Exactly! He **couldn't have** known what to expect. In fact, halfway through the dive he started spinning. He **must not have** expected that to happen.

Vanessa: So what did he do?

Lili: I'm not sure. He **might have** put out his arms and legs, maybe. Or he **could have** used his body weight in some way. Anyway, he got the dive back under control and landed safely.

Vanessa: His family **must have** been relieved.

Lili: I bet he was, too!

NOTICE!
Look at the phrases in bold in the text. What form of the verb follows each phrase?

B ANALYSE Read the conversation in Exercise A again.

Form Complete the table with the correct modals in bold from the text.

Past modals of deduction: modal + (*not*) *have* + past participle

Strong probability	Moderate probability/improbability		Strong improbability	Impossibility
(1) _____	(2) _____ (4) _____ *may not have* (3) _____ *might not have*		(5) _____	(6) _____ (7) _____

Function Choose the correct options to complete the explanation.

We use past modals of deduction to (1) _____ about the past. This may be based on evidence or on our (2) _____. The choice of modal verb depends on whether we think our deduction is very probable, moderately probable, very improbable or (3) _____.

1   a) draw conclusions   b) express regret   c) express criticism
2   a) hopes   b) assumptions   c) wishes
3   a) undesirable   b) impossible   c) illogical

WHAT'S RIGHT?
○ She must know what she was doing.
○ She must have known what she was doing.

C PRACTISE Rewrite the sentences with past modals of deduction.

1   Baumgartner almost certainly felt nervous as he waited to jump.

_____

2   I'm sure it wasn't the first time he'd made a very high skydive.

_____

3   It's possible that he made a number of practice jumps first.

_____

4   I'm sure he didn't plan it alone and I expect he had a team of people behind him.

_____

5   It's possible that he didn't know he would break the sound barrier.

_____

6   It's possible that his family didn't want him to make the jump.

_____

D 🗣 **NOW YOU DO IT** Work in pairs. Describe the photo. Use past modals of deduction to talk about what you think happened before the photo was taken.

A 🎧 **2.19** Listen and repeat the phrases with past modals. How is *have* pronounced?

Affirmative:	Negative:
must have gone	must not have gone
might have taken	might not have taken
may have been	may not have been
could have given	couldn't have given

B 🎧 **2.20** Listen and practise the sentences.

1. Baumgartner must have known the risks before he jumped.
2. He may not have known how fast he'd fall.
3. He couldn't have known exactly where he'd land.
4. He must have been very brave to do it.

LISTENING: rapid speech

⚙ The difficulty in understanding rapid speech is that people tend to run words together. If you learn some common phrases that run together, your ability to understand rapid speech will improve.

A 👥 Work in groups. Look at the photo and read the paragraph. Discuss whether you think David Blaine was in real danger.

Magician and endurance artist David Blaine risked electrocution during an amazing stunt, which he named 'Electrified: One Million Volts Always On'. Blaine managed to spend 72 hours on a 22-foot high pillar, surrounded by huge coils that generated a million volts of electricity. That million volts was aimed at Blaine, who didn't eat or sleep for the duration of the stunt. He wore a metal suit that conducted the electricity away from his body, but even so, doctors found that the stunt had caused him to have an irregular heartbeat.

B 🎧 **2.21** Listen to two people talking about David Blaine's stunt. What is Nicola's opinion of the stunt? What is Jemma's opinion?

C Listen to the conversation again. Tick the phrase in each pair that you hear.

1. a) You could have seen it! ☐
   b) You've got to see it! ☐
2. a) Why, do you think? ☐
   b) What do you think? ☐
3. a) It could have been real. ☐
   b) It couldn't have been real. ☐
4. a) He must have practised a lot of times. ☐
   b) He missed practice a lot of times. ☐
5. a) I don't know. ☐
   b) I want to know. ☐
6. a) I've got to find some photos of it. ☐
   b) I'm going to find some photos of it. ☐
7. a) I don't want to see the photo. ☐
   b) I want to see the photo. ☐
8. a) I've got to go. ☐
   b) I'm going to go. ☐

SPEAKING: speculating about events

A 🎧 **2.22** Look at the photo and listen to the news report. What speculations do the reporters make about the event?

B 🗣 Work in groups. Discuss why you think the man did this and what you think happened in the end.

HOW TO SAY IT 🗣

I think he must have / could have wanted to …
I guess he managed to / was able to …
He must not have been able to …
I imagine what might have happened was that …

C Read the news story. Were your guesses about what happened correct?

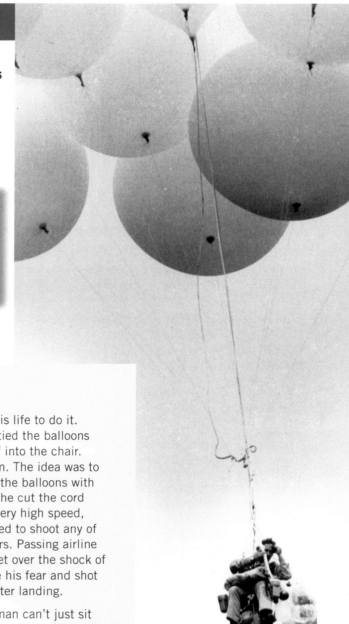

News Features

Larry Walters had always wanted to fly and was willing to risk his life to do it. One day, he bought a deck chair and 45 weather balloons. He tied the balloons to the chair, filled them with helium and then strapped himself into the chair. He brought some sandwiches, a drink and a pellet gun with him. The idea was to float up about 30 feet, enjoy the view, and then shoot a few of the balloons with the pellet gun so that he could return to the ground. But when he cut the cord holding the chair to the ground, the balloons pulled it up at a very high speed, quickly reaching an altitude of 16,000 feet! Larry was too scared to shoot any of the balloons with his gun, so he stayed sitting there for 14 hours. Passing airline pilots reported seeing a man in a deck chair. They may never get over the shock of seeing a man in a chair at 16,000 feet! Finally, Larry overcame his fear and shot a few of the balloons. He descended safely, but was arrested after landing.

When a reporter asked him why he'd done it, Larry replied, 'A man can't just sit around'. The police were unsure how to deal with Mr Walters because they didn't know what to charge him with. Police officers have to put up with people doing a lot of risky stunts, but this was definitely one of the craziest!

D 🗣 Work in pairs. Decide which of the two headlines you will each talk about. Speculate about the news story behind your headline and make notes about what you think may have happened.

DRIVER CHASES RUNAWAY BUS ON BUSY ROAD

BOY WHO SWALLOWED METEORITE LIVES

E 🏃 Independent Speaking Tell your partner what you think happened. When you have both finished talking, check the answers with your teacher.

LifeSkills

MANAGING STRESS

- Recognise the symptoms of and risk factors for stress.
- Consider different ways of relaxing.
- Develop your stress-management strategy.

A Read the article about stress. Do you ever experience stress in your life? What do you think of the advice offered in the article?

COPING WITH STRESS

Some stress is good. It prepares you for action and gives you the adrenaline boost you need for a busy modern lifestyle. However, too much stress can be bad. Have you ever suffered from any of these symptoms?

- low mood
- an inability to relax
- a short temper for no reason
- difficulty concentrating
- unexplained aches and pains
- headaches
- sleeping problems

If so, you could be suffering from stress. Stress can be caused by a number of different factors, including exams, relationship problems, pressure at work and money problems. It's important to work out what causes you stress and to develop a strategy for dealing with it when it happens, such as finding positive ways to relax or communicating with those around you. For each cause of stress, you need to ask yourself these key questions to develop a strategy that works for you:

- Can I avoid the thing that causes me stress? (*avoid strategy*)
  e.g. *If some aspects of your job cause you stress, can you say 'no' to those tasks?*
- Can I change the thing that causes me stress? (*alter strategy*)
  e.g. *If something is causing you stress, be assertive and ask for the change you need.*
- Can I change my reaction to the thing that causes me stress? (*adapt strategy*)
  e.g. *You might be putting yourself under pressure to be perfect. Maybe you need to adjust your standards.*
- Can I learn to live with the thing that causes me stress? (*accept strategy*)
  e.g. *Sometimes we just need to accept that we can't control every aspect of our lives.*

Find the right strategy for each cause of stress and you'll succeed in taking back control of your life and reducing the amount of stress in it.

B What makes you stressed? Look at each of the situations and rate them according to how stressful you find them (1 = not stressful at all, 5 = very stressful).

You have to …	1	2	3	4	5
1 speak in front of a group of people you don't know	○	○	○	○	○
2 speak to one person you don't know at a party	○	○	○	○	○
3 do a test at college or at work	○	○	○	○	○
4 make a long journey on your own	○	○	○	○	○
5 manage with little money for a while	○	○	○	○	○
6 find a new place to live	○	○	○	○	○
7 take care of children or relatives for a day	○	○	○	○	○
8 complain about something, such as service in a restaurant	○	○	○	○	○

C Compare your answers in pairs. Discuss what causes each of you stress. Are you both stressed by the same things?

D Look at the following ways of relaxing. Under each one, write *I already do this*, *I'd like to try this* or *I'm not interested in this*. Make a note of any other ways of relaxing that you do regularly.

1 _____

2 _____

3 _____

4 _____

5 _____

6 _____

7 Other: _____

E Choose one cause of stress in your life. Make notes on how you might use different strategies to cope with it. Use the example to help you. Then compare your ideas in pairs. Which strategy or strategies do you think would be most effective? Give reasons for your answers.

Cause of stress: doing exams at college

AVOID strategy
I could change to a course that uses continuous assessment instead of exams.

ALTER strategy
I wonder if I could ask my tutor about taking oral exams, which I find less stressful, rather than written exams.

ADAPT strategy
I could study more and make sure I'm fully prepared for each exam so that I don't worry about it.

ACCEPT strategy
If I tried to see exams as a chance to show what I know, maybe that would help.

REFLECT ... How can the skill of managing stress be useful to you in **Work & Career** and **Study & Learning**?

RESEARCH ...

One technique some people use for managing stress is meditation. Find out what meditation is and how it works. In your next lesson, tell the class what you have learnt.

F **Work in groups. Discuss the questions.**

1 What have you learnt about managing stress?
2 Do you think you will be able to manage stress better in the future?

Language wrap-up

1 VOCABULARY

Complete the paragraph with words and phrases from the box in the correct form. There may be more than one correct answer. (12 points)

> at risk   dare   exposed   failure   freedom   high-risk   play it safe
> risk your life   risky   run the risk   security   take a chance

Walt Disney once said, 'I dream, I test my dreams against my beliefs, I **(1)** _____ to take risks and I execute my vision to make those dreams come true'. He recognised that there was no advantage in **(2)** _____. By risking **(3)** _____, he made success possible. He **(4)** _____ on unlikely heroes, such as Mickey Mouse, and it paid off. Each of us has to decide whether to **(5)** _____ of failing or to seek **(6)** _____, even if it means accepting less. For those in business, it can sometimes feel as if you're **(7)** _____, so it's important to remember that it's not exactly a game of life and death – although it's true that your career and livelihood are often **(8)** _____. When you are **(9)** _____ to risk, it can in fact give you a great sense of **(10)** _____, as it can feel like you've got nothing more to lose. It may be this, which makes many entrepreneurs engage in **(11)** _____ behaviour away from work, such as hot-air ballooning or motor sports. Perhaps these **(12)** _____ activities give them the same excitement they get from their working lives.

> **10–12 correct:** I can use words and phrases to talk about safety and risk.
> **0–9 correct:** Look again at the vocabulary sections on pages 118 and 120. **SCORE:**   /12

2 GRAMMAR

Choose the correct options to complete the newspaper story. Some answers depend on grammatical form and others on meaning. (12 points)

Investigators have been **(1)** unable / incapable to determine the cause of the crash of an Inter-City commuter plane last Thursday. The small plane, en route from Boston to New York, did not **(2)** succeed / manage to reach the runway, and it crashed into some nearby trees. All 20 people aboard the aircraft were killed. Firefighters **(3)** succeeded in / were able to controlling the resulting fires, and no homes were damaged. Fortunately, all of the homeowners **(4)** were unable to / were able to get out of their houses with no injuries.

Lead investigator Carol Owens said that she wouldn't be able **(5)** make / to make a full statement until more facts were known. She did say that the crash **(6)** may / could not have been caused by weather because Thursday was clear and calm. She said that it **(7)** may / must have been caused by a mechanical failure, but that more information is needed. However, airline officials have stated that they feel strongly that the crash **(8)** must / couldn't have been caused by mechanical failure. 'Our mechanics are extremely good at **(9)** keep / keeping our planes in top condition. We **(10)** are able / can say with great confidence that this tragedy was not the result of poor maintenance,' said IC spokesman Jim Carr.

'It **(11)** must / might have been pilot error, but there's no clear evidence of that, or possibly a pilot medical emergency. Whatever the cause was, it **(12)** may / couldn't have been easy to control the plane and the pilot did well to avoid loss of life on the ground'.

> **10–12 correct:** I can use expressions of ability and past modals of deduction.
> **0–9 correct:** Look again at the grammar sections on pages 119 and 121. **SCORE:**   /12

SPEAKING WORKSHOP
Responding to a question asking for a choice

A 🎧 **2.23** 🎤 Listen to someone answering the question below. Make a note of the main points the speaker makes. Compare your notes in pairs.

> Some people find high-risk activities, such as mountain climbing or extreme sports relaxing. Others find quieter activities relaxing. Which type of activity do you find most relaxing? Include details and examples in your explanation.

B Listen again and complete the phrases the speaker uses to express her preferences.

1 I _____ rather do something quiet than …
2 I find quieter activities _____ extreme sports because …
3 The second reason I _____ quieter activities is …
4 Finally, quieter activities appeal _____ because …
5 I _____ to do activities that don't cause me more stress.

C You are going to answer the question in the box in Exercise D. Before you do that, make notes to answer the questions.

1 What examples of high-risk professions can you think of?
_____

2 What examples of professions with less risk can you think of?
_____

3 Which type of profession would you prefer?
_____

4 What is the first reason for your choice?
_____

5 What is the second reason for your choice?
_____

6 What is the third reason for your choice?
_____

D 🎤 Answer the question. Talk to your group or to the whole class.

> Some people would like to do a high-risk job, such as being a police officer, and would find it exciting. Others would find it stressful and would prefer a less risky profession. Which type of profession would suit you most? Include details and examples in your explanation.

HOW ARE YOU DOING?
- ○ I expressed my choice clearly.
- ○ I used good examples and provided detail in my explanation.
- ○ I gave three clear reasons for my choice.

UNIT 11 THROUGH THE LENS

IN THIS UNIT YOU

- ⚙ learn language to talk about photos and make comparisons
- ⚙ read about selfies
- ⚙ talk about the similarities and differences between two photos
- ⚙ listen to a podcast about photography
- ⚙ write a memo about photos of staff members
- ⚙ learn about giving and receiving feedback
- ▶ watch a video about how photography can help change people's perception of a country

READING
understanding text organisation

Different sentences have different functions. What functions can you think of, e.g. *providing an example*?

SPEAKING
making comparisons

What words, phrases or grammar do you know that we use for comparing one thing to another, e.g. *comparative adjectives*?

LIFE SKILLS

WORK & CAREER

giving and receiving feedback
Who do you receive feedback from in your everyday life? Do you find it a positive experience? Why or why not?

A 🗣 Work in pairs. Look at these images of people taking photos. Tick the situations you have taken photos in. Say what kind of photos you like to take and why.

B 🗣 Work in pairs. How much do you agree with the statements? Explain why.

'I can't stand having my photo taken.'
'I prefer photos of people to photos of beautiful scenery.'

GRAMMAR: verb + gerund/infinitive with a change in meaning

A LANGUAGE IN CONTEXT Read what this person says about an old family photo. Summarise the speaker's response to the photo in your own words.

Oh, I remember being in this photo! That was so long ago! My dad made us try to look natural, but we couldn't do it. Oh, look at that hair! I regret having that style now. What was I thinking? And those clothes! So old-fashioned! Everyone stopped wearing those years ago! What an embarrassing photo! Still, I'll never forget laughing and having fun with my family when we took it. We've all grown up now and are living busy lives, but it's good to stop to think about those days sometimes. You have to remember to treasure every moment with your family because time goes by so fast!

NOTICE!
Find and underline all the gerunds (*-ing*) and infinitives (*to* + verb) in the text. Which verbs do they follow?

B ANALYSE Read the text in Exercise A again.

Form Complete the table with examples from the text.

Verb	+ gerund examples	+ infinitive examples
forget	(forget that you have done sth.; have no memory of sth.) (1) _____	(forget that you need to do sth.) *Don't forget to show him the photo.*
regret	(regret that you have done sth.) (2) _____	(apologise for bad news) *We regret to inform you that your photos have been deleted.*
remember	(remember that you have done sth.; have a memory of sth.) (3) _____	(remember that you need to do sth.) (4) _____
stop	(stop an action/habit) (5) _____	(stop in order to do sth. else) (6) _____
try	(do sth. to see what result it will have) *Try cleaning the lens.*	(in the past = attempt sth. without success; in the present/future = attempt sth. you may/may not be able to do) (7) _____

Function Write *gerund* or *infinitive*.

1. not remember something you have to do: *forget* + _____
   not have a memory of something: *forget* + _____
2. feel bad about something you have to tell someone: *regret* + _____
   wish you hadn't done something in the past: *regret* + _____
3. have a memory of something: *remember* + _____
   not forget something you have to do: *remember* + _____
4. stop an action or habit: *stop* + _____
   stop so that you can then do something else: *stop* + _____
5. attempt something you may or may not be able to do: *try* + _____
   do something to see what result it will have: *try* + _____

WHAT'S RIGHT?
○ I really regret to wear that outfit!
○ I really regret wearing that outfit!

C PRACTISE Write each verb in the correct form.

1. Have you ever taken a photo you regretted _____ (*take*)? What happened?
2. Do you remember ever _____ (*have*) a family photo taken? Who was there? How did you feel?
3. Do you agree with the writer that we should stop _____ (*think*) about our family history sometimes? Do you ever look at family photos and do that?
4. Do you ever try _____ (*avoid*) having your photo taken? When? Why?

D 🎤 **NOW YOU DO IT** Work in pairs. Ask and answer the questions in Exercise C. Use as many of these verbs as you can: *forget, regret, remember, stop, try.*

A 🎙 You are going to listen to a podcast. Look at the photo and say what you think it might be about.

B 👂 **2.24** Listen to the podcast. As you listen, write a word or short phrase you hear in each gap.

1   Jack went to an exhibition of work by

_____.

2   Penny says we often assume photos only appear on _____ these days.

3   Jack was most _____ by Judy Anderson's photo of a homeless man.

4   Nothing takes _____ from the man and his expression.

5   The photo is also a comment on the area's recent

_____.

C   VOCABULARY: DESCRIBING PHOTOS
Listen again and label the photos with words from the box. One of the words can be used more than once.

background   focus   foreground   landscape   portrait   side   subject

1   a _____
2   in the _____
3   out of _____ (*opposite*: in focus)
4   the _____ of the photo

5   a _____
6   on the left-hand _____
7   on the right-hand _____
8   in the _____

D 🎙 **VOCABULARY: DESCRIBING PHOTOS**
Work in pairs. Choose one of the photos in Exercise C and describe it to your partner. Say what you like or don't like about it. Then exchange photos and listen to your partner describe the other photo.

SPEAKING: making comparisons

⚙ We may be in a situation where we need to make a choice between two or more things. By comparing and contrasting, we can judge the things against each other and make a better decision.

A 🗣 **Work in pairs. Look at the photos. Make notes on what the photos have in common and what the differences are between them.**

Things the photos have in common

both show people posing for photos

_____

_____

_____

_____

Things that are different between the photos

the first shows a family, the second shows a group of friends

_____

_____

_____

_____

B 👂 **2.25 Listen to two people comparing the photos in order to choose one to illustrate an article. Tick the points they make against the notes you made in Exercise A. Make a note of any points they mention that you didn't.**

C VOCABULARY: MAKING COMPARISONS

Listen again and complete the sentences with a word or phrase from the box. In one of the gaps, two words are possible.

| alike in contrast in that point of difference similarity unlike whereas while |

1 Both photos are _____ because they're both photos of groups of people.
2 The first is a family portrait and looks like it's been taken by a professional, _____ the second shows someone taking a selfie with their friends.
3 Another _____ is that the people are posing and smiling in both photos.
4 However, maybe the first situation is a little formal for my article, _____ the second situation is much more informal.
5 Another _____ is the reason they're having their photo taken.
6 _____, the second group want a photo they can send to friends or put online to show people what a good time they're having.
7 Both photos are similar _____ the people want to record this moment in their lives, but the second one is more modern.
8 It'll appeal to younger people, _____ the first one.

D 🗣 **VOCABULARY: MAKING COMPARISONS**

Work in pairs. Take turns choosing one of these sets of photos and comparing them.

A LANGUAGE IN CONTEXT Read the opinions. Who do you most agree with?

THE GREAT DEBATE

Home   Archive   About us   Links

Here at The Great Debate, we ask two people to comment on a current issue and then invite you to join the debate! This week, the topic is 'edited photos' and joining us are fashion photographer Shannon Atkins and mental-health campaigner Connor Rourke. Add your comments below.

Shannon Atkins

The vast majority of images we see every day are edited in some way **because of** the demands placed on photographers by the clients. They want their product to be presented in the best way, whether it's a new clothing line, a new perfume or a new car, **so** people want to go out and buy it. **Moreover**, consumers themselves want edited photos. Who wants to see celebrities with pimples and a few extra pounds? I edit the unattractive aspects out of my fashion images **due to** the expectations of both clients and consumers, and I'm not ashamed of that. **Besides that**, I think my job is to give people images to aspire to, to show them a perfect ideal to aim for. Most people don't want reality. They want dreams.

Connor Rourke

I'm very concerned about the number of photos we see these days that have been edited. We are surrounded by images that have been altered to make the subject seem more attractive. **As a result** of this heavy editing, these images present an unrealistic idea of beauty. **Furthermore**, they imply that we ordinary people with our ordinary lives and ordinary bodies are inadequate. **As a consequence**, young people, in particular, feel like failures because they will never match the ideal. This can lead to very low self-esteem. **In addition to** these problems, these images can also make us unhappy with our partners, the people around us and the lives we lead.

NOTICE!

Look at the words in bold in the text. Which of the words have similar meanings?

B ANALYSE Read the opinions in Exercise A again.

Form Complete the rules with the words and phrases in bold from the text.

Connectors of addition	Connectors of cause and effect
and, also, _____, _____, _____, _____	because, _____, _____, _____, _____, _____, therefore

Function Choose the correct options to complete the sentences.

1 Connectors of addition / cause and effect are used to add further points or to provide more information in support of a point.

2 Connectors of addition / cause and effect are used to show how one thing makes another happen, or how one thought follows logically from another.

WHAT'S RIGHT?

◯ She looked perfect in the photo but it was all because heavy editing.

◯ She looked perfect in the photo but it was all because of heavy editing.

C PRACTISE Rewrite each pair of sentences as one sentence. Use the words and phrases in brackets. Add any other words you need.

Many people cannot live up to the ideal they see in images. They get depressed.

1 (because of, fact) _____

2 (result, not being able) _____

Models are made to appear more beautiful. They are often also made to appear thinner.

3 (and, besides that) _____

4 (and, furthermore) _____

D 🎧 NOW YOU DO IT Work in pairs. Discuss the questions. Use connectors of addition and of cause and effect to explain your opinion.

1 Are images around us edited too much? Give reasons for your opinion.

2 What do you think the expression 'the camera never lies' means? Do you agree? Why or why not?

In a well-organised text, different sentences have different functions. Some sentences introduce a new topic, some give additional information or supporting details and some argue for or against an idea. Recognising the function of sentences improves your understanding of the text.

A Read the article. Do you agree with the writer's views on selfies? Explain why or why not.

The selfie ▭ ⚡ ☁ 🖼

¹ The selfie has become the defining document of the modern age. In the world of social networking, no event, whether life changing or mundane, can truly be said to have happened unless the participants have taken a photograph of themselves doing it.

² Selfies are visual diary entries, offered to the world as evidence that you were in a certain place at a certain time. ᵃ They are also, in some ways, a perfect reflection of the digital age, being usually pointless and ephemeral. ᵇ No one treasures someone else's selfie.

³ The selfie is the modern postcard. It says: 'I am here'; it possibly also says: 'Wish you were here'; it frequently says: 'Don't you wish you were here? Because then your life would be as glamorous/popular as mine'.

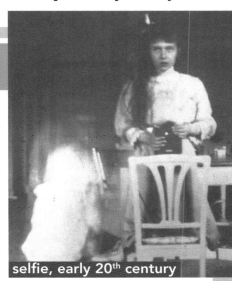

selfie, early 20th century

⁴ The selfie feels new, but people have been taking photographs of themselves since the invention of the camera. ᶜ The first documented case of a teenager taking a selfie was in 1914, when Russia's Grand Duchess Anastasia Nikolaevna, then aged 13, took her own photograph using a Kodak Brownie and sent it to a friend with a letter that read: 'I took this photo of myself looking at the mirror. It was very hard as my hands were trembling'. The instant self-portrait, instantly self-published, is one of the fastest-growing internet phenomena. ᵈ According to a survey, two-thirds of Australian women aged 18–35 take selfies, which are usually then posted on Facebook. According to another, nearly a third of all photographs taken by people aged between 18 and 24 are selfies.

⁵ So what does it say about us, this need to picture ourselves to others, however briefly, however little the rest of the world cares? Inevitably, some sociologists are worried (as sociologists usually are). Some link the selfie-craze to an obsession with looks and the objectification of the body.

selfie, early 21st century

⁶ This seems ridiculous to me. ᵉ Human beings have been picturing themselves, trying to hone their self-images, and showing off to their friends for centuries. The citizens of Pompeii had their portraits painted on their walls, the Roman equivalent of Facebook, to impress the neighbours. The Victorian selfie was the studio portrait, a ritual requirement of middle-class life. The growth of photography brought a boom in self-photography, but the relationship between sitter and photo was always interrupted by a mirror: today's technology enables photographic self-portraits in which the camera is invisible.

⁷ Today we take photos of ourselves faster, more frequently, and with greater self-irony, but the selfie says what the self-portrait has always said: this is me, in my world, with the background and friends that define me.

B Read the article again. Match the underlined sentences (a–e) in the article to the functions (1–5).

This sentence …

1 summarises what comes before it. _____
2 presents a further explanation of an important idea. _____
3 provides evidence against a point of view mentioned. _____
4 provides evidence in support of a claim. _____
5 gives a specific example of something mentioned. _____

C Choose the correct options to complete the sentences.

1 The writer says that people take selfies …
  a) because diaries and postcards are old-fashioned.
  b) because other people want to see what they are doing.
  c) as a way of proving that they really did something.

2 According to the writer, the selfie …
  a) is more popular than ever before.
  b) is mainly popular in Australia.
  c) is only popular among young people.

3 The writer thinks that sociologists …
  a) are right to be worried about selfies.
  b) are obsessed with appearances.
  c) worry too much about this kind of thing.

D 🎧 Work in pairs and answer the questions.

1 Do you ever take selfies? If so, why and in which types of situations?
2 Why are selfies more popular now than ever before?
3 Are there situations where it's not appropriate to take selfies? Where would you not take a selfie?

PRONUNCIATION: stress timing

A 🔊 **2.26** Listen to the quotations about photography. Notice how the underlined stressed syllables fall in a regular rhythm and how the syllables between are said very quickly.

> 'You <u>don't</u> make a <u>photograph</u> just with a <u>camera</u>. You <u>bring</u> to the act of pho<u>tog</u>raphy all the <u>pictures</u> you have <u>seen</u>, the <u>books</u> you have <u>read</u>, the <u>mu</u>sic you have <u>heard</u>, the <u>people</u> you have <u>loved</u>.'
> Ansel Adams, American photographer (1902–1984)

> 'You can <u>look</u> at a <u>picture</u> for a <u>week</u> and never <u>think</u> of it a<u>gain</u>. You can <u>also</u> look at a <u>picture</u> for a <u>second</u> and <u>think</u> of it <u>all</u> your <u>life</u>.'
> Joan Miró, Catalan Spanish artist (1893–1983)

B 🔊 **2.27** 🎧 Practise saying the quotations using a regular rhythm like the examples above. Underline the syllables that you think should be stressed. Listen and check your answers.

> 'What I like about photographs is that they capture a moment that's gone forever, impossible to reproduce.'
> Karl Lagerfeld, German fashion designer, artist and photographer (1933–)

> 'The camera is an instrument that teaches people how to see without a camera.'
> Dorothea Lange, American photographer (1895–1965)

WRITING: a memo

A 🔊 **2.28** Your manager Erica needs new images from staff members for the company website. Listen to the phone message and make a note of what she tells you.

B Read the description of a memo. Write an email memo to staff members in your notebook based on your notes. Start by completing the details at the top of the email.

> A memo is a short letter or email that is sent to people in an organisation. It is often used to pass on information or report on meetings. A memo should be direct and clear and use a neutral tone.

To:	All staff members
From:	_____
Subject:	_____

Dear all,

LifeSkills

GIVING AND RECEIVING FEEDBACK

Giving feedback
- Start by making at least a couple of positive comments.
- Give the other person a chance to respond.
- Use friendly language and positive body language.

Receiving feedback
- Listen with an open mind.
- Ask questions to fully understand the feedback.
- Stay calm and consider the validity of any criticism.

A 🎧 **2.29** Listen to the feedback session. Do you think the manager gives feedback well? Does Paul receive the feedback well? Explain what they do well or badly.

B 🗣 Work in groups. You work as a member of a team in a public relations company. Read the email from your manager and discuss the questions.

1 What two elements need to be included in the campaign?
2 What steps does your manager want you to take?

From: Kaewa@mastermail.mac.wd

Subject: Local tourism campaign

Hello everybody,

As you probably know, the number of tourists visiting our local area has been falling in recent years. It's not clear whether this is due to increasing prices or other factors. However, the local government is eager to reverse this trend, so they've approached us for ideas.

We need to design a whole campaign, and it needs to be visual. We need to really use the beauty of the local area in images for adverts, both in the traditional media and online, and we need to come up with some good slogans for the campaign. Think of as many ways of promoting the area as you can, and I'm sure we'll come up with something powerful between us.

Work with your own team first to come up with good ideas. Then I want you to present your ideas to another team and listen to their constructive feedback. That will guide you in improving your ideas.

I'd like to see what you've come up with in a few days. I'll contact you to arrange a meeting.

Regards,
James Kaewa
Project Manager

C As a group, discuss the ideas. Say what you like or dislike about them and decide which ones you might be able to use in your campaign. Make a note of any other ideas.

- organise a competition for photos taken of the area by local people and use the best ones
- hire a professional photographer to take photos of local sights
- create social media pages with lots of images of different kinds
- do a survey with local people to see what they think
- make a short professional film about the area to go online
- use local people to make a short film
- create a poster campaign with an interesting slogan

D Using ideas from your discussion, and other ideas of your own, make notes to plan your local tourism campaign. Give as much detail as you can.

E Work with another group. Group A, describe your campaign to Group B. Explain how you think it will boost local tourism. Group B, listen and make notes. Then give Group A feedback on their ideas. Follow the steps below. Finally swap roles.

1 Comment on what you liked about the other group's ideas.
2 Comment on any problems you can see with the other group's ideas. Allow the other group to respond.
3 Try to suggest ways to improve the ideas.

F In your group, improve your ideas. Take into account the feedback you received. Then present your ideas to the whole class.

Key features of the campaign

HOW TO SAY IT

We thought ... was a really good idea. In addition, we liked ...
Can you tell us why you decided to ...?
Have you thought about ...? Also, ...
Do you think ... might be better?
I see your point, and I could change things so that ...
Yes, I understand, but the reason I did that was ...

G Discuss the questions.

1 What did you learn about giving and receiving feedback?
2 How well do you usually respond to feedback? Do you think what you've learnt will change your reaction in the future? Why or why not?

REFLECT ... How can the skill of giving and receiving feedback be useful to you in **Self & Society** and **Study & Learning**?

RESEARCH ...

Find out how your local area is advertised to tourists. What images and slogans are used?
Think of ways in which the image of your area could be improved. In the next lesson, report back to the class on what you have found.

Language wrap-up

1 VOCABULARY

Choose the correct options to complete the sentences. (12 points)

1 I can't tell what's in the background because it's out of / off focus.
2 One similar / similarity between the photos is that they were both taken in exotic locations.
3 I'm a big fan of portrait / landscape photos of mountains, lakes and beautiful sunsets.
4 This photo carries a lot of emotion, alike / unlike this one, which is very cold.
5 One mark / point of difference between the photos is the time of day they were taken.
6 I have a wonderful portrait / landscape of an old man. You can almost see what he's thinking.
7 The subject / object of the photo is a young girl playing with her pet dog.
8 The two photos are similar from / in that they both show problems within families.
9 In / By contrast to the first photo, the second shows people enjoying their free time.
10 On the left-hand part / side of the photo, there's a sign, but I can't read what it says.
11 I'm planning to study photography, whereas / otherwise my brother is going to study law.
12 In the background / foreground, close to the camera, there's a young child.

> **10–12 correct:** I can describe photos and make comparisons.
> **0–9 correct:** Look again at the vocabulary sections on pages 131 and 132. **SCORE:** /12

2 GRAMMAR

A Complete the sentences with the correct form of the verbs in brackets. (6 points)

1 I'll never forget _____ (take) my grandfather's photo for the last time.
2 I tried _____ (get) my old camera to work, but I couldn't work out how.
3 As we walked along the bridge, James stopped _____ (take) a photo.
4 Don't forget _____ (send) a photo with your passport application.
5 I'll always regret _____ (get) rid of our old family photo albums.
6 I wish people would stop _____ (take) selfies all the time!

B Complete the paragraph with the words and phrases from the box. There may be more than one correct answer. (6 points)

> as a consequence   as a result   because   besides that   due to   in addition to

Henri Cartier-Bresson's photographs demonstrate that he truly was the father of street photography. **(1)** _____ of his work, street photography with a 35mm camera became the standard of photojournalism. This is **(2)** _____ the fact that he showed that great art could be produced by capturing 'the decisive moment'. This is when the photographer is looking at a scene and **(3)** _____ the elements in it come together perfectly, they feel they must take a photo. **(4)** _____, the phrase 'the decisive moment' has entered the vocabulary of all photographers. **(5)** _____ popularising this phrase, he also showed that it is possible to find great beauty in ordinary life. **(6)** _____, he brought out the beauty of the city he loved – Paris.

> **10–12 correct:** I can use verbs + gerund/infinitive with a change in meaning. I can use connectors of addition and connectors of cause and effect.
> **0–9 correct:** Look again at the grammar sections on pages 130 and 133. **SCORE:** /12

WRITING WORKSHOP

A Read the email report. What problems does the writer identify? What recommendations does she make?

| To: | John Delaney | Subject: | The company website |
| From: | Maria Murray | | |

Introduction
As requested, I have carried out a review of the company website. In particular, I was asked to consider the images. My findings and recommendations appear below.

Overall design
The website was redesigned five years ago. As a consequence, it is badly in need of an update. Visitors to the website are able to read about our products and can order them online. However, at the moment they are not able to share what they find with their friends on social networks. In contrast, our competitors have much more up-to-date sites in that they are well connected to social networks.

Company image
The current images on the website are very formal and professional. They consist mostly of photos of staff members at work or in a professional studio. This gives the website a formal feel, and as a result of this, it isn't very attractive to our younger customers, who are more likely to react better to a more modern company image.

Suggestions for improvement
In terms of the overall design, we need to modernise the website. One key part of that is having better links to social media. In addition to that, it's essential that we update the staff profile photos. I suggest we ask all staff to provide informal selfies, which would make the company image far more fun and modern.

B Read the report again and answer the questions.

1 How does the writer clearly show what this is and who it is for?
2 How does the writer clearly show which particular topic she is discussing?
3 Why is it important in this kind of report to clearly show who it is for and what topics are covered?
4 How formal is the report? Why?

C You are going to write a similar report. Before you write it, read the instructions and make notes to answer the questions.

You work in your local tourism office. Your manager has asked you to write a report about tourism in your area and how it might be improved. Identify any areas that need improvement and make suggestions.

1 Complete the opening of your report:
   To: _____   Subject: _____
   From: _____
2 What two problem areas could you talk about? What problems are you going to identify?
   _____
   _____
3 What suggestions are you going to make to address those problems?
   _____
   _____

D Use your notes to write a report of approximately 200 words.

HOW ARE YOU DOING?
○ I have used an appropriate format for a report.
○ I have used an appropriate tone.
○ I have identified areas for improvement and made suggestions.

UNIT 12 BRIGHT LIGHTS, BIG CITY

IN THIS UNIT YOU

- learn language to talk about cities and city life
- listen to people discuss tourist sites
- write a letter of complaint about a city tour
- read an extract from a guidebook about Fez, Morocco
- talk about cities of the future
- learn about plagiarism
- ▶ watch a video about life in Belfast, Northern Ireland

WRITING
a letter of complaint

When you write a letter or email of complaint about a product or service, what information do you think you should include?

LISTENING
rapid speech

How easy is it to understand native English speakers? What kinds of things cause difficulties for you? Do you have any techniques that help you?

LIFE SKILLS

STUDY & LEARNING

recognising and avoiding plagiarism
What is plagiarism and why is it important to understand what it is?

A Read the list and tick the criteria you think are important in defining a 'great' city. If there are other things that you think are essential to a great city, add them to the list.

A great city should be/have …
- [ ] an international airport
- [ ] a world-famous landmark or tourist attraction
- [ ] the country's financial centre
- [ ] the seat of government
- [ ] a centre for arts and culture
- [ ] a successful sports team
- [ ] an efficient public transport system
- [ ] a top university
- [ ] a multicultural population
- [ ] other: _____

B 🗣 Work in groups. Think about the most important city in your country. Is it the capital city? According to the criteria you chose in Exercise A, would you define it as a great city? Why or why not?

I agree that our most important city is the capital. It has an international airport, but the transport system isn't that great because it doesn't have an underground …

GRAMMAR: connectors of contrast

A LANGUAGE IN CONTEXT Look at the photo. Can you guess which country and city the writer is visiting? Read the extract from a travel blog to check your answer.

I've finally arrived, and I'm feeling OK <u>despite</u> the long flight! The weather is beautiful even though spring is just beginning. Today, I walked around the city and took photos of the jacaranda trees with their beautiful purple flowers. Although Pretoria is full of jacarandas, the trees are not native to South Africa. Just two jacarandas were imported from Rio de Janeiro in 1888, but later many more trees were planted along Pretoria's streets. They are gorgeous; nevertheless, they are a non-native species and some ecologists want to get rid of them. In spite of the fact that the trees are an invasive species, I find myself hoping that they are allowed to stay to continue to enhance the beauty of this attractive city.

NOTICE!
Look at the underlined word in the text. What two ideas are being contrasted in this sentence?

B ANALYSE Read the extract in Exercise A again.

Function Answer the question in your own words.
What do we use words like *but*, *nevertheless* and *despite* for? _____

Form Complete the table with connectors from the text. Then answer the questions below.

Position	Examples
beginning of second clause, after a comma	*Just two jacarandas were imported from Rio de Janeiro in 1888,* **(1)** _____ *later many more trees were planted along Pretoria's streets.*
beginning of second clause, after a full stop or semicolon; comma after the connector	*They are gorgeous;* **(2)** _____ *, they are a non-native species …*
beginning of first clause, clause is followed by a comma / beginning of second clause, no comma	**(3)** _____ *Pretoria is full of jacarandas, the trees are not native …* *The weather is beautiful* **(4)** _____ *spring is just beginning.*
beginning of first or second clause, followed by a gerund phrase, noun phrase or *the fact that*	*In spite of / Despite having to work, I'm having a great time.* *I'm feeling OK* **(5)** _____ *the long flight.* **(6)** _____ *the trees are an invasive species, I find …*

7 Which connectors can go at the beginning of the first or the second clause or phrase?

_____ _____ _____ _____

8 Which connectors have to go at the beginning of the second clause or phrase? _____ _____

C PRACTISE Choose the correct options to complete the sentences.

1 In spite of / However the tourist crowds, Rio de Janeiro is an amazing city.
2 San Francisco is one of the world's best cities even though / despite it can be very windy!
3 But / Although Diane lives in Sydney, she's never been to the Opera House.
4 Travelling abroad is expensive. Nevertheless, / Despite, you can find some bargains online.
5 Personally, I couldn't live in a city however / though I know it must be exciting.
6 My favourite city has to be Delhi, in spite of / but it can be really chaotic!
7 Despite / Nevertheless hating the cold, I loved Stockholm.
8 But / Even though Alberto speaks Catalan, he's never visited Barcelona.

WHAT'S RIGHT?
○ In spite we got really lost, we had an amazing day.
○ In spite of the fact that we got really lost, we had an amazing day.
○ In spite of getting really lost, we had an amazing day.

D **NOW YOU DO IT** Work in pairs. Tell your partner about a popular city or landmark that you've visited, but don't say the name of the place. Your partner will try to guess the place. Use connectors from the table in Exercise B to express contrasting ideas.

I visited … in …, but …
In spite of the fact that …, …

It was …; however, …
Although it's a popular place/landmark, …

WRITING: a letter of complaint

When you write a letter of complaint, use a formal, polite style. Also, make sure you explain the problem clearly, including specific details about the product or service and the problems with it. You're more likely to get a positive response to your complaints if your letter is clear and polite.

A Read the letter of complaint about a city tour. Underline four complaints. Then underline the writer's request.

Dear Sir/Madam:

I am writing with regard to a city tour that I took with your company on 12ᵗʰ July this year. My wife and I booked the tour because we thought the price was reasonable and because it included some of the landmarks of Bangkok that we wanted to see. However, we were very disappointed with it for a number of reasons.

First of all, it lasted only three hours despite being advertised as a five-hour tour, and we didn't visit Wat Pho or the Grand Palace even though these were included on the itinerary. Furthermore, they gave us only 30 minutes at The Golden Mount, but the itinerary said we would have an hour there. Finally, although the tour guide said he spoke good English, he wasn't easy to understand.

For these reasons, I request a refund for the cost of the tour. I enclose the tickets and a copy of my receipt for $88 as proof of payment.

I look forward to hearing from you.

Yours faithfully,

James Thompson

B Read the letter again. What is the writer's purpose in each of the three main paragraphs? What specific details does he include in each paragraph?

C VOCABULARY: FORMAL LETTERS
Write the words or phrases the writer uses to do the following.

1 open his letter _____
2 say why he is writing _____
3 say that he didn't like the tour _____

4 list his main complaints _____
   _____ _____
5 ask the person to reply _____
6 close his letter _____

D **VOCABULARY: FORMAL LETTERS**
Work in pairs. Make a list of things that could go wrong on a tour of your city. Then write a formal letter of complaint to a tour company saying 1) what you were unhappy about and 2) what you want the tour company to do.

E Now work with another pair. Read their letter and make suggestions for possible ways to improve the following things:

Content	Language		
organisation of paragraphs	grammar	vocabulary	use of formal language
details	spelling	punctuation	use of connectors

A 🗣 Work in pairs. Have you ever been to Fez in Morocco? If not, say what you imagine it to be like. Then read the guidebook to see if your ideas were correct. If you have been there, read the guidebook and say whether it describes Fez as you know it.

Fez, founded around 790 AD, is located in the geographical **heart** of Morocco and is also considered by many to be the cultural heart of the country. The main attraction in this ancient **settlement** is the medieval medina, the old **village** at the centre of the city. It has been inhabited since the 10th century and still bustles with crowds of people involved in everything from the spice **trade** to selling street food. The medina of Fez is an important archeological **site** and is the most complete medieval town still in existence. In fact, it is a UNESCO World **Heritage** site. The Fez medina forms a working model of daily life from when civilisation was still young.

A guided tour is the easiest way to tackle Fez, but the brave can take on the narrow **alleys**, risking getting lost and having to haggle with a local to be guided back out. The noise of buying and selling is often interrupted by the cries of mule drivers pushing heavy carts that warn shoppers to get out of the way. The most stunning **views** over the ancient walled city are from the ruined Merenid tombs on a hilltop. From here, it is possible to see some of the magnificent palaces, green-roofed holy places and the Karaouine Mosque. Fez is secretive and shadowy, but captivating and colourful at the same time. It is an important part of world heritage, as well as of the national heritage of Morocco.

B VOCABULARY: DESCRIBING PLACES

Match the nouns in bold in the text with the definitions (1–8).

1 the things you can see from a particular place: _____
2 the art, buildings or traditions that are important to a country and its history: _____
3 the central part of something: _____
4 a place where something interesting happened; an important building or other construction: _____
5 the activity of buying and selling things: _____
6 a very small town: _____
7 a place where people have come to live: _____
8 small passages between buildings: _____

C VOCABULARY: DESCRIBING PLACES

Complete the noun collocations (1–8) with words from Exercise B. Look back at the text in Exercise A to check. There may be more than one correct answer.

1 old / historic / tiny _____
2 coastal / mountain / ancient _____
3 narrow / dark / old _____
4 religious / mystical / archeological _____
5 waterfront / rooftop / stunning _____
6 religious / cultural / national / world _____
7 spice / gold / cloth _____
8 cultural / commercial / geographical _____

D 🗣 Work in groups. Take turns describing a city you know for your group to guess. Use words and phrases from Exercise C where possible.

A: *This is an ancient city on an island near here.*
B: *Is it …?*
A: *No. It's a coastal city, and it has an important archeological site.*

It is not necessary to understand every single word in a conversation, or even every sentence, so don't worry when you hear a word or several words that you don't recognise. Focus on what you do understand.

A Look at the photos. Where do you think each one was taken?

B 🔊 **2.30** Listen and match the extracts from a guided tour to the photos. Listen for key details and ignore anything that is too fast to understand.

Extract 1: ___   Extract 3: ___
Extract 2: ___   Extract 4: ___

C 🔊 **2.31** Listen to the guided tour, this time with comments from participants. Ignore anything you don't understand. Choose *T* (true) or *F* (false). Where were the photos taken?

1	The man and the woman agree that the first area looks very much like Mexico.	T / F
2	Brixton Market has existed since the 1800s.	T / F
3	The guide thinks that visiting his city is a bit like taking a world tour.	T / F
4	They have Indian food for lunch.	T / F
5	The last area on the tour is Chinatown.	T / F
6	The tourists like the international aspect of the city.	T / F

D 🗣 Work in pairs. Listen to the guided tour again. Then discuss what you understood and what you didn't understand. Did you understand the main topics and ideas?

GRAMMAR: ways of talking about the future

A LANGUAGE IN CONTEXT Read about a city of the future. Would you like to live in a city like this? Why or why not?

CITY OF THE FUTURE
MASDAR CITY, ABU DHABI

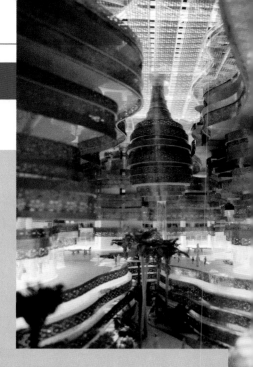

Thousands of people in Abu Dhabi in the UAE (United Arab Emirates) are moving to a new city soon. The government has started building a carbon-neutral city, and on completion in 2025, it will have approximately 50,000 residents. The city is going to function entirely on solar, wind and hydrogen power. There won't be any fuel-powered cars in Masdar; people will travel on electric trains. Some people might also have small electric cars that run on tracks. Several countries are starting to build eco-cities or communities, and some will be finishing them in the last years of this decade, but Masdar City may be the first completely carbon-neutral city.

NOTICE!
Find and underline the verb forms that are used to refer to the future in the text. Which form can be used for either the present or the future?

B ANALYSE Read the text in Exercise A again.

Function Complete the rules with the words from the box. Then complete the examples with words from the text.

> future continuous   going to   ~~may, might or will~~   present continuous

Function	Examples
Use (1) _may, might or will_ to make predictions about the future.	... it (2) _____ approximately 50,000 residents. Masdar City (3) _____ the first completely carbon-neutral city.
Use (4) _____ to make predictions about the future and to talk about intentions.	The city (5) _____ function entirely on solar, wind and hydrogen power.
Use (6) _____ to talk about fixed arrangements and plans.	Thousands of people in the UAE (7) _____ to a new city soon.
Use (8) _____ to talk about events in progress at a particular time in the future.	... some (9) _____ them in the last years of this decade.

The future continuous is formed: *will/won't/may/might + be + -ing* form

It can be used with (*by*) *this time tomorrow / next week*, etc, and *when*.

By this time next year, we may be living in Masdar City.
I will be waiting for you when you arrive in Abu Dhabi.

WHAT'S RIGHT?
○ This time tomorrow, I'll be flying to Rome.
○ This time tomorrow, I'll fly to Rome.

C PRACTISE Choose the correct options to complete the sentences.

1 By July, I'm working / I will be working in the new office.
2 I'm going / I'll go on holiday on Friday. Can you drive me to the airport, please?
3 I think Tom will visit / is visiting Dan when he's in New York.
4 This time next month, we are getting ready / will be getting ready to move to Perth.
5 I might be working / might work when you call, so wait for me to answer.
6 Heather will fly / is flying to Berlin on Monday.
7 The new city will look / will be looking very impressive.
8 By this time tomorrow, I'll drive / I'll be driving down to Buenos Aires.

D 🗣️ **NOW YOU DO IT** Think of predictions, plans and intentions for your life at the points in the future listed below. Use different future forms to tell a partner about them.

- this time tomorrow
- in about two years
- next week
- ten years from now
- by next summer
- when you're 50

A: *This time tomorrow, I'll be travelling to the beach for my holiday.*
B: *Next week, I'm visiting my aunt in Leeds.*

PRONUNCIATION: connected speech

A 🎧 **2.32** Listen to the phrases and compound words. How are they connected? What happens to the final consonant sound of each word?

next time
good day
electric car
will live

love Venice
Club Bayview
same manager

B 🎧 **2.33** Listen to the sentences, paying special attention to the underlined phrases. Then practise saying the sentences using connected speech.

1 The weekend is the <u>best time</u> to travel.
2 We <u>will live</u> in a city where <u>electric cars</u> run on tracks.
3 They <u>love Venice</u> and had a <u>great trip</u> there last year.
4 They might also <u>visit Turin</u> <u>and Dolo</u> <u>next time</u>.
5 <u>Club Bayview</u> has had the <u>same manager</u> for a long time.

SPEAKING: talking about cities of the future

A You are going to talk about what you think cities of the future will be like. First, use the guide opposite to make some notes about your ideas.

B 🎧 **2.34** Listen to three people talking about what they imagine cities of the future will be like. Match each speaker to the correct statement. Were any of the notes you made in Exercise A similar to what the speakers said?

Speaker 1   a)   thinks that rural areas will disappear.
Speaker 2   b)   thinks cities are going to become more environmentally responsible.
Speaker 3   c)   thinks that most people will live below ground in the future.

- Very different from today's cities?
  yes / no
- More / less environmentally responsible than cities now?
  yes / no
- If so, how?
- Type and location of buildings and homes:

- Transport:
- Population distribution:
  more urban / more rural / the same
- Other ideas:

C 🗣️ Work in pairs. Say which of the ideas (a–c) mentioned in Exercise B you most agree with and which ideas, if any, you disagree with.

D 👥 Independent Speaking Think about your ideas from Exercise C and the notes you made in Exercise A. Add any additional points you want to include. Then describe your vision to your partner.

LifeSkills

RECOGNISING AND AVOIDING PLAGIARISM

- Understand what plagiarism is.
- Learn to recognise plagiarism in your own work or others' work.
- Learn and use strategies for avoiding plagiarism.

A Read the definition of *plagiarism*. In small groups, discuss the questions.

1 For what purposes or in what situations do people have to write texts?
2 Where might the information for different types of texts come from?
3 Is it always wrong to use material from someone else's work? Why or why not?
4 What are the possible consequences of plagiarising someone's work?

> **plagiarism** /ˈpleɪdʒəˌrɪz(ə)m/ (*n.*) [UNCOUNTABLE]
> taking someone else's work, ideas or words and using them as if they were your own. Plagiarism also includes borrowing facts, statistics, photos or even song lyrics without giving credit to the source they came from. Because we use the internet as a source of information (which means we have access to so many different people's ideas), it's easy to find that you've plagiarised someone without actually meaning to. Recognising what constitutes plagiarism is a necessary starting point in learning to avoid it.

B How much do you know about what constitutes plagiarism? Work in pairs and take the online quiz.

Is it plagiarism if you …

1 copy and paste a paragraph of text from a website into your work?	YES	NO
2 take someone else's text, but change a few of the words and sentences around?	YES	NO
3 copy a diagram or other data from a source and provide a reference for the source?	YES	NO
4 use another author's ideas as your own ideas?	YES	NO
5 include a fact in your work which is general knowledge?	YES	NO

SUBMIT >

C Match the strategies for avoiding plagiarism (1–4) to the definitions (a–d).

1 paraphrasing
2 quoting
3 referencing/citing
4 summarising different sources

a) mentioning the sources of the information that you have included in your written work
b) using several different texts on a topic and synthesising the information from all of them
c) rewriting what someone has written or said using your own words
d) using quotation marks (' ') around words that you have taken directly from another source and listing the source

D Work in pairs. Read the extract from an article on global urbanisation. Then read texts 1–4 below and decide which one plagiarises the original and why.

> The world is becoming increasingly more urbanised with people leaving rural areas in favour of cities. By the end of the first decade of the 21ˢᵗ century, more than half of the world's population was living in cities, and this trend is projected to continue, especially in Asia and Africa. There are many advantages to urbanisation, for example, cities offer more job opportunities and better infrastructure such as transport links, services and hospitals. However, rapid growth without adequate planning and resources can cause the types of problems seen in the world's biggest cities – inadequate housing, increased crime, and pollution of air, water and soil.
>
> **J.E. Short, PhD**

1 As the world shifts from rural to urban economies, cities are undergoing massive changes. Cities now contain over half of the world's population, and adaptation to this new population model is not easy. People move to cities to find jobs and to take advantage of the services that urban areas offer, but because this change is happening so quickly, cities often cannot cope with the rapid growth and this can result in a number of serious problems which can affect both society and the environment.

2 Most countries in the world are becoming more urban as people move from rural areas to cities. By 2010, over 50% of the population of the world lived in cities, and cities are continuing to grow, particularly in Africa and Asia. Urbanisation can be positive because there are more jobs in cities, and people have more access to services like transport and health care. The disadvantage is that cities often grow too quickly, causing problems such as pollution, lack of suitable places for people to live and higher crime rates.

3 In his article titled **Urbanisation: A Fact of Life**, economist J.E. Short discussed the pros and cons of global urbanisation. He says that while cities do offer people more opportunities than rural areas, there are many problems associated with rapid urban growth. However, he feels that with proper planning and designation of resources, problems such as inadequate housing, increased crime and pollution can be controlled.

4 More and more people around the world are leaving rural areas and moving to cities. This is understandable, as people tend to feel that cities offer more opportunities for education and jobs. However, too often urban growth is fast, unplanned and unregulated, and the result can be chaos. According to economist J.E. Short, '… *rapid growth without adequate planning and resources can cause the types of problems seen in the world's biggest cities …*'.

HOW TO SAY IT

Even though this writer has used some of the same words, …
I think / don't think this writer has plagiarised because …
The writer has/hasn't used … although …
Despite …, this writer has …

E Work in pairs. Discuss how the writers of the other three texts have avoided plagiarism. Say which of the strategies in Exercise C they used.

F Work in groups. Discuss the questions.

1 Have you ever been in a situation when you may have accidentally plagiarised, e.g. by copying and pasting from the internet?
2 What would you do differently now to avoid plagiarism in a similar situation?

 REFLECT … How can the skill of recognising and avoiding plagiarism be useful to you in **Self & Society** and **Work & Career**?

 RESEARCH …

Choose a city you want to know more about and do research on it. Use the information you find to write a short report about the city. Use the techniques in this section to ensure you do not plagiarise any content.

Language wrap-up

1 VOCABULARY

Complete the text with the words and phrases from the box.
Then choose the correct options. (10 points)

> Dear Madam   Despite the large numbers of people   I am writing with regard to
> I look forward to hearing from you   Sincerely

To: Young, Sarah
From: Harper, Zena
Subject: Celebrations

(1) _____,

(2) _____ the local celebrations that took place recently. I thought the event was great and even though the weather wasn't very good, I was glad so many people came.

First of all, may I congratulate the organising committee on their decision to hold the celebrations in the **(3)** heart / alleys of the city – it really gave visitors the chance to see our cultural **(4)** settlement / heritage at its best. We had a stunning **(5)** site / view of the firework display from the main square.

(6) _____, it was easy to get in and out of the city.

I'm attaching some photos of the evening that you might like to include on your website. Some of them were taken at the archeological **(7)** alley / site and others were taken from our **(8)** village / settlement ten miles from the city at the start of the evening. Please let me know if you have any problems downloading them.

(9) _____.

(10) _____,

Zena Harper

8–10 correct: I can use formal written language in letters and describe places.
0–7 correct: Look again at the vocabulary sections on pages 143 and 144. **SCORE:**   /10

2 GRAMMAR

Write the appropriate future forms of the verbs in brackets and choose the correct options to complete the diary entry. (10 points)

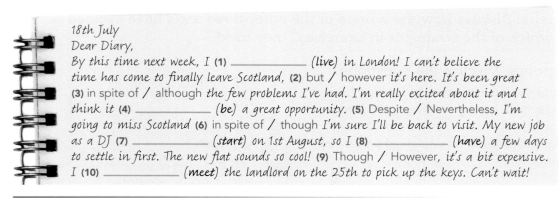

18th July
Dear Diary,
By this time next week, I **(1)** _____ (live) in London! I can't believe the time has come to finally leave Scotland, **(2)** but / however it's here. It's been great **(3)** in spite of / although the few problems I've had. I'm really excited about it and I think it **(4)** _____ (be) a great opportunity. **(5)** Despite / Nevertheless, I'm going to miss Scotland **(6)** in spite of / though I'm sure I'll be back to visit. My new job as a DJ **(7)** _____ (start) on 1st August, so I **(8)** _____ (have) a few days to settle in first. The new flat sounds so cool! **(9)** Though / However, it's a bit expensive. I **(10)** _____ (meet) the landlord on the 25th to pick up the keys. Can't wait!

8–10 correct: I can use connectors of contrast and talk about the future.
0–7 correct: Look again at the grammar sections on pages 142 and 146.   **SCORE:**   /10

SPEAKING WORKSHOP

A 🎧 **2.35** Listen to someone talking about what she thinks her city will be like in the next century. Answer the questions.

1   Does the speaker think Dallas will be completely different in the 22nd century from how it is now?
2   What aspects of 22nd century Dallas does she talk about?
3   In what area does she think there will be the most changes? The fewest changes?

B Listen again. Make a note of the words and phrases the speaker uses for the following purposes.

To express contrast	To express a reason or result	To express an opinion
however	*because (of)*	*I think*
_____	_____	_____
_____	_____	_____
_____		

C You are going to talk about what you think your city will be like in the 22nd century. Use the format below to make some notes.

Introduction to the areas you are going to talk about
Point 1:
•   things you think will change and how
•   things you think won't change much and why
Point 2:
•   things you think will change and how
•   things you think won't change much and why
Point 3:
•   things you think will change and how
•   things you think won't change much and why

D 🎙 Talk to your group or class about your city in the 22nd century. You can refer to your notes, but you should not read.

HOW ARE YOU DOING?
○ I talked about at least three aspects about a city of the future.
○ I used correct phrases to express contrasting ideas, results or opinions.
○ I used correct future verb forms.

Grammar reference

REVIEW OF PAST TENSES

Form	Function	Examples
past simple -ed, irregular forms (*was, had,* etc)	used to describe a completed event, action or state in the past. It is usually the main tense used to talk about the past.	*I grew up in Bradford.* *They spoke to us in a different language.*
past simple with *did* for emphasis *did* + infinitive	used to describe a completed event, action or state in the past and is used for emphasis, often for contrast	**A:** *You didn't find it difficult to settle in when you came to the UK, did you?* **B:** *Not really, but I did feel a sense of culture shock at first.*
past continuous *was/were* + –ing form	used to describe actions or states in progress at a particular time in the past. It is often used to describe background action (e.g. the weather).	*Two years ago, I was living in Canada and researching the customs of indigenous communities.*
past perfect *had* + past participle	used to describe a completed event, action or state that took place before another past event, action or state. It is used to talk about things that happened before the main action.	*We practised the traditional activities that our parents had taught us.*

1 Choose the correct options to complete the sentences.

1 Emily had / was having a bath when her mobile phone rang / was ringing.
2 She learnt / had learned the language of her ancestors even though no one spoke / had spoken it for 50 years.
3 I don't do much sport now, but I had played / did play a lot of football when I had been / was at school.

2 Complete the sentences with the correct past tense form of the verbs in brackets.

1 We _____ (*not get into*) the concert because the tickets _____ (*sold out*).
2 I _____ (*see*) Jane earlier. She _____ (*read*) in the library.
3 When he got home, Jack _____ (*open*) the letter he _____ (*receive*) that morning.

WOULD, USED TO, BE + ALWAYS + -ING

Form	Function	Examples
would (always/never) + infinitive without *to*	used to talk about habits or customs in the past	*Sara would never remember to buy milk on her way home.*
(always/never) *used to* + infinitive	used to talk about habits or customs in the past, or to express something that was true in the past, but is no longer true	*The wind always used to blow really hard in Auckland.* *When I was younger, I used to have short hair.*
be + *always* + *-ing* form (present or past continuous)	used to talk about habits or customs in the present and past	*They are always laughing and joking.* *He was always singing.*

1 Find the mistake in each sentences. Rewrite the sentences correctly.

1 I used struggle with my sense of identity when I first came to the UK.

_____

2 Jessica would never to arrive on time for meetings.

_____

3 They are always try to meet people from different backgrounds.

_____

2 Complete the sentences with the verbs in brackets and _always_, _never_ or _used to_.

1 Where is he? The meeting began ten minutes ago. He
_____ (run) late.

2 The school director usually had lots of activities planned. The students
_____ (get) bored.

3 Amy had her hair cut. She looks really different; she
_____ (have) long hair.

UNIT 2

VERBS WITH STATIVE AND DYNAMIC USES

Function Some verbs are rarely used in continuous forms. They are called stative verbs because they usually refer to states or conditions which continue over a period of time, e.g. _know_, _prefer_ or _agree_. However, some stative verbs are frequently used in continuous (dynamic) forms to convey a different meaning.

Verb	Stative use (simple verb form)	Dynamic use (continuous verb form)
be	(permanent state, general truth) _Lucy is married._	(acting, behaving) _Michael is being really weird._
have	(possession, characteristics) _I have five minutes before lesson starts._	(causing, experiencing) _I'm having problems with my car._
see	(notice, observe, understand) _Do you see what I mean?_	(meet or date) _They've been seeing each other for a while._
think	(have an opinion) _I think it's a good idea._	(the process of thought) _I was thinking about it all day._

1 Choose the correct options to complete the sentences.

1 Do you see / Are you seeing that sign on the wall? It says 'No smoking'.
2 Maria is / is being really thoughtful at the moment.
3 We think / are thinking about where to go on holiday.

2 Complete the sentences with _have/see/be_ in the correct stative or dynamic form.

1 Alex and I _____ really happy in our new home.
2 I _____ much money at the moment. Could we stay home this evening instead of eating out?
3 'Susanna, _____ anyone now, or are you single?'

REPEATED AND DOUBLE COMPARATIVES

Form	Function	Examples
comparative + *and* + comparative *more and more* + multi-syllable adjective *less and less* + multi-syllable adjective	**Repeated comparatives** are used to describe something that is changing.	As a result of social media, it has become easier and easier to maintain friendships around the world. Global corporations are becoming more and more powerful. These days, it is less and less common for people to spend their whole lives in the same job.
the + *more* (+ noun) + verb phrase … *the* + comparative + verb phrase … *the* + comparative + *the* + noun + verb phrase …	**Double comparatives** are used to describe how two things are changing at the same time, or how one thing changes as a result of a change in something else.	The more you study, the more you learn. The more food you buy from local farmers, the easier it is to support the local economy. The more expensive the item, the fewer people will buy it.

1 Put the words in the correct order to form sentences.

1 are / multinationals / less / in / up / more / developed / countries / and / setting / more / .

_____

2 more / face-to-face / have / rely / the / we / less / social media, / on / interaction / we / the / .

_____

3 the / more / world / globalised / the / foreign / resemble / more / each / cities / other / becomes, / the / .

_____

2 Write sentences with a repeated comparative (RC) or double comparative (DC) using the prompts and any other words you need.

1 average temperatures / in the world / become / warm / every year (*RC*)

_____

2 difficult / class / you need to study (*DC*)

_____

3 good / healthcare / long / life expectancy / in a country (*DC*)

_____

UNIT 3

REPORTED SPEECH – MODAL VERBS AND PAST PERFECT

Form		Examples
No tense change	past perfect → past perfect	'I hadn't added him as a friend on Facebook.' He said that he hadn't added him as a friend on Facebook.
modal change	*may* → *might* *will* → *would* *can* → *could* *must* → *had to*	'I may have to work part-time in the future.' She admitted that she might have to work part-time in the future. 'Candidates must do a presentation in the job interview.' They stated that candidates had to do a presentation in the job interview.
no modal change	*might* → *might* *would* → *would* *could* → *could* *should* → *should*	'Could you help me download a new app?' She asked him if he could help her download a new app. 'Celebrities should use their fame to help others.' He claimed that celebrities should use their fame to help others.

1 **Choose the correct options to complete the sentences.**

1 'I must come up with some new ideas.'
I explained that I must / had to come up with some new ideas.

2 'They will assume we can do the task.'
She said that they will / would assume we could / can do the task.

3 'Would you like some coffee?'
I asked him if he would / will like some coffee.

2 **Complete the reported speech sentences.**

1 'I would never miss the final of The X Factor.'
She told me _____.

2 'If I had known, I would have gone.'
Bill said _____.

3 'We should read this best-selling book.'
They admitted _____.

REPORTED SPEECH – OPTIONAL BACK-SHIFTING

Function	Examples
Back-shifting is optional when reporting … **a general truth** 'The Arctic is warming much faster than the Antarctic.' **something that is still true at the moment of reporting** 'The Hanshin Tigers are this year's champions.' **future possibilities or plans** 'The 2020 Olympic Games will be held in Tokyo.'	The article said that the Arctic **is** warming much faster than the Antarctic. The article said that the Arctic **was** warming much faster than the Antarctic. He announced that the Hanshin Tigers **are** this year's champions. He announced that the Hanshin Tigers **were** this year's champions. The IOC declared the 2020 Olympic Games **will** be held in Tokyo. The IOC declared the 2020 Olympic Games **would** be held in Tokyo.
Back-shifting is necessary when reporting **something that is no longer true** 'We're having a New Year's party.'	(On 3rd January): He told me they **were having** a New Year party.

1 **Choose the correct options to complete the sentences. Both options may be correct.**

1 'Ellen and Craig are getting married today.'
She said that Ellen and Craig are / were getting married that day.

2 'More and more people are buying organic food.'
The manager reported that more and more people are / were buying organic food.

3 'Daft Punk will be in the spotlight at next week's Grammy awards.'
The journalist commented that Daft Punk would / will be in the spotlight at next week's Grammy awards.

2 **Complete the sentences. Use back-shifting where appropriate.**

1 'Globalisation is a threat to many indigenous communities.'
He stated _____.

2 'I don't eat meat anymore.'
She declared _____.

3 'Unemployment figures are going to decrease next year.'
The government claimed _____.

NOUN CLAUSES AS OBJECTS

Form	Examples
what = the thing(s) that	*Psychologists are interested in **what makes people happy**.*
how = the way that	*Do you know **how we can cheer Julia up**?*
when = the time that	*Maria still remembers **when you surprised her with a bunch of flowers at work**.*
where = the place that	*I'm not sure **where I can find more information**.*
why = the reason that	*He explained **why he didn't answer your text**.*

1 Underline the noun clauses in the sentences. Then match them to the purpose (a–c).

1 Do you know why no one was interested in the talk today?
2 I think people often feel pessimistic about how the world is changing.
3 I think he'll be happier when he starts his new job.

a) the way that
b) the time that
c) the reason that

2 Complete the sentences with the missing question word.

1 I was fascinated by _____ we learnt in the lesson.
2 Are you trying to decide _____ to go for your anniversary?
3 Thanksgiving is _____ many people choose to visit their families.

REVIEW OF CONDITIONAL FORMS

Form	Function	Examples
third conditional If + past perfect, *would(n't)* have + past participle	used to talk about unreal situations in the past	*If he hadn't taken a year off before going to university, he wouldn't have discovered his true passion.*
second conditional If + past simple, *would(n't)* + verb	used to talk about things the speaker feels are unreal or unlikely in the present or future	*If you were friendlier, you'd be more popular.*
first conditional If + present simple, *will (won't)* + verb	used to talk about things that the speaker thinks are likely or possible in the future	*If she goes to the lessons, her English will definitely improve.*
zero conditional If + present simple, present simple	used to talk about things that are generally true	*If I have time, I go to the gym three times a week.*

1 Find the mistake in each sentence. Rewrite the sentences correctly.

1 If we finished early, we usually go for coffee.

_____

2 If the company doesn't make a loss this year, salaries would increase.

_____

3 He said he would come if he would finish work on time.

_____

2 Write conditional sentences with the words in brackets.

1 I / more outgoing / I / get / job in sales (unreal situation)

_____

2 people / often / less happy / they / focus on / material goods (general truth)

_____

3 team members / get on well / project / complete / on time (likely)

_____

THE PASSIVE

Function We use the passive when the action is more important than the person doing the action, or when we don't know who is doing the action.

Tense	Form	Examples
present simple passive	*is/are* + past participle	*Modern buildings are designed to withstand heavy rains.*
past simple passive	*was/were* + past participle	*Many homes were destroyed by the floods last year.*
present continuous passive	*is/are being* + past participle	*Traffic is being diverted due to roadworks.*
present perfect passive	*has/have been* + past participle	*Tourists have been informed of severe delays on major routes.*
past perfect passive	*had been* + past participle	*We had already been told about the next press conference.*

1 Complete the sentences with the correct passive form of the verbs in brackets.

1 In the last few days, dates for the summer music festival _____. (*confirm*)
2 Possible causes of climate change _____ at the moment. (*discuss*)
3 Most of the region's infrastructure _____ before heavy rains a few weeks ago. (*rebuild*)

2 Rewrite the sentences in the correct passive form.

1 Researchers are carrying out studies into laughter therapy.

_____

2 In the last few years, more and more companies have outsourced jobs.

_____

3 The website has announced Britney Spears' comeback tour.

_____

EXPRESSIONS OF PURPOSE

Form	Function	Examples	Formality
to + infinitive *in order (not) to /* *so as (not) to* + infinitive	used to express why someone does or uses something	*I showed my students a meditation technique* **to** *help them relax.* **In order to** *register, please bring some ID with you.* *Please turn off your mobile phone* **so as not to** *disturb other visitors.*	neutral more formal very formal
for + gerund (*-ing*)	used to express the use or purpose of a thing, especially when the thing is the subject of the verb	*We'll rent a car* **for** *sightseeing.*	neutral
so (that) + noun + clause	used to express why someone does or uses something	*We bought rain barrels* **so (that)** *we could collect rainwater.*	neutral

1 Cross out the two incorrect options.

1 My friend didn't get the job, so I took him to see a film for / to / so that cheer him up.
2 I turned the volume down at midnight to / so as not to / for wake up the neighbours.
3 Use these scissors for / so as to / so that opening the wrapping.

2 Complete the sentences with an expression of purpose. There may be more than one correct answer.

1 Write down a reminder _____ forget your appointment.
2 _____ work well on a team, you need to be a good communicator.
3 We can use the internet _____ booking a last-minute flight.

UNIT 6

BE USED TO / GET USED TO

Form	Function	Examples
be + used to + noun / gerund	used to talk about things we are / are not already familiar with	I'm used to a live audience. He wasn't used to performing for so many people.
get + used to + noun / gerund	used to talk about the process of becoming familiar with something	He's getting used to his new job. She had to get used to wearing a suit.

1 Jack has gone back to university after working. Match the sentences (1–3) to the meanings (a–c).

1 He's getting used to writing essays.
2 He's used to working long hours.
3 He's not used to long lectures.

a) He's not familiar with this.
b) He's in the process of becoming familiar with this.
c) He's familiar with this.

2 Complete the sentences with the correct form of *be/get used* to and the verbs in brackets.

1 I was a teacher for years, but I retired last week. I _____ (not, have) so much free time!
2 I had to get up at 6.30 every morning. So it's taking me a while to _____ (wake up) late.
3 At first it felt strange to spend so much time at home because I _____ (work) long hours in school.

VERB + OBJECT + INFINITIVE

Form	Verbs	Examples
verb + noun + infinitive	advise, allow, ask, encourage, expect, force, get, invite, need, order, permit, persuade, tell, want, warn, would like	They persuaded me to open a Twitter account.
negative verb + noun + infinitive		The company doesn't encourage staff to work from home.
verb + noun + *not* + infinitive		He asked me not to invite his ex-girlfriend to the party.

1 Find and correct the mistake in each sentence.

1 The emergency workers told people do not stay in their homes if they began to flood.
2 Teachers don't expect that you to speak perfect English.
3 Airlines warned to passengers not to carry liquids over 100 ml in their hand luggage.

2 Complete the second sentence so that it has a similar meaning to the first. Use the verb in brackets.

1 Meteorologists convinced people that it's better to avoid unnecessary trips this weekend.
Meteorologists _____ (persuade) take unnecessary trips this weekend.
2 Colleges tell freshers they don't have to take part in initiation ceremonies.
Colleges _____ (not expect) take part in initiation ceremonies.
3 In some companies, employees are permitted four personal days each year when they don't have to work.
Some companies _____ (allow) take four personal days off work each year.

POSSESSIVE APOSTROPHE

Form	Possessive 's examples	Possessive ' examples
singular common/proper nouns singular proper nouns ending in *s*	*London's best park* *the bus's new route* *Luis's house*	*Luis' house*
plural nouns	*The children's school*	*The students' schedule*
compound nouns Separate ownership Joint ownership	*Carla's and Max's noses* *Carla and Max's house*	
double (two consecutive nouns)	*My friend's parents' house*	
with gerund	*The shop's opening is on Friday.*	*The boys' shouting gave me a headache.*

1 Find and correct the mistake in each sentence.

1 I suppose if Caleb's and Joanna's mum had called, she would have left a message.
2 Do you have Max brother's phone number?
3 The mens' football team organises games every Sunday.

2 Write 's in the correct place(s) in the sentences.

1 The dog barking is getting louder and louder.
2 Would you mind looking at Julia and Adrian contracts?
3 I wonder if Chris and Ben sister is coming to the party.

PAST PERFECT VS PAST PERFECT CONTINUOUS

Tense	Form	Function	Examples
past perfect	*had* + past participle	used to describe a completed event, action or state that took place before an event, action, state or time in the past	*Beyoncé had released several albums when she began recording with Jay Z.*
past perfect continuous	*had + been +* gerund	used to emphasise the duration of an event, action or state that continued up to another event, action, state or time in the past	*By the time her friend arrived, she had been waiting for 45 minutes.*

1 Choose the correct options to complete the sentences.

1 I had been having / had a really weird dream when the alarm clock woke me.
2 Susie has finally bought her ticket to Japan! She had been talking / talked about buying it for months.
3 I got to the cinema late, but the film hadn't started / been starting yet.

2 Find the mistake in each sentence. Rewrite the sentences correctly.

1 Every time he checked his inbox, he was disappointed to see that she still hadn't been replying.

_____

2 Unfortunately, the band had played for 30 minutes when we arrived, but we heard a few songs.

_____

3 I had never really been thinking about living abroad until I saw the advert for this job in Spain.

_____

WOULD RATHER AND *WOULD PREFER*

Form	Function	Examples
would rather (not) + infinitive	used to express the subject's preference about their own actions	*I'd rather have coffee.* *She'd rather not have coffee now.*
would prefer (not) + infinitive with *to*		*We'd prefer to have coffee.* *I'd prefer not to have coffee now.*
would rather + subject + (negative) verb in past tense	used to express a preference about the actions of the subject and someone else, or someone else alone	*The manager would rather customers paid by card.* *The manager would rather they didn't pay in cash.*
would prefer + object + (not) + infinitive with *to*		*The manager would prefer customers to pay by card.* *The manager would prefer them not to pay in cash.*

1 Find and correct the mistake in each sentence.

1 Farmers would prefer consumers buy products that promote fair trade.
2 We'd rather you come with us.
3 I would rather to get there by lunchtime.

2 Complete the second sentence so it has a similar meaning to the first.

1 I'd like to come up with my own ideas for a website instead of contracting a designer.
   I would prefer _____.
2 I'd be happier if you didn't post photos of me on social media sites.
   I'd prefer _____.
3 We would like richer countries to cancel poorer countries' debt instead of giving them financial aid.
   We would rather _____.

NOUN CLAUSES AS SUBJECTS

Form	Examples
Form 1: Question word is the subject: **What/Who** + verb + noun/adjective	**What <u>is</u> clear** is that young people are finding it harder to get a job these days.
Form 2: Question word is the object: **What/How/Who/Where** + noun + verb	**Where a child <u>grows up</u>** will influence his/her development.

1 Choose the correct options to complete the sentences.

1 What / Where you choose to stay in the city will depend on your budget.
2 What / Who you meet at university will influence how hard you study.
3 How / Where you get there is up to you – you can go by car, by train or by bus.

2 Put the words in the correct order to form sentences.

1 finished / the test / was / how / you / quickly / amazing / .

_____

2 decided / the / government / what / unfair / was / .

_____

3 win / predict / to / is / hard / who / will / .

_____

GERUNDS AFTER PREPOSITIONS

Form	Examples	
verb + preposition (+ gerund)	*care about, complain about, fond of, insist on, look forward to, object to, worry about*	*We're looking forward to seeing you this weekend.*
adjective + preposition (+ gerund)	*bored with, capable of, excited about, good at, happy about, interested in, responsible for*	*Anna's interested in learning more about the country.*

1 Complete the sentences with prepositions.

1   Is he good _____ playing football?
2   She always complains _____ doing the housework.
3   We're really excited _____ moving to our new house.

2 Complete the sentences with the words from the box and prepositions.

> capable   looking forward   worry

1   The world is _____ producing enough food for everyone.
2   I always _____ giving presentations; I'm terrible at public speaking!
3   She is _____ designing her own home next year.

VERB + GERUND

Form		Examples
have + object + gerund	objects: *a good time / a hard time / difficulty / trouble / fun*	*Sam was having a hard time adjusting to the long hours of his new job.*
verb of perception + object + gerund	verbs: *find / notice / hear / feel / listen to / imagine / watch / see / observe*	*They found him watching TV downstairs.*
spend/waste + expression of time + gerund	time: *days / years / my time / a long time / most of your time / your life*	*I spent years studying for my postgraduate degree.*
sit/stand/lie + expression of place + gerund	place: *there / at your desk / on the sofa / around*	*The crowd just sat listening to the music all afternoon.*

1 Put the words in the correct order to form sentences.

1   for / imagine / day / hours / can't / training / I / five / every / .

_____

2   homework / you / difficulty / having / the / understanding / are / ?

_____

3   work / long / commuters / waste / hours / travelling / to / distances / .

_____

2 Rewrite each pair of sentences as one sentence. Use the verbs in brackets followed by a gerund.

1   I heard a sound. My brother arrived home. (*hear*)

_____

2   James repaired an old property. This took him many years. (*spend*)

_____

3   The girls stood on the beach. At the same time they watched the sunset. (*stand*)

_____

EXPRESSING ABILITY

Form	Examples	
verb + infinitive with to	be able, be unable, manage	I won't be able to help you redecorate tomorrow.
verb + infinitive	could/couldn't, can/can't	She couldn't call you back because she was driving.
verb + gerund	be good at, succeed in, be capable of, be incapable of	I'm pretty good at singing.

1 Complete the sentences with the correct form of the words from the box. Add any other words you need.

1 Not many people _____ to work full-time and study.
2 They said they _____ come because they're taking care of Ella's dog.
3 I always have to help them. They _____ doing it themselves.

> be able
> capable of
> couldn't

2 Rewrite the sentences with the words in brackets.

1 A few years ago, I successfully ran a half marathon. (*manage*)

_____

2 Do you think you will be able to raise £1,000 for charity? (*succeed in*)

_____

3 Sam can design websites. I saw some of her work and it was fantastic. (*good at*)

_____

PAST MODALS OF DEDUCTION

Form modal + *(not) have* + past participle

Strong probability	Moderate probability/ improbability	Strong improbability	Impossibility
John must have heard some good news this morning. He can't stop smiling.	I can't find my glasses. I might/could/may have left them at home.	Sarah must not have come to work. I haven't seen her all day.	Julia can't/couldn't have eaten her lunch. Her sandwich is still on her desk.

1 Complete the sentences with *might/may/could, must* or *can't/couldn't*.

1 Susan got the teaching job. She _____ have impressed the interviewer.
2 They _____ have discussed the new project. The team didn't know anything about it.
3 One possible explanation is that he _____ have forgotten about the meeting.

2 Complete the sentences with the correct form of past modal verbs and the verbs in brackets.

1 Sally _____ (*get on*) well with Steve last week because they're going out again.
2 My brother _____ (*go*) out last night because he doesn't have any money.
3 Where's Owen? I'll check my phone; he _____ (*send*) a text.

VERB + GERUND/INFINITIVE WITH A CHANGE IN MEANING

Verb	Gerund examples	Infinitive examples
forget	(have no memory of sth) I'd completely forgotten seeing that film when I was a child.	(forget that you need to do sth) I forgot to reserve tickets for the cinema and now they're sold out for this evening.

regret	(regret that you have done sth)	(apologise for bad news)
	I regret spending so much money.	We regret to inform you that your account has been suspended.
remember	(have a memory of sth)	(remember that you need to do sth)
	I definitely remember texting Jane earlier because I had to look for her number.	I remembered to text Jane because Mark reminded me.
stop	(stop an action/habit)	(stop in order to do sth else)
	I stopped eating gluten a few months ago.	I stopped to eat my sandwich because I was hungry.
try	(do sth to see what result it will have)	(in the past = attempt sth without success; in the present/future = attempt sth you may/may not be able to do)
	Try going to the gym more if you want to lose weight.	I tried to go to the gym but it was closed.

1 Choose the correct options to complete the sentences.

1   I regret to eat /eating so much at lunch. I feel really tired now.
2   I tried to mend / mending the washing machine, but I think I made it worse.
3   Don't you remember to book / booking an appointment with the dentist? It's in your calendar.

2 Rewrite the sentences using the correct form of the words in bold.

1   I've try / **call** / work several times but nobody answers.

_____

2   I remembered / **post** / that letter for you. It should get there by tomorrow.

_____

3   Do you think you could stop / **eat** / chocolate for a week?

_____

CONNECTORS OF ADDITION / CONNECTORS OF CAUSE AND EFFECT

Form	Function	Examples	
connectors of addition	used to add further points or provide more information in support of a point	and, also, besides that, furthermore, moreover, in addition	I like reading and listening to music. This forest is an area of natural beauty. Besides that, it is home to many wild animals. The new supermarket will be bad for local businesses. Furthermore, it will also be bad for the environment.
connectors of cause and effect	used to show how one thing makes another happen, or how one thought follows logically from another	so, therefore, because of, as a result (of), as a consequence, due to	She loves playing tennis. Therefore, she plays as often as possible. The ice cream melted because of the heat. As a result of not studying, I failed my exams.

1 Choose the correct options to complete the sentences.

1   We need to improve local transport. In addition / Therefore, we need to create new work opportunities in the area.
2   A lot of processed food products today contain high amounts of fat. As a consequence / Furthermore, this is usually saturated fat.
3   There have been many forest fires in Western Australia as a result of / in addition extreme temperatures.

2 Rewrite each pair of sentences as one sentence using words from the box and any other words you need. Omit any words you do not need.

| because of   Furthermore   Therefore |

1   It's important to enjoy what you do. Earning a large salary should not be the most important factor when choosing a career. _____

2   It is claimed that anorexia is increasing. A possible reason is the presence of very thin models in magazines. _____

3   Some studies find that children are more productive when they cooperate with others. Collaborative work increases self-esteem. _____

UNIT 12

CONNECTORS OF CONTRAST

Position	Connector	Examples
beginning of second clause, after a comma	but	New York isn't the capital city, but it is the cultural capital of the USA.
beginning of second clause, after a full stop or semicolon; comma after the connector	however nevertheless	I'm not really enjoying the story of the book I'm reading. However, I do like the author.
beginning of first clause, clause is followed by a comma beginning of second clause, no comma	although even though	Although the talk only lasted 15 minutes, it was very informative. The talk during the excursion was very informative even though it only lasted 15 minutes.
beginning of first or second clause, followed by a gerund phrase, noun phrase or *the fact that*	despite in spite of	Despite his qualifications, David is finding it hard to get a job. Despite passing all his exams, David decided not to go to college and got a job instead. In spite of the fact he's a qualified chef, David's finding it hard to get a job.

1 Complete the sentences with the words from the box.

| Despite   Even though   Nevertheless |

1   _____ there was a transport strike in her city, Mia got to work on time.
2   My brother says he doesn't really enjoy going to the cinema. _____, he goes all the time.
3   _____ complaining about his job all the time, Adrian never looks for a new one.

2 Complete the sentences with a connector of contrast. Use the correct punctuation.

1   _____ her idea for an eco-café didn't take off at first, she persevered and is now opening her second one.
2   We warned him not to go hiking in the bad weather. _____, he ignored our advice.
3   He only speaks a few words of Spanish _____ having lived in Peru for five years.

WAYS OF TALKING ABOUT THE FUTURE

Form	Function	Examples
future simple *will* *won't* + infinitive *may (not)* *might (not)*	used to make predictions about the future	*People won't travel on diesel trains in the cities of the future.*
going to *be + going to + infinitive*	used to talk about intentions or predictions	*The World Cup hosts are going to build three new stadiums.*
present continuous *be + –ing* form	used to talk about fixed arrangements and plans	*I'm starting my new job on Monday. Can you give me a lift?*
future continuous *will* *won't + be + -ing* form *may (not)* *might (not)*	used to talk about events in progress at a particular time in the future It can be used with (by) *this time tomorrow / next week* and *when*.	*By this time next week, we will be living in our new house.*

1 Choose the correct options to complete the sentences.

1 I won't be able to come on Saturday; I'm having / I will have friends over for dinner.

2 I don't think people will use / are using cars in cities in ten years.

3 This time next year, consumers will be designing / will design their own clothes and shoes.

2 Complete the sentences with the words given and the correct future form.

1 What are you doing this weekend? I / stay / hotel / Paris.

_____

2 By this time tomorrow, we / sit / on / a sunny beach.

_____

3 In the future, I think most schools / use / digital notebooks.

_____

Audioscript

1.01 I = Interviewer, D = Dylan

I: Today I'm talking to Dylan Drummond about how he defines who he is. Dylan is 28 and married. He's Scottish, and he lives in Nagoya in Japan. Dylan, how long have you lived in Japan?

D: For almost two years.

I: When you were living in Scotland, which factors were most important to your sense of personal identity?

D: Well, my social group was always very important to me. My friends always played a bigger part in creating my identity than my family, I'd say.

I: Why do you think that was?

D: I think it's because we grew up together and shared the same life goals. And we dressed the same, followed fashion, you know. That was very important to me when I was younger.

I: What about other aspects of your life?

D: I was always really interested in music and belonged to my local bagpipe band. That was a big part of who I was and I loved taking part in shows. It made me very proud to be Scottish.

I: I see. Did anything else influence your personal identity?

D: Erm … I'd say that my career has helped me define who I am. Social status was never particularly important to me, but I always wanted to have a good career. I was very pleased when I finally qualified and could call myself an architect.

1.02 I = Interviewer, D = Dylan

I: OK, Dylan. Let's move on to talk about your life now and how moving to another country has affected your sense of identity. Was it a shock to move to Japan?

D: Oh, yes, in many ways. My wife is Japanese – we met at university – and so she tried to prepare me for life here, but it was still a shock at first. Everyone faces culture shock when they move to a country that's so different, and of course it affects who you are.

I: And how would you say you've changed?

D: I've definitely become more aware of other people's opinions. In Scotland, I just did what I wanted to, but here people pay much more attention to what other people think. You have to be careful not to shock the neighbours!

I: So are the most important identity factors on your list the same as they were when you were in Scotland?

D: No. Well, my friends are still important, of course, and we stay in touch through social media, but other things have changed. For example, my music is not a main factor in who I am any more.

I: And why has that changed?

D: The type of music I played was very Scottish and there's no similar tradition here in Nagoya. But that's been replaced by other interests, such as photography, and I belong to the local camera club.

I: That's interesting. So apart from your hobbies, what things do you consider most important to your identity now?

D: Well, back home, my family background was not really a big part of my identity. My family wasn't particularly close, and as we grew up, my brother and sister and I didn't really keep in touch very much. Here in Japan, it's very different. Family values are much more important, and I've learnt to respect the idea of family far more. My wife and her family have taught me a lot, and it's interesting to see how living here is affecting the identities of our two young children.

I: I'm sure it's going to be interesting to watch them grow up. Dylan, thank you very much for talking to us today.

D: My pleasure.

1.03 A = Anna, S = Sean, B = Bettina, M = Matt

A: How important is it to be an individual, to express your personal identity? Sean?

S: I think it's really important to be yourself. If we don't have a strong sense of our own identity, then it's as if we were all made in a factory.

B: Well, yes, to a certain extent, but don't you think we have to respect the people close to us, like our family?

S: Yes and no. Family members should respect each other, but that also means respecting each other as individuals. I don't think your family should ever force you to dress or act in a certain way.

B: I'm sorry, but I just don't think that's true. I think parents have the right to expect their kids to conform to certain family values.

M: And what about at work? For example, you have really long hair, Sean, but if you get an office job, that might not be appropriate.

S: I just don't think a job should force you to go against who you are. I would never take a job that wouldn't let me be myself.

B: I'm afraid I can't agree. People have to make compromises. My older brother was always saying that he would never change because of a job, and he would make fun of people who did. But then he got an office job and he had to start wearing a suit!

A: Sean, do you think you lose your individual identity if you change your hair or clothes?

S: Well, you don't change who you are, but you're letting other people put pressure on you to do what they want you to do.

M: In a way, you're right, but if you think life is going to be exactly the way you want it, you're just going to be disappointed.

B: I couldn't agree more. And it isn't sensible to do things that offend other people just to show how individual we are.

S: Yeah, but …

1.06

1

I think that globalisation is having a beneficial effect. I mean, it's easier for countries to export goods and that means some of the world's poorer countries can develop their economies. In some Asian countries, there's been huge economic growth in recent decades and the standard of living has increased dramatically.

2

But is that always the case? It seems to me that multinational companies increase their profits by, like, setting up factories in poorer countries because the workers aren't paid very much. I think it's unfair that there's such inequality; the company owners become millionaires, while the majority of people live in poverty.

3

That's a good point. And multinational companies are completely taking over – you know, you see the same fast-food restaurants, coffee shops, and supermarkets wherever you go. And small independent companies don't stand a chance.

4

Yeah, I completely agree. I kind of think it's sad that regional cultures are disappearing and countries are becoming more similar to each other. The same music and films dominate popular culture everywhere and it all starts to look the same.

5

I know what you mean, but don't you think that globalisation also has some positive effects? For example, it's so much easier to communicate with people in other countries. The internet facilitates information sharing and … well … that helps everyone.

1.07

A: Everyone agrees that people are becoming increasingly interconnected through the use of social media. We can communicate with more people and we can communicate wherever we are. But what do people actually think about it? What do they think are the advantages and disadvantages? We're here in a local shopping centre to find out.

Hello. We want to know what people think about social media. Do you use any sites regularly, and what are their advantages and disadvantages?

B: Oh yeah, I love using social media – my favourite is Twitter. The best thing about it is that I can send short messages all day long and I get tons of messages from my friends, so it's like a conversation going on all the time.

A: How about you? Do you use a lot of social media?

C: Yes, I like to share pictures and videos on Flickr. It's really great because when I went on holiday to India last summer, I could show my friends all the fascinating places I was going to. It's getting easier and easier to send and share information. I think it's great.

A: Excuse me. What do you think about social media?

D: I don't use it very much. I think there are lots of advantages, but I think it's too easy for people like companies and advertisers to get hold of your personal information. It's not a good idea to put all that stuff on the web – you just don't know how they're going to use it, do you?

1.09

1

There are many **vast** new emerging markets.

2

We **do** want to take part in the global conversation.

3

There's a rapid **pace** of development.

4

Large companies can **drain** skilled workers.

5

There is a new international **coal** agreement.

1.10

This is a photo of a modern-looking café that is popular with young people. There are lots of people in the background, and the café looks really busy. In the foreground is a group of three young women, sitting in a row. The young woman on the left is using her laptop and the young woman in the middle is on her tablet. They're both smiling, so they're probably not studying. Maybe they're reading emails from friends, or maybe they're watching videos. The young woman on the right is on her mobile phone and she's using a tablet at the same time. She's smiling too, so she's probably chatting to a friend. They're sitting close together so they probably know each other, but they aren't talking or looking at each other at all. They all seem to be very involved with their electronic devices.

UNIT 3 Fame and fortune

1.11

In the late 1990s, an American journalist called James Ulmer devised a scale to find out how valuable film stars are to any film they work on. It takes into account factors such as talent and willingness to promote a film. He called it 'the Ulmer Scale', and it is widely used in the industry. But now this term is being used to rank celebrities in terms of how famous they are. So, at the top of this scale are people on what is called the 'A-List'. Those are people who have been very famous for a long time, like Daniel Day-Lewis, as well as the hottest stars of the moment, such as Keira Knightly. A-listers are often famous celebrities like actors or singers, but they can also be people who are not exactly celebrities, but who are famous. For example, they might run a global company – like Bill Gates.

Or they could have broken a world record, such as Usain Bolt, or written a best-selling novel – someone like J K Rowling.

And then further down this list are the celebrities who aren't quite as well-known – the B-listers. They tend to be famous in their own country or profession, but may not be known to the general public around the world. A good example would be someone like, uh, Leona Lewis. She won the X Factor in the UK and is also well-known in Europe, but she isn't an international star – at least not yet. Or they might be people who are famous, but not in an 'I'm-a-celebrity-look-at-me!' kind of way. These are people who have done incredibly important things, such as discover a cure for a disease, or come up with an amazing new invention, like, Sir Tim Berners-Lee, who invented the World Wide Web, but who don't get on the front pages of celebrity magazines.

And the ones who are even less valuable on the social scene are, of course, the C-listers. This group might include people who've done something like appearing on a reality TV show, causing a scandal somewhere, or just inheriting a fortune. They might not really have a particular talent, but we see them in the media a lot.

Of course, the whole idea of using the Ulmer Scale for ranking people in terms of their social value is completely subjective, based on opinions and not on any real factors, but it's interesting to many people anyway.

1.14

Conversation 1

A: I sometimes feel sorry for celebrities. Imagine being chased by the paparazzi every time you left the house.

B: You feel sorry for them? Really? Most of them seem happy with the publicity when it suits them!

A: Well, what I meant was, it can't be easy living in the public eye, that's all.

Conversation 2

A: I think a lot of very famous people lose a sense of reality, don't you?

B: I'm not sure I understand what you mean …

A: What I'm trying to say is that they forget how to behave in a normal way.

Conversation 3

A: It seems to me that rock stars and celebrities are never happy.

B: Of course they are! You're not telling me that these people wake up in the morning worrying where their next million is coming from?

A: Maybe I'm not making myself clear. I'm not necessarily talking about money. Look at the number of famous people who have personal problems when they're at the peak of their careers.

Conversation 4

A: Downsides? Yes! Imagine having all that fame and all that money and not knowing who your real friends are anymore. I think being famous must be awful. I'd hate it.

B: Seriously?

A: OK, maybe I should rephrase that. I wouldn't hate *all* of it, but I don't think it'd be easy …

Conversation 5

A: So you're saying that celebrities don't enjoy their fame?

B: Actually, that's not what I meant. I didn't mean that celebrities never look for fame. A lot of celebrities love all that attention. But I was talking about famous people who don't really enjoy the celebrity part of their jobs. You know, the ones who always try to avoid reporters and photographers. They really just want to have normal lives, and they're not going around looking for attention.

A: Oh, right. I see what you're saying.

Conversation 6

A: It's people like Jay Z and Beyoncé I feel really sorry for. I mean, all that pressure to perform, to keep your fans happy, to try and keep the paparazzi off your back long enough to spend time quietly with your family. I think fame comes at a price. Put it that way.

B: Did you say that you felt sorry for them?! I think it would be great! You'd have loads of money, a private jet, you could do anything and go anywhere.

1.15   T = Tanya, El = Elaine, B = Bob, Ev = Evan

T: Good morning, everyone. We're here today to discuss my proposal to cut the Lifestyle and Entertainment section from the paper. Who would like to start the discussion?

El: I'm afraid I disagree. We get dozens of letters to the editor each week with comments about articles in the L&E section. In fact, last week we got 50 letters related to that section. If L&E disappears, we're going to get lots of complaints.

B: Yes, but we get hundreds of letters about the news stories and editorials, far more than we get for L&E. We have to cut something, and I agree with Tanya that L&E should go. People want to read real news.

Ev: I don't know. Do we have good data on who our readers are? Tanya, I know you gave us some facts and statistics on newspaper readership, but those are generalisations for the whole country. I'm not sure the numbers would be the same for our local paper. I think people in our community want a newspaper that offers a variety of content.

El: Yes, and also, several national surveys have shown that when young people *do* read the newspaper, they tend to read the L&E sections. If we cut that section, we'll lose any young readers that we have!

B: But look at the facts, Elaine. First, the population is getting younger. Second, newspaper sales are getting smaller. I think the reason is that most young people do not get their news from newspapers.

T: OK. You all have some good points. Why don't we investigate further before making a decision? Let's talk to a large sample of our subscribers and find out who reads the paper and what they read. Here's what we want to know: First, how many people in the family read the paper, and how old are they? Second, what sections of the paper does each person read? Based on that information, we can decide whether to cut the L&E section, or any other sections. Do you agree? Fine. I'll design the survey and we can discuss it at the next meeting. Now, is there any other business?

UNIT 4   Ups and downs

1.16

Good morning, and welcome to today's lecture. This is the third in this series of psychology lectures, and today we're going to be looking at happiness, or more specifically, the relationship between wealth and happiness. Does having more material wealth increase or decrease your happiness?

1.17

Good morning, and welcome to today's lecture. This is the third in this series of psychology lectures, and today we're going to be looking at happiness, or more specifically, the relationship between wealth and happiness. Does having more material wealth increase or decrease your happiness? It would seem to be common sense that more money will make us happier. Most of us aim to increase our income throughout our lives, to enable us to buy more material goods, such as a car or our own home, or provide the resources to raise a family and so on. And we think that all of this will make us happy. If we didn't think money would make us happy, why would anyone try to get rich?

Well, as expected, the results of an international study confirm the idea that, in general, people with higher incomes feel more satisfied with their lives. This was the case when comparisons were made between people in different countries, as well as between different income groups within the same country.

However, other surprising research has indicated that people with higher incomes are not necessarily happier than those who earn less.

Although these two studies seem to contradict each other by saying, on one hand, that wealthier people are more content, and on the other hand, that wealthier people aren't happier, both offer some very interesting insights into the connection between wealth and happiness. Nevertheless, the first thing to consider is the possible explanations for the differences in the findings of these two studies.

The most crucial factor is the terminology used. Quite simply, 'satisfaction' and 'happiness' are different things. Various factors have an influence on happiness, and 'satisfaction' is just one element of happiness.

So why do people with higher incomes experience lower levels of happiness? A recent study has investigated this question. Research suggests that in addition to satisfaction, another element of happiness is enjoying the simple things in life, like a beautiful sunny day or a good coffee. People with lots of money can purchase lots of positive life experiences, like exotic holidays and expensive meals, and as a result, they may enjoy everyday pleasures less.

Another issue is thought to be …

1.22 A = Alex, L = Luke

A: How was the workshop you went to last week?

L: Oh, yeah! The positive thinking workshop? Yes, well, I was really sceptical at first. I mean, how can someone teach you how to be positive? But I thought, why not give it a go?

A: And? Are you happier?

L: You know, it was better than I thought it would be … to start off with, we all had to think of one aspect of our lives that we want to improve. I chose the problem I had at work, you know, about that promotion? If I'd taken that extra training course, I would've been promoted! But because I hadn't taken the course, they gave the job to someone else.

A: Yeah, that was a tough situation.

L: So, when we had chosen our situation, we had to explain it to a partner and explain all the reasons why it was bad and why it was absolutely impossible to do anything about it.

A: OK …

L: And then I had to swap roles with my partner, and he had to pretend to be me and explain my situation to me as if it was his problem.

A: I see! But how does that help?

L: Well, that's the interesting part. Every time he said a negative thing, I had to say something positive.

A: Hmm … and did that work?

L: Well, it was a bit strange hearing someone talking about my problem. But after a while, it did make me think about it in a different way, and I came up with one or two ideas about how to change things.

A: And did they work?

L: I don't know yet – I'm going to try them out today!

A: Well, good luck – and tell me how it works out!

1.23

Although many people believe that money is the key to happiness, I don't really agree. Personally, I think family and friends are more important. There are two main reasons why I think this.

First of all, it's clear that a person can have lots of money and plenty of 'stuff' – they can own houses and cars and nice clothes – but in the end they are not necessarily happier. Let me give you an example. My friend's grandfather worked for a big financial company. He had a good position there and made a lot of money, but he spent all his time working and never had time to enjoy the money he made or spend any time with his family or friends. When he was old, no one came to visit to him, and he became very lonely and depressed.

My second reason is that money is very temporary but friends and family last a lifetime. For example, I once had a neighbour who had a lot of money, but one day her house burnt down in a fire. She lost all her possessions. Just like that. But friends and family are always there for you whether you are up or down. Relationships with other people are therefore more important to happiness, in my opinion, because they last longer. They aren't necessarily damaged by things like economic crises, or losing your job.

To sum up what I've been saying, I don't believe money can bring us happiness by itself. Spending too much time worrying about money just takes time away from your relationships with family and friends who are more likely to make you happy in the long run.

UNIT 5 Something in the water

1.26 RH = Radio Host, J = Jenny

RH: This week is Stop Water Poverty week. My guest today is Jenny Bryant, spokesperson for the charity Water Watch. Jenny, first, please tell us generally what water poverty is, what Water Watch does and what appeal you're making this week.

J: Sure. Hello. There are 884 million people in the world living without access to clean water, and 5000 children die every day because of this. A lack of sufficient clean water to meet your basic needs is known as water poverty. Water Watch aims to prevent water poverty and provide communities worldwide with clean drinking water, but we can't do it without your help. As you said, this week is Stop Water Poverty week, and we are making an appeal to the public to donate money. Even a small donation can make a huge difference to people's lives and help in the fight against water poverty.

RH: What are some of the specific goals of Water Watch?

J: Well, Water Watch has several different goals, Lucas. The primary purpose of the organisation is to prevent water poverty, of course, but we also work to improve hygiene, education, and the standard of living of the people in the regions we are active in.

RH: OK, so what does that mean in practical terms?

J: Well, for example, in many parts of Africa, girls don't get access to an education because they have to travel long distances in order to collect water for their families. And as adults, women spend up to 12 hours per day searching for water or looking after children who are sick because of diseases caused by water pollution. So we're investing money to increase the number of taps in these areas. The aim is that no villager should be further than half a mile from their nearest source of clean tap water and that no child should die from a disease that's easily preventable.

RH: And is there a reason why our attention is being drawn to this now with Stop Water Poverty week?

J: Yes, absolutely! Climate change has made a bad situation much worse. The amount of rainfall has been affected by rising temperatures so that many parts of the world see no rain from one season to another. Some areas are experiencing severe drought, and this can cause famine because farmers cannot grow enough food to feed all the people in the region. In areas that do experience a regular rainy season, there have been floods, and crops have been badly damaged.
So famines can be caused by too little water or too much water. There's an urgent need to act quickly to end this crisis. That's where the public comes in …

RH: OK. I was just going to ask you what people can do to help.

J: Water Watch is a charity. It doesn't receive any government funding. The only money we get is from public donations. In order to prevent many, many more people from dying, we need to raise £25 million. This seems like a lot, but there are around 25.5 million households in the UK, and if every one of them donated only £1, we'd reach our target. We are also looking for more volunteers. We already have about 3500 volunteers around the world, but we need more! Training is offered to all our volunteers whether they are actively working in the affected countries or offering their services here. You can give a donation or sign up to volunteer on the Water Watch website, or call us at 0800 …

1.27

A: Wow, I was really moved by that documentary about water pollution. I think we should do something to help Pure Water Action. They're doing amazing work for people who don't have access to clean water.

B: Yeah, I agree. Let's get involved! I'd suggest donating some money to Pure Water Action.

A: Well, we don't have much money at the moment, so we wouldn't be able to donate very much. We could try to raise money, though.

B: OK. How would we do that?

A: Well, we could get sponsored by people to run a marathon or something and then send the money. Maybe that would take too long to arrange, though. There's always a jumble sale. You know, we could ask people to donate things like household items, books, clothes, unwanted gifts, that kind of thing, so that we can sell them. Then we send the money we make to Pure Water Action.

B: I'm not sure we could charge much for stuff if it wasn't in good condition. What if we do some volunteering instead?

A: Yeah. Volunteering's another option – and you'd feel more involved in the whole issue. Do you know much about what they expect you to do?

B: Not really, but we could find out.

A: Yeah. Let's look online …

1.28

My family – my husband, my five children, and I – live in a small village in Ethiopia. There are about 30 people who live here. Most of the men are farmers. My day starts at about 5 a.m. I get my eldest daughter, Ashmi, out of bed. Her job is to go and collect the water from our nearest waterstand, which is two kilometres away. It takes her about two hours because she often has to wait while other villagers get the water they need. When she gets home with the water, I can begin making the tea and the food for the family's breakfast. Ashmi is very young, so she can carry only 10 litres of water at a time. Sometimes I ask her to get extra water in the evening, especially if it hasn't rained and my husband needs water for washing. As for washing ourselves and our clothes, well, I go with Ashmi and the baby twice a week to the river and we wash there. It's not very clean, but we don't have enough water from the waterstand for all our needs.

UNIT 6 Living traditions

1.30

Interview 1

A: Excuse me. I'm doing some interviews for KT FM. Can I talk to you for a minute?

B: Yeah, sure. What about?

A: We want to know if people think it's important to maintain traditions.

B: Do you mean like traditional weddings and things like that?

A: Yes. Do you think traditions are an important part of our society?

B: Well, I think they used to be more important, but I think a lot of people, especially young people, don't really care about a lot of old traditions.

A: What about you, personally?

B: No, I'm not into all that traditional stuff, like formal weddings.

A: Why not?

B: They're not relevant to today's society. Young people aren't used to dressing formally and going through rituals that don't make much sense to them. We want to do things in more creative, interesting ways.

A: OK, thanks for sharing your opinion.

B: That's OK.

Interview 2

A: Do you think it's important for society to maintain traditions?

C: It depends on what you mean. We need traditions, but they can't stay the same. All traditions in all societies change over time, and I don't think we can expect new generations to keep doing things in exactly the same way they were done in the past.

A: So you don't object to changes in traditions like weddings, graduation ceremonies, or other traditional ceremonies?

C: No. I'm a university lecturer, and every year I love seeing what the students do at the graduation ceremony. They do some pretty non-traditional things, but the essence of the ceremony, the joy of it, stays the same. Each generation has to make the tradition relevant to themselves and to their lives.

A: Thank you for your comments.

C: You're welcome.

Interview 3

A: How important do you think it is for a society to maintain certain traditions from generation to generation?

D: I think that traditions are one of the things that give society, and groups within a society, a sense of history and continuity.

A: And do you think young people feel the same way? I mean, are they interested in maintaining traditions?

D: Some are, but for the most part, no. Look at the city history festival, which we've had every year in this city for the last 40 years. Young people aren't interested in it. They think it's boring. Nowadays, young people avoid getting involved in anything to do with history or traditions. It's a shame because the traditions will be lost soon.

A: Thank you for your opinions.

D: That's all right.

Interview 4

A: Do you think traditions are important and should stay the same, or is it OK for old traditions to change or disappear?

E: Well, I know that most people my age aren't really interested in keeping traditions, but I think it's important.

A: Why is that?

E: Traditions are important in order for our society to maintain its identity, and also so that there are connections and similarities between one generation and another. For example, if I were getting married, I would want to have a really traditional wedding, just like my parents' wedding, you know, with a white dress, and dancing, and everything. I suppose some people might think that was old-fashioned, but that's what I believe and that's what I'm used to.

A: Thanks for talking to me.

E: You're welcome.

1.34

Speaker 1

I had never thought about personal rituals, but I suppose I do have some. For example, I allow myself to eat exactly three biscuits while I watch the news in the evening. That's because I love biscuits, but I have to be careful not to eat the whole packet! What else? Oh, before I go to bed, I always have to plan out the next day. If I don't, I don't sleep well. I write down the things I have to do the next day. In the morning, I go over my list, and that makes me feel prepared for the day.

Speaker 2

Let's see. I do have some rituals, I think. I always go through my post while I eat breakfast, and I line it up in three piles – bin, urgent things, and other things. Of course, I don't do anything about it, but at least I feel organised! Oh, and I always get a coffee at the same café on my way to work every day. I get the same thing every day – a large latte. I drink it on the way, and I finish it just as I arrive at the office.

Speaker 3

My working life can be very varied, and every day can be different, but I do have one ritual. You might think it's a little strange, though! OK, here it is … I always put on all of my work clothes for the next day before I go to bed. Well, I mean I try on the clothes to see how they look. I don't sleep in them!

1.35

Well, let me see. Both photos show something connected to the idea of tradition. While the first photo is of a traditional meal, the second is of a traditional dance. One thing the photos have in common is that they both show people doing an activity together. In the first one it's a family, while in the second they might be from the local village or neighbourhood. The photos are similar because in both of them the people are enjoying themselves in a traditional way. In the first, they might be eating special food to celebrate a festival. In the second, it might be a dance they do on a particular day of the year. In contrast to the first photo, the second photo shows people in unusual costumes, which is probably a kind of traditional dress. The first photo is a more relaxed situation and the people are wearing their usual clothes.

I think these traditions are important to these people because they remind them of their history, either their family history or their national history. These traditions bring them together and remind them what they have in common with each other and with other people around them.

UNIT 7 Designed to please

2.01 RH = Radio Host, T = Tony, M = Marianna

RH: OK … we're talking about celebrity designers. What do you think of celebrities who bring out their own ranges of products? We've got our next caller on the line, and it's Tony. Hi, Tony. What do you want to say?

T: Hi. I just wanted to say that I'm not a big fan of celebrity designers. I just don't really rate them very highly. These days, it seems that anyone whose career takes off decides to produce a line of clothes, or a perfume. Look at people like Lady Gaga, or Gwen Stefani. They might be great singers, and yes, they are trendsetters when it comes to fashion, but does that mean they can come up with good ideas? It doesn't. I also think that some of them are cheating the public, in a way. I think a lot of the time they don't even draw up the designs themselves. Somebody else does it and the celebrity just puts their name on it.

RH: Thanks for your opinion, Tony. Next, we've got Marianna on the line. Marianna, I think you've got a different opinion.

M: Yes, I disagree with the last caller. I think it takes real talent to create new designs that catch on, and some celebrities have that talent. Look at Victoria Beckham, for example, or Penélope Cruz. Millions of young women look up to them for what they've achieved. When you're famous, you spend a lot of your time thinking about producing the right look, and that means you understand the effects that clothes have on people and you know about the latest trends. Even if a celebrity doesn't actually create a design, they choose it because it fits their style. And if you like that person's style, then you can look like that, too.

RH: OK. Well, thanks for all your calls. We'll hear some more of your opinions after the next song.

2.05

I've been here for nearly two years now. Before I started here, I'd been working in much smaller companies, and they didn't really have an annual performance review. You know, a meeting where they ask you how you feel about what you've done well. Here, though, they rate your performance every two years, and I'm really not looking forward to it. I've been talking to some of the others, and I know they're going to ask me about things like leadership and showing initiative. I'm really not sure what I'm going to say in answer to that. I need to come up with some good ideas over the next few weeks.

There's a conference next week. I don't really want to go, but maybe it would be a good opportunity for me to show initiative. I'm not sure how, though. There must be lots of ways. I need to think of a few and then go to my boss with some suggestions.

And the following week we've got to attract new clients. But how? The managers really didn't give us very much guidance on that. I'm sure they're waiting to see how we do on that task just before our performance reviews. So I need to come up with something good. But what?

UNIT 8 A fair deal?

2.07

Good morning, and welcome to today's lecture about fair trade. I'd like to start by saying a little about what the fair-trade movement is, before looking at its history, its successes, and criticisms of the system.

2.08

Fair trade is an attempt to avoid exploitation and inequality in business between the developed and the developing world. The developed world relies on products from developing countries and spends huge amounts of money on products like tea, coffee and sugar. The companies selling these products make plenty of money, but, very often the people who actually produce them live in poverty. In other words, the farmers who grow coffee or tea only receive a very small part of the price you pay in the supermarket. Buying fair-trade products means that the people who produce them receive a fair price.

The next point I'd like to discuss is the change in focus of fair trade. From the 1960s until the 1980s, fair trade was mostly about buying handmade objects, such as traditional fabrics or jewellery. However, by the 80s, many of these objects started to seem old-fashioned. At the same time, international prices of products like coffee and tea were falling, making life very difficult for the producers. Most fair-trade organisations shifted their focus to agricultural products, and today, fair-trade products include not only tea and coffee but also cocoa, honey, bananas, sugar and cotton.

Now, let's move on to how fair trade works. You are probably familiar with the way fair-trade products are labelled. Each has a symbol that shows that they have been approved by an organisation, so the buyer knows they are making a fair-trade purchase.

The most familiar to most people is the organisation simply called Fairtrade. The key point about the symbols is that they allow fair-trade products to be easily identified in supermarkets. Customers don't have to wonder which coffee is fair trade and which isn't, and they don't have to go to a special shop. They can buy their fair-trade coffee at the same time as they buy their other groceries. This has made fair-trade products much more popular, and the organisation works with 1.3 million people in more than 70 developing countries.

Let's turn our attention now to some of the criticisms of fair trade. Producers may benefit in the short term, but some economists say that fair trade actually makes the situation worse in the long term. They argue that fair-trade products introduce a high price for goods such as coffee. This encourages the producers to grow more, so then there is too much coffee, and the price generally drops. This makes life even harder for the coffee producers. Now, I'd like to look in detail …

2.10

If we want our society to be fair, we have to help poor people. I believe this for three main reasons.

First of all, a fair society is one where everyone has enough food. Some people live on very little money every day and they can't afford to buy enough food for their families. The government should provide benefits so that no one goes hungry. We should all have the right to enough food.

Second, we should remember that anyone can lose their job and then be unemployed. In a fair society we take care of the poor because we know that one day we could be in that situation ourselves. We should help people now so that we can get help when we need it.

Finally, we all have a responsibility to help the next generation. Many children are born into poor families. In a fair society we should give them the chance for a good education. In that way, the society of tomorrow will be better off than the society of today.

2.12

The problem is that the rents in her city are very high. She complains that the rents go up every year and soon she won't be able to afford to live in the city.

This problem is very common in many cities. In my opinion, there are a couple of ways to solve this problem. First, landlords need to stop raising the rent so much. I think it would be good to limit their increases to just one or two per cent per year. Also, they should have to explain why they want to increase the rent. If they don't have a good reason, the rent should stay the same.

Secondly, what the local authorities should do is use taxes from rich people to provide low-rent housing for people who are on low incomes. Then people can save up enough money to buy their own homes, instead of spending everything on high rents.

These are two possible ways to solve the problem of high rents in the city.

2.13 M = Moderator, DC = Dr Carson, DB = Dr Banks

M: Hello, everyone, and welcome to the third session of the Conference on Healthy Children. Our two guest speakers this morning are Dr Jane Banks and Dr Leo Carson. They are both educational psychologists, and they will present opposing theories on the effects of competition on children and adolescents. After their presentations, they will take questions. Dr Carson?

DC: Good morning. We all know that competition is a fact of life, but is competition healthy? Recently there has been an increase in the number of studies that have led me to conclude that competition is terrible, especially for children. Think about it: in our society, personal value is measured by how many competitions a person wins – in sports, for jobs, to get into the best universities. Schools award gold stars or other prizes for top marks in exams and tests, so even getting an education becomes a competition. Very few people can be winners, and if you are not a winner, what are you? A loser. Competition makes children anxious and unable to concentrate well. 'Winners' become more aggressive, and they often feel ashamed or angry when they don't win. 'Losers' become discouraged and often stop trying because they feel that they won't win anyway. The solution? We need to experiment with ways to teach children to work *with* others, not against them. Cooperative games and projects produce feelings of high self-esteem and the satisfaction of being part of a group. Thank you.

DB: Good morning, everyone. My colleague has some legitimate concerns about competition, and I agree that there are some negative effects when competition is taken to extremes. However, I would argue that there is, in fact, healthy competition and that it is necessary for children to grow into well-rounded adults. As Dr Carson mentioned, competition is a fact of life. We compete in sports, for jobs – even for the person we want to marry! While it's true that competition can produce anxiety and damage self-esteem in some young people, there is no proof that competition is bad for the majority of people. In fact, a number of psychologists have conducted research and recorded results that indicate that when children are not allowed to experience failure, they respond very negatively to failure later on. Competition helps young people develop important life skills such as problem-solving, recognising strengths and weaknesses, creating strategies and, perhaps most importantly, knowing how to win and how to lose. Thank you.

2.16

A: I read an interesting study on how young adults' success in both sport and education is affected by the amount of peer support they receive. When young adults receive praise and encouragement from their teammates or classmates, there's an increase in self-esteem, which results in higher motivation, which in turn, results in higher achievement. The conclusion is that praise has a positive effect, even when the person's performance wasn't great.

B: I'm not convinced. There are plenty of other studies that indicate the opposite, which is that excessive praise has no effect, or even a negative effect, on performance. We all know when we've done well, and if we haven't, then having people say 'Well done!' is actually insulting. There is also a theory that too much praise results in decreased effort. If people are praised for basically just turning up, then they start to think that's good enough and they stop trying to improve.

2.21 N = Nicola, J = Jemma

N: Hey, Jemma, did you hear that David Blaine almost got electrocuted?

J: Nicola, he's an illusionist! He's really good at making people think he's risking his life when he isn't.

N: No, this really happened! Here's the video. You've got to see it!

J: OK, OK, play it.

N: Look, that's a million volts passing through him. What do you think?

J: It couldn't have been real. He must have practised a lot of times before they filmed it. And what's that metal suit he's wearing?

N: I don't know. He looked scared to me. I'm going to find some photos of it.

J: OK, but I think it was all fake. He might have found a way to just get the electricity to go right around him.

N: Look! Here's a photo after the stunt. See? He needs help walking! And I heard that the doctors at the hospital found that he'd developed an irregular heartbeat. Look at how exhausted he is!

J: I don't know, but I don't want to see the photo. Look, I've got to go.

2.22

A: Wait 'til you see this next clip, just in from Jane McCormack. Here we go …

B: What's that guy doing?

A: Well, apparently he managed to ascend to an altitude of 16,000 feet in a deck chair by tying balloons to it.

B: Are you kidding?! Why would anyone want to do that?! Look, he even took his lunch with him!

A: Who knows why people do the things they do? He may have always wanted to be a pilot, but couldn't get a licence.

B: So he decided to fly a deck chair. Why did he have a pellet gun?

A: No idea. He might have wanted to shoot at birds. Stay tuned for the story of Larry and his deck chair, right after the commercial break.

2.23

In general, I would much rather do something quiet than an exciting extreme sport. There are three main reasons for that. First, I find quieter activities much more relaxing than extreme sports because of the danger involved in activities such as mountain climbing. Unlike some people, I don't like the idea of putting my life at risk for no reason. Relaxation for me means reading a book or watching TV, not risking serious injury. The second reason I tend to prefer quieter activities is that my job is very active – I work outdoors with horses. I might have had a hard week, so on my days off, I like to watch films or meet friends, and I don't really have the energy for extreme sports. Finally, quieter activities appeal to me more because they reduce the amount of stress in my life. Some people like the excitement that more stress brings, but I don't. I much prefer to do activities that don't cause me more stress.

UNIT 11 Through the lens

2.24 J = Jack, P = Penny

J: Hello, and welcome to *Click*, the number 1 photography podcast, with all the latest news from the world of photography, and this is Episode 23, with me, Jack Wood, as usual.

P: And me, Penny Green. So, what have you been up to this week, Jack?

J: It's been such a busy week, Penny. I did a very special wedding shoot, and I'm going to be talking a little bit more about that later, and I attended the opening of an exhibition of local photographers. Wow, I was blown away by the level of talent we have in our local area!

P: I know! It's easy to think that photography these days is all selfies and snapshots on social media, isn't it? But some people are really putting a lot of effort into their work. Did you have a favourite?

J: There were lots of great shots in the exhibition, including some fantastic landscapes of the local area, but I think the one that really impressed me the most was a picture by a local woman, Judy Anderson. It's a portrait of a local homeless man. In the foreground, you can see his dog, and, on the left-hand side, a small sign. The man, the dog and the sign are all in focus, so you can see them clearly and that's where your eye is drawn. In the background, there are people moving around, but it's out of focus, so you can't really tell what's happening. That means they don't take your attention away from the subject – this man who lives on the streets. The photographer has managed to capture his expression and, for me, it makes me wonder about what his story might be, where he came from, how he ended up on the streets. It also says a lot about the recent economic problems that we've been facing around here, so it's like a piece of local history.

P: That sounds really interesting, and I believe that exhibition runs until the end of the month, so go along to the Mayweather Gallery to see some great examples of local work. Now, Jack, tell us about this wedding. I thought you said you'd never do another wedding.

J: Ha. I did, but this one was a little different.

2.25 B = Becky, K = Kumiko

K: Hi, Becky. What've you got there?

B: Oh, just a couple of photos for an article I'm writing. I need to choose one to go with the article, which is called 'The Art of Photography'. I'm just comparing them and trying to choose.

K: Well, the two photos are alike because they're photos of groups. The first is a family portrait and looks like it's been taken by a professional, while the second shows someone taking a selfie with their friends. Everyone's taking selfies these days!

B: Yeah, that's right. And I talk about the selfie phenomenon in my article. Another similarity is that the people are posing for the camera and smiling in both photos. However, maybe the first situation is a little formal for my article, whereas the second situation is much more informal. The people in the second photo seem more natural than in the first, and that would fit with the article well. Another point of difference is the reason they're having their photo taken. The first group of people probably want a photo they can put on the wall at home. In contrast, the second group want a photo they can send to friends or put online to show people what a good time they're having. I think the second one's going to suit the article better, isn't it?

K: Yes, I think so. Both photos are similar in that the people want to record this moment in their lives, but the second one is more modern. It'll appeal to younger people, unlike the first one. I'd go for the photo of people taking a selfie.

2.28

Hi, this is Erica. I just wanted to see if you could send a memo around to everyone about the images for the website. We've decided to do things a little bit differently this year, so instead of having a professional photographer, we're going to get everyone to do a selfie, you know, to give the website a much more modern feel. They need to take a shot of themselves in a situation that means something to them – in the kitchen, cooking or out on their bike, that kind of thing. And they should email it to you, so you can check it before we use it. In addition to that, we need them to write a few sentences about themselves, their interests and hobbies, just to give the website a human face. Can you ask them to do that, please? Oh, and we need everything before the 22nd of the month. Thanks! Bye.

2.29 M = Manager, P = Paul

M: Thanks for coming in today, Paul. I just wanted to give you some feedback on your presentation the other day. Now, don't worry! The first thing to say is that everyone thought you did a very good job, particularly since you had such a limited time to prepare.

P: OK … thanks.

M: And we thought you had some very good ideas. We liked your suggestions for increasing sales. You've given us something to think about. What did you think about the presentation?

P: Um … well … I thought it went OK, you know. I mean, I did my best and I really didn't have very much time to prepare for it because the last speaker dropped out.

M: Yes, I understand that. Now, I'd like to move onto one or two ideas to improve your presentations in the future. There's always room for improvement, and I've made a few notes. First of all, you seemed pretty nervous. It's important to relax and be confident, you know.

P: That was because of the rush to get things done. It was Damian's fault, really. He was giving the presentation, then he felt ill, and so I had to quickly …

M: Yes, as I said, we understand that. Still, just try to relax a little bit more next time. Besides that, there were one or two problems with the technology. I know computers can be tricky, but you didn't seem to have any idea how to solve the problems.

P: It's that IT woman, Sylvia. She never explains things to me, and I keep asking her for more help. I don't think I should have to work it out for myself.

M: Well, I know Sylvia is very busy with a lot of people. All I'm saying is that I'd like you to be more familiar with the computer next time. I think that's all. Thanks again for coming to see me, and I look forward to your next presentation.

P: Oh, OK. Great. Thanks.

UNIT 12 Bright lights, big city

2.30

1

You're going to want to take some photos here, I imagine. It's one of the most colourful areas in London. It's called Neal's Yard, and as you can see, all of the windows and doors, and some of the buildings, are painted bright, happy colours. I think it looks a bit like some photos I've seen of Mexico, with all those brilliant colours!

2

Brixton Market. The market started up in the late 19th century, and today it's the best place to buy African and Caribbean goods and produce. A lot of African and Caribbean immigrants live in this area, and apart from the market, there are lots of nice restaurants and shops where you can get things from those countries.

3

Yes, that's the great thing about London; you can visit several countries in different parts of the world all in the same day! It's almost lunchtime now. Would you like to have some of the best Chinese food in the world? This is the place for it – Chinatown, London!

4

I'm glad you liked the Chinese food. OK, big change of scenery here. This area is called Southall. As you probably know, London has a very large Indian population, and many people from India live in this area.

2.31

A: You're going to want to take some photos here, I imagine. It's one of the most colourful areas in London. It's called Neal's Yard, and as you can see, all of the windows and doors, and some of the buildings, are painted bright, happy colours. I think it looks a bit like some of the photos I've seen of Mexico, with all those brilliant colours!

B: Yes, it does kind of remind me of Mexico, with all the little shops and bright colours.

C: I don't know. The colours do look like what you'd see in Mexico, but the architecture is completely different, of course. You're right that it doesn't really look like London, but not that much like Mexico, either.

A: We're in a very different area of London now, called Brixton. I think you'll very much enjoy seeing Brixton Market. As you can see, it's an enormous street market…

C: Oh, that's amazing. What did you say it's called?

A: Brixton Market. The market started up in the late 19th century, and today it's the best place to buy African and Caribbean goods and produce. A lot of African and Caribbean immigrants live in this area, and apart from the market, there are lots of nice restaurants and shops where you can get things from those countries.

B: Oh, look at this! Looks like we've travelled from Africa to China!

A: Yes, that's the great thing about London; you can visit several countries in different parts of the world all in the same day! It's almost lunchtime now. Would you like to have some of the best Chinese food in the world? This is the place for it – Chinatown, London!

C: Great! Of course, we have amazing Chinese food in LA, but we've got to try Chinese food in London, right?

B: Yeah, sounds good!

A: I'm glad you liked the Chinese food. OK, big change of scenery here. This area is called Southall. As you probably know, London has a very large Indian population, and many people from India live in this area.

B: It's so interesting 'cause LA is a pretty international city – a lot of people from China and all over Latin America, especially, but London seems to have folks from everywhere! In this area, I feel like I'm actually in India!

A: Of course, India was a British colony for many years, so people from India have been coming to live here for a long time. There are also lots of families from Pakistan, Bangladesh and other Asian countries.

C: I think that's what makes London such a fascinating city. Every area is different, with different food, different languages, everything.

A: Oh, yeah. Name just about any country, and there are people here from there!

2.34

Speaker 1

Whenever I think of cities of the future, I think of some of the futuristic cities that already exist or that some countries will be building in a few years. The main characteristic of all of these cities is that they are environmentally responsible. One example is Pangyo, in South Korea. It's an eco-friendly planned community near Seoul. It has lots of green areas, and it is extremely energy efficient. I think Pangyo and communities like it will be the models for the cities of the future. The emphasis is going to be on creating cities that are carbon neutral and use natural sources of energy like the sun and the wind. This has to happen if we want to continue living on the Earth. We all like modern conveniences like air-conditioning and cars; nevertheless, if we don't make our cities greener, they may become uninhabitable in the near future.

Speaker 2

By the 23rd century, I think most city dwellers will be living below ground. I don't say that because I think it's a good idea, but I think all of the world's biggest cities will be too crowded, and there'll just be nowhere else to go. I imagine that future cities will have enormous areas that serve different purposes. So, for example, there might be a large central area with office buildings, shopping centres and things like that. There will be tunnels that go from the business centre to different areas where people live. I'd like to think some cities above ground will stay as they are in spite of the fact that people no longer live there. These cities could become memorials to the past. Maybe people will even go on holiday there and talk about how they didn't like the climate or the food, or how strange life in the past was!

Speaker 3

My idea of a city of the future is really just the same as a city of the present day – except there'll be lots more people, more cars and fewer green places to escape to. I honestly don't think that 200 years into the future we will be driving flying cars or living in underwater cities. However, I think the spaces we live and work in will definitely change. Gardens may disappear completely, and more and more people will be moving into small houses and flats. The biggest change is going to be in rural areas. In fact, there won't be any rural areas anymore, just a lot of mega-cities with suburbs between them. Farms are going to disappear, so all of our food will be artificial. I'm really glad I won't be around to see it!

2.35

I live in Dallas, which is already a very modern city. Of course, lots of things will be changing between now and the 22nd century, mostly because of new technologies that we can't even imagine yet. However, I think that many things will be pretty similar to the way they are now. I'm going to talk about three areas: entertainment and going out, architecture and transportation.

I'm starting with architecture because that relates to the whole appearance and lifestyle of the city. We already have lots of skyscrapers in downtown Dallas, and I believe those buildings will still exist in the next century because they're very functional. I mean, there are lots of buildings still around from the last century, right? I think the main change will be that more and more people will want to live in the city, and as a result, the downtown area will get much bigger. The new buildings will probably all be built from environmentally friendly materials. I think they'll renovate old buildings, so they will be much greener. I'm sure that houses and apartments will all be 'green' and 'smart' by the 22nd century, but apart from that, I don't think there will be any huge changes in architecture.

The area that I imagine may have the least changes is entertainment and going out. The main changes in this area will definitely be related to new technologies. For example, movies might be holograms so that you feel that you're actually in the movie instead of just watching it on a screen. Sort of like 3D but even more real! In spite of the new technologies, I don't think people are really going to change what they like to do for entertainment. People will still be going to the movies, going out to eat and go dancing or to listen to music.

The area of transportation is where I believe the biggest changes may happen. We already have a light rail system in Dallas, but I think it will grow to cover a larger area, and it will become much faster. Nevertheless, I think people will still have cars; people in Texas love their cars! But I imagine that car designs are going to change a lot. The other day I saw a prototype of a car that can fold up to fit into a very small parking space! I'm also sure that cars will be completely automatic by then, so drivers won't actually drive. They'll just programme their destination and the car will drive itself. Finally, there will be no need for oil or gasoline because all vehicles will run on natural resources.

Irregular verbs

Infinitive	Past simple	Past participle
be	was/were	been
become	became	become
begin	began	begun
break	broke	broken
bring	brought	brought
build	built	built
buy	bought	bought
catch	caught	caught
choose	chose	chosen
come	came	come
cost	cost	cost
cut	cut	cut
do	did	done
draw	drew	drawn
drink	drank	drunk
drive	drove	driven
eat	ate	eaten
fall	fell	fallen
feed	fed	fed
feel	felt	felt
find	found	found
fly	flew	flown
get	got	got
give	gave	given
go	went	gone
grow	grew	grown
hang	hung	hung
have	had	had
hear	heard	heard
hit	hit	hit
hold	held	held
hurt	hurt	hurt
keep	kept	kept
know	knew	known
leave	left	left
let	let	let
lose	lost	lost
make	made	made
meet	met	met
pay	paid	paid
put	put	put
read	read	read
ride	rode	ridden
ring	rang	rung
rise	rose	risen
run	ran	run
say	said	said
see	saw	seen
sell	sold	sold
send	sent	sent
set	set	set
sing	sang	sung
sit	sat	sat
speak	spoke	spoken
stand	stood	stood
stick	stuck	stuck
take	took	taken
teach	taught	taught
tell	told	told
think	thought	thought
throw	threw	thrown
understand	understood	understood
wake	woke	woken
wear	wore	worn
win	won	won
write	wrote	written

Pronunciation symbols

Vowels

ı	did
e	bed, neck
æ	bad, hand
ɒ	box
ʌ	but, mother
ʊ	book, good
ə	banana, computer
iː	feed
ɑː	father
ɔː	tall
uː	boot, food, student
ɜː	shirt, birthday
eı	date, table
aı	cry, eye
ɔı	boy
əʊ	comb, post
aʊ	about, how
ʊə	tour
eə	their
ıə	here, near

Consonants

p	park, happy
b	back, hobby
t	tea
d	die
k	came, kitchen, quarter
g	game, go
f	face, photographer
v	vegetable
θ	thing, maths
ð	then, that
s	city, summer
z	please, goes
ʃ	she, shop
ʒ	leisure
h	hot, who
tʃ	chicken, watch
dʒ	jacket, orange
m	men
n	sun, know
ŋ	sung, singer
w	week, white
r	rain, writer
l	light, long
j	yes, use, music

Grammar review answer key

1
1 I've <u>already</u> taken all my holiday days this year. / I <u>haven't</u> taken all my holiday days yet.
2 He didn't <u>use</u> to be a troublemaker at school.
3 Did you use <u>to</u> give presentations in your old job?
4 You should help your mother, <u>shouldn't</u> you?
5 <u>Happiness</u> is important in life.
6 By the time I arrived, he <u>had left</u> the office.

2
1 been
2 yet
3 used
4 aren't
5 had
6 didn't

3
1 's/has been retraining
2 's/has been studying
3 's/has applied / 's/has been applying
4 's/has been pushing
5 's/hasn't had

4
1 Could you tell me if you give refunds without a receipt?
2 Do you know what other models you have?
3 I would like to have someone create a website for me. / I would like to have a website created for me.
4 I need to get my hair cut. / I need to get a haircut.
5 Mark wishes (that) his friend wouldn't (always) talk through films.

5
1 too long
2 dissatisfied
3 frustrating
4 so
5 supposed

6
1 Mark said (that) he had worked on the/that project for a long time
2 The bank's business advisor told Harry (that) they / the bank would give him a loan when the business plan was accepted
3 My aunt told me (that) the/that song reminded her of her school days
4 Mike and Naomi asked me where I was / we were going to take them to lunch tomorrow / the next/ following day
5 My manager asked me if I thought many customers had been dissatisfied with the sound quality.

7
1 must
2 might/could
3 could/might
4 might/could
5 can't

8
1 'd/had bought
2 hadn't felt
3 had advertised
4 wouldn't have turned up
5 'd/had studied

9
1 using
2 sending
3 to read
4 feeling
5 starting
6 registering

10
1 *The Grapes of Wrath*, which is a famous American novel, is set during the Great Depression.
2 There is a great restaurant in Bologna where you can eat the best minestrone soup.
3 The Burj al Khalifa, which is the world's tallest building, is over 2716 feet high.
4 Jennifer Lawrence, who won Best Actress at the 2013 Oscar Award Ceremony, had wanted to be a doctor. / Jennifer Lawrence, who had wanted to be a doctor, won Best Actress at the 2013 Oscar Award Ceremony.

11
1 advisable/good to check
2 should have worn
3 understandable to feel
4 shouldn't have sent
5 good/advisable to see
6 should have told

12
1 Dan called. Did you <u>call him back</u>?
2 ✓
3 What about your essay? Did you <u>hand it in</u>?
4 Did you <u>run into Jonas</u> at the café this afternoon?
5 ✓
6 That music is too loud. Can you <u>turn it down</u>

Language wrap-up answer key

1 Vocabulary

A 1 family
2 identity
3 sense
4 life
5 social
6 sense

B 1 status
2 group
3 humour
4 sensitive
5 sense
6 sensible

2 Grammar

1 was always doing
2 would be waiting
3 used to
4 had asked
5 used to
6 found
7 used to tell
8 would say
9 did try
10 would forget
11 am always asking
12 used to embarrass

1 Vocabulary

1 economic growth
2 multinational
3 facilitate
4 generating
5 profits
6 dominated
7 regional
8 value
9 support
10 campaign
11 promote
12 boost

2 Grammar

1 Do you think
2 have
3 The more connected
4 are having
5 more and more
6 see
7 easier and easier
8 The more
9 the better
10 is
11 more and more common
12 am thinking

1 Vocabulary

A 1 caused
2 written
3 inherited
4 runs
5 discovered
6 broke
7 coming up with

B 1 makes it big
2 ambition
3 dwindles
4 in the spotlight
5 washed-up

2 Grammar

Suggested answers:

1 The manager said (that) I/we had to wear a tie if I/we wanted to get into the club. /
The manager said (that) I/we have to wear a tie if I/we want to get into the club.

2 Rachel commented (that) people had to be very self-confident to be an actor. /
Rachel commented (that) people have to be very self-confident to be an actor.

3 Vicky asked if/whether the film industry would change a lot in the near future. /
Vicky asked if/whether the film industry will change a lot in the near future.

4 Anton revealed (that) he had seen lots of celebrities around here/there. /
Anton revealed (that) he has seen lots of celebrities around here/there.

5 Sonia told me (that) she could help me find an agent. /
Sonia told me (that) she can help me find an agent.

1 Vocabulary

1 depressed
2 emotions
3 pessimistic
4 mood
5 enjoyment
6 wealth
7 content
8 distracted
9 optimistic
10 well-being
11 appreciate
12 pleasures

2 Grammar

A 1 when I went to a laughter workshop
2 what happened at work the other day
3 why you aren't happy
4 how stress can affect our state of well-being

B 1 hadn't
2 wouldn't
3 were
4 would
5 have
6 helps
7 have
8 will invite

UNIT 5

1 Vocabulary

A 1 put; up against
2 are as much about; as
3 range from; to
4 make; worth
5 market; as
B 1 floods
2 diseases
3 hygiene
4 water pollution
5 famine

2 Grammar

A 1 The environment has been affected by climate change.
2 Our water supply was cut off (by the water company) last week.
3 Before we bought the house, the cellar had been damaged by a flood.
4 I'm being charged £5 for this bottled water!
5 Water usage is limited in some areas.
B 1 for
2 as to / (that) you
3 so (that)
4 In order / So as
5 to

UNIT 6

1 Vocabulary

1 initiation
2 freshers
3 ritual
4 symbolic
5 mascot
6 written down
7 cross off
8 work out
9 gone over
10 lined up

2 Grammar

1 get
2 you to live
3 to stay
4 not to
5 used
6 him
7 expect you
8 to settle
9 to go
10 get
11 to take
12 you to stay

UNIT 7

1 Vocabulary

1 innovative
2 come up
3 unique
4 personalised
5 manufacture
6 miniature
7 template
8 top quality
9 affordable
10 take
11 catch
12 bring

2 Grammar

1 father's
2 Beatles'
3 parents'
4 had already designed
5 had been working
6 had opened
7 had launched
8 mother's
9 Stella's
10 had been creating
11 athletes'
12 had been

UNIT 8

1 Vocabulary

1 poverty
2 refugees
3 right
4 afford
5 underprivileged
6 unemployed
7 live on
8 responsibility
9 injustice
10 humanitarian
11 foundations
12 Ambassadors

2 Grammar

A 1 would rather
2 to provide
3 we didn't send
4 start
5 to organise
6 them
B 1 the world needs is more tolerance and understanding
2 some countries are poorer than others is because of global trade issues
3 most help is needed is in schools and hospitals
4 receives the most aid is decided by the international community /
decides which countries receive the most aid is the international community
5 you've just lost your job is the worst time to think about training
6 we need to focus on is getting help to people who need it most

UNIT 9

1 Vocabulary

A 1 feeling of
2 desire for
3 thrill of
4 joy of
5 will to
6 agony of
B 1 experiment
2 measure/test
3 research
4 theory
5 test
6 concluded

2 Grammar

1 in
2 have
3 saying
4 of
5 feel
6 increasing
7 of running
8 having
9 with
10 around
11 for
12 to

UNIT 10

1 Vocabulary

1 dare
2 playing it safe
3 failure
4 took a chance
5 run the risk
6 security
7 risking your life
8 at risk
9 exposed
10 freedom
11 risky/high-risk
12 risky/high-risk

2 Grammar

1 unable
2 manage
3 succeeded in
4 were able to
5 to make
6 could
7 may
8 couldn't
9 keeping
10 can
11 might
12 couldn't

UNIT 11

1 Vocabulary

1 out of
2 similarity
3 landscape
4 unlike
5 point
6 portrait
7 subject
8 in
9 In
10 side
11 whereas
12 foreground

2 Grammar

A 1 taking
2 to get
3 to take
4 to send
5 getting
6 taking
B 1 As a result / As a consequence
2 due to
3 because
4 As a result / As a consequence
5 In addition to
6 Besides that

UNIT 12

1 Vocabulary

1 Dear Madam
2 I am writing with regard to
3 heart
4 heritage
5 view
6 Despite the large numbers of people
7 site
8 village
9 I look forward to hearing from you
10 Yours faithfully

2 Grammar

1 will be living
2 but
3 in spite of
4 will be / is going to be
5 Nevertheless
6 though
7 is starting
8 will have / am going to have
9 However
10 am meeting / am going to meet

Grammar reference answer key

UNIT 1

1 1 was having, rang
  2 learnt, had spoken
  3 did play, was
2 1 didn't get into, had sold out
  2 saw, was reading
  3 opened, had received

1 1 I used **to** struggle with my sense of identity when I first came to the UK.
  2 Jessica would never **arrive** on time for meetings.
  3 They are always **trying** to meet people from different backgrounds.
2 1 is/'s always running
  2 never used to get / would never get
  3 used to have

UNIT 2

1 1 Do you see
  2 is being
  3 are thinking
2 1 are
  2 don't have / haven't got
  3 are you seeing

1 1 More and more multinationals are setting up in less developed countries.
  2 The more we rely on social media, the less face-to-face interaction we have.
  3 The more globalised the world becomes, the more foreign cities resemble each other.
2 1 Average temperatures in the world are becoming warmer and warmer every year.
  2 The more difficult the class, the more you need to study.
  3 The better the healthcare, the longer the life expectancy in a country.

UNIT 3

1 1 had to
  2 would, could
  3 would
2 1 She told me (that) she would never miss the final of *The X Factor*.
  2 Bill said (that) if he had known, he would have gone.
  3 They admitted (that) they should read this/that best-selling book.

1 1 were
  2 (both are correct)
  3 (both are correct)
2 1 He stated (that) globalisation is/was a threat to many indigenous communities.
  2 She declared (that) she doesn't/didn't eat meat anymore.
  3 The government claimed (that) unemployment figures are/were going to decrease next year / the following year.

UNIT 4

1 1 Do you know <u>why no one was interested in the talk today</u>? (c)
  2 I think people often feel pessimistic about <u>how the world is changing</u>. (a)
  3 I think he'll be happier <u>when he starts his new job</u>. (b)
2 1 what
  2 where
  3 when

1 1 If we **finish** early, we usually go for coffee.
  2 If the company doesn't make a loss this year, salaries **will** increase. /
If the company **hadn't made** a loss this year, salaries would increase / would have increased.
  3 He said he would come if he **finished** work on time.
2 1 If I were more outgoing, I would get a job in sales. /
I would get a job in sales if I were more outgoing.
  2 People are often less happy if they focus on material goods. /
If people focus on material goods, they are often less happy.
  3 If team members get along, the project will be completed on time. /
The project will be completed on time if team members get along.

UNIT 5

1 1 have been confirmed
  2 are being discussed
  3 was rebuilt / had been rebuilt
2 1 Studies into laughter therapy are being carried out (by researchers). / Studies are being carried out into laughter therapy (by researchers).
  2 In the last few years, more and more jobs have been outsourced.
  3 Britney Spears' comeback tour has been announced (on the website).

1 1 for, so that
  2 to, for
  3 so as to, so that
2 1 in order not to / so as not to / so that you don't
  2 To / In order to
  3 for

UNIT 6

1 1 b
  2 c
  3 a
2 1 'm/am not used to having
  2 get used to waking up
  3 had been used to working / was used to working

1 1 The emergency workers told people **do** not to stay in their homes if they began to flood.
  2 Teachers don't expect **that** you to speak perfect English.
  3 Airlines warned **to** passengers not to carry liquids over 100 ml in their hand luggage.
2 1 persuaded people not to
  2 don't expect freshers to
  3 allow (their/the) employees to

1 1 Caleb and Joanna's
2 Max's
3 men's

2 1 The dog's
2 Julia's and Adrian's
3 Chris and Ben's

1 1 been having
2 been talking
3 started

2 1 Every time he checked his inbox, he was disappointed to see that she still **hadn't replied**.
2 Unfortunately, the band **had been playing** for 30 minutes when we arrived, but we heard a few songs.
3 I **had never really thought** about living abroad until I saw the advert for this job in Spain.

1 1 Farmers would prefer consumers **to buy** products that promote fair trade.
2 We'd rather you **came** with us.
3 I would rather **get** there by lunchtime.

2 1 I would prefer to come up with my own ideas for a website instead of contracting a designer.
2 I'd prefer you not to post pictures of me on social media sites.
3 We would rather richer countries cancelled poorer countries' debt instead of giving them financial aid.

1 1 Where
2 Who
3 How

2 1 How quickly you finished the test was amazing.
2 What the government decided was unfair.
3 Who will win is hard to predict.

1 1 at
2 about
3 about

2 1 capable of
2 worry about
3 looking forward to

1 1 I can't imagine training for five hours every day.
2 Are you having difficulty understanding the homework?
3 Commuters waste hours travelling long distances to work.

2 1 I heard my brother arriving home.
2 James spent many years repairing an old property.
3 The girls stood on the beach watching the sunset. / The girls stood watching the sunset on the beach.

1 1 are able
2 couldn't
3 aren't / are not capable of / 're/are incapable of

2 1 A few years ago, I managed to run a half marathon.
2 Do you think you will succeed in raising £1,000 for charity?
3 Sam is good at designing websites. I saw some of her work and it was fantastic.

1 1 must
2 can't/couldn't
3 might/may/could

2 1 must have got on
2 can't/couldn't have gone
3 might/may/could have sent

1 1 eating
2 to mend
3 booking

2 1 I've tried calling work several times but nobody answers.
2 I remembered to post that letter for you. It should get there by tomorrow.
3 Do you think you could stop eating chocolate for a week?

1 1 In addition
2 Furthermore
3 as a result of

2 1 It's important to enjoy what you do, and therefore earning a large salary should not be the most important factor when choosing a career.
2 It is claimed that anorexia is increasing because of the presence of very thin models in magazines.
3 Some studies find that children are more productive when they cooperate with others, and furthermore, collaborative work increases self-esteem.

1 1 Even though
2 Nevertheless
3 Despite

2 1 Although / Even though / In spite of the fact that / Despite the fact that
2 However/Nevertheless
3 despite / in spite of

1 1 I'm having
2 will use
3 will be designing

2 1 What are you doing this weekend? I'm staying / going to stay in a hotel in Paris.
2 By this time tomorrow, we'll be sitting on a sunny beach.
3 In the future, I think most schools will use / are going to use / will be using digital notebooks.

Macmillan Education
4 Crinan Street
London N1 9XW
A division of Macmillan Publishers Limited

Companies and representatives throughout the world

ISBN 978-0-230-45767-6

Text, design, and illustration © Macmillan Publishers Limited 2015
Written by Mickey Rogers, Steve Taylore-Knowles, Joanne Taylore-Knowles
and Ingrid Wiesnieska
The authors have asserted their rights to be identified as the authors of
this work in accordance with the Copyright, Designs, and Patents Act 1988.

This edition published 2015
First edition published 2010

All rights reserved; no part of this publication may be reproduced,
stored in a retrieval system, transmitted in any form, or by any means,
electronic, mechanical, photocopying, recording, or otherwise, without
the prior written permission of the publishers.

Designed by emc design limited
Cover design by emc design limited
Cover photograph by Getty Images/Paul Bradbury(foreground), Getty Images/
ipbb(background)
Picture research by Susannah Jayes and Emily Taylor

The publishers would like to thank the following educators and institutions who
reviewed materials and provided us with invaluable insight and feedback for the
development of *Open Mind*:
Petra Florianová, Gymnázium, Praha 6, Arabská 14; Inés Frigerio, Universidad
Nacional de Río Cuarto; Alison Greenwood, University of Bologna, Centro
Linguistico di Ateneo; Roumyana Yaneva Ivanova, The American College
of Sofia; Táňa Jančaříková, SOŠ Drtinova Prague; Mari Carmen Lafuente,
Escuela Oficial de Idiomas Hospitalet, Barcelona; Alice Lockyer, Pompeu
Fabra University; Javier Roque Sandro Majul, Windmill School of English; Paul
Neale, Susan Carol Owens and Beverley Anne Sharp, Cambridge Academy of
English; Audrey Renton, Dubai Men's College, Higher Colleges of Technology,
UAE; Martin Stanley, British Council, Bilbao; Luiza Wójtowicz-Waga, Warsaw
Study Centre; Escuela Oficial de Idiomas de Getxo; Cámara de Comercio de
Bilbao; Universidad Autónoma de Bellaterra; Escuela Oficial de Idiomas EOI
de Barcelona; University of Barcelona; Escuela Oficial de Idiomas Sant Gervasi,
Isidro Almedarez, Deniz Atesok, Monica Delgadillo, Elaine Hodgson, Mark
Lloyd, Rufus Vaughan-Spruce, Kristof van Houdt, Rob Duncan, James Conboy,
Jonathan Danby, Fiona Craig, Martin Guilfoyle, Rodrigo Rosa.

The authors and publishers would like to thank the following for permission
to reproduce the following material:
Extract from 'Science gets the last laugh on ethnic jokes' by Kathleen Wren
originally published on NBCnews.com.
Material from 'Why 'selfie' is the word of the year' by Ben Macintyre. Originally
published on the Times online website on 20th November 2013. Reprinted with
permission.
Figures adapted from 'Press Release: Bottled Water Sustains Strength' by the
Beverage Marketing Corporation. www.beveragemarketing.com/
Material adapted from 'Would you pay $55 for bottled water?' by John Fuller
originally published on How Stuff Works. http://www.howstuffworks.com/

The authors and publishers would like to thank the following for permission
to reproduce their photographs:
Alamy/Allstar Picture Library pp38(tml),84(tm,tr), Alamy/Marc Anderson
p141(bl), Alamy/Lee Avison p129(tl), Alamy/Mario Babiera p64(bl), Alamy/
Patrick Batchelder p140, Alamy/Blend Images pp31(tr), 48, Alamy/Blue Jean
Images p132(tl), Alamy/BSIP SA p47, Alamy/james cheadle p69(4), Alamy/
Bill Cheyrou p33(cr), Alamy/ClassicStock p14, Alamy/Neil Cooper p62, Alamy/
Matt Dayka p16, Alamy/Design Pics Inc. p92(bcr), Alamy/DP RF p93(tr), Alamy/
Dundee Photographics p32(cr), Alamy/epa european pressphoto agency b.v.
p105(cl), Alamy/FALKENSTEINPHOTO p81(bl), Alamy/foodfolio p26(cr), Alamy/
Andrew Fox p45(2), 63(3), Alamy/fStop Images GmbH p104(cr), Alamy/I.
Glory p147, Alamy/Horizons WWP p69(6), Alamy/imageBROKER p51, Alamy/
Image Source Plus p79(A), Alamy/D Johnson p79(B), Alamy/Robert Kneschke
p9(1), Alamy/Alistair Laming p145(B), Alamy/B Lawrence p141(tc), Alamy/
MBI pp60(cl),132(bl,br), Alamy/Tom Merton p33(tr), Alamy/Aiva Mikko p81(tr),
Alamy/Pixellover RM 9 p24, Alamy/Vova Pomortzeff p69(5), Alamy/Purestock
p53, Alamy/RubberBall p86, Alamy/Ian Shaws p65(b), Alamy/Adrian Sherratt
p57(5), Alamy/Ian Shipley ARC p73, Alamy/Paul Solloway pp12,13, Alamy/
Mele Stemmermann p125(6), Alamy/Devon Stephens p96(cl), Alamy/Jochen
Tack p21(3), Alamy/Matjaz Tancic p46(3), Alamy/Tetra Images p117(cm), Alamy/
Mark Thomas p33(bcr), Alamy/UpperCut Images p61, Alamy/Gregg Vignal
p117(tr), Alamy/wales_heritage_photos p69(2), Alamy/Wavebreak Media ltd
p80(cl), Alamy/Jim West p21(2), Alamy/Charlotte Wiig p145(D), Alamy/Zooner
GmbH p112(cml); Anouska Hempel Design pp87; Arte Luise Kunsthotel p91;
Corbis pp46(br),129(cl), Corbis/PIYAL ADHIKARY p93(bl), Corbis/Adrianko
p89, Corbis/Aflo p104, Corbis/All Canada Photos/Paul Zizka p127(tr), Corbis/
arabianEye/Patrick Eckersley p55, Corbis/GAETAN BALLY p105(br), Corbis/
Phil Banko p56, Corbis/Blend Images/JGI/Tom Grill p125(1), Corbis/Blend
Images/Mike Kemp p45(6), Corbis/Blend Images/John Lund/Marc Romanelli
p109, Corbis/Sam Diephuis p119, Corbis/Galeries/Brian Shumway p101(cl),
Corbis/Karl-Heinz Haenel p20, Corbis/Lindsay Hebberd p68(br), Corbis/
Hero Images pp9(4),29,125(5),132(tr), Corbis/Image Source pp97,125(3),135,
Corbis/Maskot p40(cr), Corbis/Volker Möhrke p149, Corbis/Lori Adamski-
Peek p9(3), Corbis/Marcus Prior p99, Corbis/Martin Puddy p141(cl), Corbis/
Radius Images pp36,107, Corbis/Reuters/CARLO ALLEGRI p68, Corbis/
Reuters/HOWARD BURDITT p95(cr), Corbis/Tomas Rodriguez p134(cr), Corbis/
Sajjad/Xinhua Press p58, Corbis/Ken Seet p98, Corbis/Hugh Sitton p93(br),
Corbis/Svenja-Foto p141(tr), Corbis/Sylvain Sonnet p116, Corbis/Les Stone/
Sygma p63(1), Corbis/Studio Eye p81(br),Corbis/Keren Su p91(cr), Corbis/Ada
Summer p133, Corbis/Topic Photo Agency p77, Corbis/Betsie van der Meer
p117(cr), Corbis/Visuals Unlimited, Inc./Carol & Mike Werner p110, Corbis/
Arman Zhenikeyev p125(4); **Ecoscene**/Chinch Gryniewicz p57(4); ©Fairtrade
Foundation p96(tr); **Getty Images**/AFP p85(br), Getty Images/Daniel Allan
p129(bl), Getty Images/alohaspirit p33(tcr), Getty Images/andresr p9(2), Getty
Images/asiseei p131(tr), Getty Images/Daniel Berehulak p81(tl), Getty Images/
ADEK BERRY p38(tl), Getty Images/chris Bott p17(bcr), Getty Images/Mark
Bowden p76, Getty Images/Paul Bradbury p39, Getty Images/Cavan Images
p131(bl), Getty Images/Chabruken p117(cl), Getty Images/Alan Copson
p141(bm), Getty Images/Cultura RM/Christin Rose p132(bm), Getty Images/
Csondy p45(5), Getty Images/Mark Cuthbert p35(tcl), Getty Images/damircudic
p88(b), Getty Images/Louis Debenham p117(tl), Getty Images/Richard Drury
p64(br), Getty Images/EMMANUEL DUNAND p122, Getty Images/Echo
p125(2), Getty Images/Amanda Edwards p35(tcm), Getty Images/John Elk
p120, Getty Images/Evening Standard p34, Getty Images/John Fedele p44(cr),
Getty Images/Fertnig p20(cr), Getty Images/Lisa Gange p75, Getty Images/
Justin Geoffrey p130, Getty Images/GordonsLife p11, Getty Images/Bartosz
Hadyniak p65(tr), Getty Images/Mike Harrington pp56(cr),115, Getty Images/
Leon Harris p72(t), Getty Images/Matthew Horwood p111, Getty Images/laflor
p124, Getty Images/Image Source p19, Getty Images/ImagesBazaar p88tr,
Getty Images/Ivan Ivanov p112(tr), Getty Images/Johner Images p45(4), Getty
Images/A.J James p9(5), Getty Images/Chris Jongkind p8, Getty Images/
Jupiterimages p33(cl), Getty Images/Nancy Kaszerman p84(tr), Getty Images/
Christopher Kimmel p140(cr), Getty Images/Wilfred Krecichwost p136(cr),
Getty Images/Clarissa Leahy p49, Getty Images/Kristina Lindberg p60(tl), Getty
Images/ Anna Lubovedskaya p41, Getty Images/Hector Mandel p116(cm),
Getty Images/Nino Mascardi p63(2), Getty Images/Marianna Massey p35(tcr),
Getty Images/Kevin Mazur p84(tl), Getty Images/Jamie McCarthy p84(tl),
Getty Images/Ryan McVay p8(cr), Getty Images/P.Medicus p136(b), Getty
Images/Chris Mellor p143, Getty Images/Ethan Miller p85(tr), Getty Images/
Jeff J Mitchell p72(b), Getty Images/Dave Nagel p46 (tr), Getty Images/Danny
Nebraska p52(tr), Getty Images/Tom Nevesely p118, Getty Images/Douglas
Pearson p144, Getty Images/Jose Luis Pelaez p108, Getty Images/Spencer
Platt p21(1), Getty Images/polygraphus p22, Getty Images/Claude Robidoux
p131(br), Getty Images/Amanda Rohde p51(br), Getty Images/Eleanor Scriven
p128, Getty Images/Zen Sekizawa p45(1), Getty Images/kristian sekulic
p132(cr), Getty Images/Margo Silver p17(cl), Getty Images/Wayne Simpson
p129(cl), Getty Images/Andy Smith p128(cr), Getty Images/SONNET Sylain
p32, Getty Images/Matthew Spolin p145(c), Getty Images/Justin Sullivan
pp40(b),81(cl), Getty Images/svetikd p94, Getty Images/Karwai Tang p35(bcr),
Getty Images/Tempura p136(tr), Getty Images/Tang Ming Tung p129(cr), Getty
Images/Matthias Tunger p31(b), Getty Images/Betsie Van der Meer p17(cr),
Getty Images/Klaus Vedfelt p129(br), Getty Images/Visuals Unlimited, Inc./
Carol & Mike Werner p110, Getty Images/Westend61 p28, Getty Images/
Willowpix p17(bcl), Getty Images/Xinhua Press/wangle p21(1), Getty Images/
yulapopkova p33(tl), Getty Images/Zero Creatives p52(b), Getty Images/
zhouyousifang p80; **IMAGE SOURCE** pp10,60(tcl),141(tl); **Mary Evans
Picture Library**/London Fire Brigade p37; **Photoshot** p69(1), Photoshot/
africanpictures.net p57(1), Photoshot/Anka Agency p142, Photoshot/Imago
p121(br), Photoshot/TIPS p23, Photoshot/UPPA p105(bl), Photoshot/Xinhua
p105(cr); **Plain Picture**/Frank Herfort p92; **Press Association Images**/
Sean Dempsey/PA Archive p83, Press Association Images/RANDY MUDRICK/
AP p123; **Rex Features** p35(cr),104(tl), Rex Features/Everett Collection
p100, Rex Features/Imaginechina p82, Rex Features/Ben Rowe p145(A),
Rex Features/LAURENTVU/TAAMALLAH/SIPA p43, Rex Features/JAY
NEMETH/SPORTSANDNEWS/SIPA p112(tr), Rex Features/Ray Tang p95(tl),
Rex Features/Tom Watkins p104(tr); **Reuters Picture Library**/Jumanah El-
Heloueh p146; **Thinskstock**/alice-photo p141(br), Thinkstock/Aydin Bacak
p45(3), Thinkstock/KatarzynaBialasiewicz p101(cr), Thinkstock/Michael DeLeon
p152(tl), Thinkstock/Antonio_Diaz p25(tm), Thinkstock/Digital Vision p103,
Thinkstock/Fuse p74, Thinkstock/Jupiterimages p44, Thinkstock/mastaka
p15, Thinkstock/miflippo p57(3), Thinkstock/Monkey Business Images p70,
Thinkstock/Monticello p112(br), Thinkstock/Nirian p57(2), Thinkstock/Mohamed
Osama p59, Thinkstock/phaendin p71, Thinkstock/Howard Sayer p127(bl),
Thinkstock/triloks p148, Thinkstock/VvoeVale p145(c).

These materials may contain links for third party websites. We have no control
over, and are not responsible for, the contents of such third party websites.
Please use care when accessing them.

Printed and bound in Spain by Edelvives

2018 2017 2016 2015
10 9 8 7 6 5 4 3 2 1